Social Transformations Of The Victorian Age

A Survey Of Court And Country

by

T. H. S. Escott

Double9 BOOKS

Social Transformations Of The Victorian Age

A Survey Of Court And Country

by T. H. S. Escott

ISBN: 978-93-71813-57-0

Published by

DOUBLE 9 BOOKS

2/13-B, Ansari Road
Daryaganj, New Delhi – 110002
info@double9books.com
www.double9books.com
Tel. 011-40042856

ABOUT THE AUTHOR

Thomas Hay Sweet Escott was a journalist and editor who was born in Taunton to Hay Escott of Launton. He earned his B.A. in 1865 and M.A. in 1868 from Queen's College, Oxford. Early in his career, he served as a lecturer in logic at King's College London and later as deputy professor of classical literature. His work as a journalist began in 1866 when he became a leader writer for The Standard. In 1882, he took over as editor of The Fortnightly Review, but a severe health breakdown in 1886 led to his resignation and many years of semi-retirement. After a long period of poor health and inactivity, he resumed writing in 1894, contributing over 100 articles and publishing several books until his death. He was well connected in literary circles, forming friendships with notable figures in literature and history. He was married twice and had three children from his first marriage. His works reflected his deep engagement with English society, politics, and culture, and his writing spanned both journalism and books on national life and character.

CONTENTS

PREFACE

It may be well very briefly to explain the relation in which the present work stands to a survey, not a history, of modern England undertaken by the same author some years ago. That earlier work was originally published by Messrs Cassell and Co. in two volumes. It was reprinted, first by them, secondly by Messrs Chapman and Hall, in a single volume. Into that re-issue of his *England: Its People, Polity, and Pursuits* (the labour of revision being much lightened by the obliging help of Mr Francis Drummond), the author introduced certain references to social or legislative changes effected since the original edition of the work appeared. Without organic disturbance of its plan, and risk of consequent confusion to the reader, it would have been impossible to bring down that book to the year 1897. The writer does not in the following pages pre-suppose any knowledge of his former book on the part of the readers of his present one. He has, however, held himself absolved from the duty of repeating in this book minute accounts of institutions fully described in its predecessor. Such repetition seemed the more undesirable because the earlier book is still in wide circulation here; while it has been translated into several European languages, and has been adopted as a text book in the higher grade State schools of Germany,[1] and of other countries. The method of workmanship adopted in *Social Transformations of the Victorian Age* is identical with that pursued in the case of *England, Etc.*

This new book being, like its predecessor, not a history, but a series of different views from a common standpoint, the sketches of national life and character as well as of national institutions at work, have in all cases been made from personal observation; supplemented by the assistance of the highest experts in their different departments to whom the writer had access. Often, he is glad to say, the same private friends who helped him in the seventies have been able to renew that help in the nineties. Thus, Sir Charles Dilke, Sir Robert Herbert, Mr Mundella, Mr Archibald Milman of the House of Commons, and Mr Albert Pell have generally and specifically repeated the assistance lent to him twenty years earlier. In most cases it is hoped the assistance given has been acknowledged in its proper place. In many cases the advantages of this service extend beyond any particular passage. In all which relates to the new schemes of local government the writer is particularly indebted to Mr Henry Chaplin or members of his staff; to Sir Henry Fowler; to Sir Charles Dilke; to the Rev. J. Charles Cox,

LL.D., of Holdenby, as in ecclesiastical matters to the Rev. A. L. Foulkes of Steventon, and to the Rev. H. W. Tucker, D.D., of the Society for the Propagation of the Gospel. In references to certain phases of social history, especially about the early railway period, he has learned much from Lord Carlingford, Mr Markham Spofforth, Mr J. C. Parkinson, and from Sir W. H. Russell. And finally he would specially thank several gentlemen of the Education Department, as well as the Vice-President himself, Sir John Gorst. It is hoped that, as in the case of the writer's *England*, so in that of his new book, the collaboration of those who are, in their different provinces, experts, has ensured a more uniform accuracy than in a volume dealing with such a variety of subjects would otherwise have been attainable.

T. H. S. E.

CHAPTER I
TWO EPOCHS OF VICTORIAN SOCIETY CONTRASTED

Difference between English society in the earlier and later years of the Queen's reign illustrated from the composition of Hyde Park crowds, first, when the Park was a playground for the Royal children, and a parade ground for social celebrities, secondly, as it has become since. Different generations of Victorian Royalty. Great noblemen, Lord Lansdowne, Lord Eglinton, Lord Shrewsbury, Lord Shaftesbury, The Duke of Wellington. Statesmen, Earl Grey, Sir Robert Peel. Other celebrities, social, or intellectual, or literary. The dandies, some of them sketched by Thackeray, Morgan O'Connell, the original of 'The O'Mulligan,' Alfred Montgomery, Alexis Soyer, Lord Adolphus Fitzclarence, 1848-51. Tall forms of Thackeray and Jacob Omnium overtopping the crowd. The editor of the *Times*, J. T. Delane, on horseback. The absence in later days of eminent individuals like these; the old editor and the new. A. W. Kinglake among the last riders in Hyde Park of veterans who write. Commerce in the Park and in society represented by 'King' Hudson before and after his fall. Lord Tollemache, of Peckforton, the last of great nobles familiar to English crowds.

As it is to-day, so, during the earlier years of the present reign, both before and after the Great Exhibition of 1851, Hyde Park was the social parade ground, not only of the capital, but of the Kingdom. Then, as now, its human panorama was the representative reflection of the social conditions not less than of the typical personages of the era.

Throughout the later forties or the fifties, the loungers from the provinces were certainly not less numerous in Hyde Park than to-day. Foreign visitors were beginning to be a feature in the Metropolitan summer. But the scale on which the London season half a century ago was observed was so small as to resemble but faintly its successors known to the present generation. Society scarcely exceeded the dimensions of a family party. Hyde Park itself seemed a Royal pleasure ground first, a popular resort afterwards, to which strangers were, as to the Park at Windsor, admitted by favour of the first Constitutional Sovereign, to behold the pastimes of the rising generations of Royalty. The little boy and girl, steering their ponies through the maze of carriages, horses, or pedestrians, were the Prince of Wales and the Princess Royal. Observers noted with appreciative criticism the progress made from day to day by the young riders. Other of the Queen's descendants of age still more tender, followed with their parents in an open carriage, the exact build of which had been introduced by the Prince Consort, and were manifestly being instructed by their father or mother in the art of acknowledging gracefully the respectful salutations of spectators.

The company crowding the Park, and most familiar to London onlookers differed from the crowds of succeeding decades, first, in the monotony of its composition, secondly, in the commanding ascendancy of some among the individuals whom it numbered. This was a kind of feudal age in our social development. The monarch was surrounded by subjects, the splendour of whose station, or the lustre of whose endowments caused them to shine forth in their exalted firmament, with a light of their own not reflected by, though comparable with, that of Royalty itself. Two noblemen, during the first quarter of a century of the Queen's reign, one Scotch, the other English, seemed to eclipse the rest of the peerage. The Earl of Eglinton, of the period now referred to, was famous, even among Englishmen, from the tournament held some years earlier in 1839 at Eglinton Castle, and described by Mr Disraeli in his last novel, *Endymion*. The lady who had been the Queen of Beauty upon the occasion, the Duchess of Somerset, was then a synonym for all which women envy or men admire. When she appeared in Hyde Park, the crowd gazed at her carriage with the awed admiration that they bestowed on those born to thrones. North of the Tweed, Lord Eglinton summed up to his adoring countrymen, in his own person, all the influence, the dignity, the splendour, the power, and all the other attributes of greatness with which the principle of birth could be endowed. What Lord Eglinton was in Scotland, or to the natives of Scotland in London, Lord Lansdowne[2] had long been to all classes of Englishmen, not more in his native county than in London. Here, during the earlier Victorian seasons, he was conspicuous in Hyde Park, generally by his perfect demeanour of high breeding, specially by this blue coat and voluminous white neck investment. After him, slowly riding on a horse whose familiarity can best be expressed to readers of to-day by comparing it with that sometime attained by the white cob of Mr Lowe, Lord Sherbrooke, there appeared, in the blue coat and white trousers of the old régime, the figure before whom all heads instinctively uncovered, the great Duke of Wellington. On horseback, also, were two other men, second only in eminence to the Duke himself, Lord Palmerston, and Sir Robert Peel. The first still wore his years lightly and was as much at home in the saddle as in the House of Commons. Sir Robert Peel, still a remarkably handsome man, had the enthusiasm of the equestrian. Those who can recall the loose connection between Bishop Samuel Wilberforce and the steed which he bestrode, can form an idea of the 'seat' of the great Sir Robert.

Next to the representatives of the reigning family and to the statesmen who were the props of the young Queen's throne, the attention of the Hyde Park crowd was fixed upon a little group of gentlemen, remarkable for the perfection of their toilettes, and for the special attention manifestly bestowed upon their hair, not as to-day cut down to the scalp, but falling gracefully over the white collar. These were the dandies. The last of the tribe has not long passed away. But as a race they have left no successors. The late Mr Alfred Montgomery had for his associates Count Alfred D'Orsay, whose Christian name was perpetuated by a dandies' club. 'The Alfred' flourished in Albemarle Street till a decade or two since. Its founder survived till the nineties, Alexis Soyer, high priest of the mysteries of the fine art of cookery as well as the original of Thackeray's 'Mirobolant' in *Pendennis*. Others who sat for their portraits to the novelist were well known in the fashionable section of the Hyde Park crowd. Morgan John O'Connell, a leader of dandies, was of course there. There, too, was that other O'Connell, known by his friends as Lord Kilmarlcock, from whom Thackeray never denied that he had taken the traits of The O'Mulligan. Possibly, too, there might have been seen here Mr Arcedeckne, whom the same novelist has immortalised in 'Harry Foker,' and who thus early in the Victorian era prefigured the social friendship since grown more common between the gentlemen who live to labour, and their comrades who live to enjoy. Still more noticeable among the Hyde Park loungers on foot, standing not far from D'Orsay and Montgomery were the two inseparables, the then Sir George Wombwell and Lord Adolphus, better known as 'Dolly,' Fitzclarence, the latter curiously like Lawrence's picture of George IV.

The editor of the *Times*, J. T. Delane, scarcely less powerful in the social and political system than in his own office, would have been mistaken, by those who did not know him personally, for the plain country gentleman whose life he liked to lead. His square, neatly compacted figure, with cleanly shaven upper lip, and penetrating, but pleasant, expression of eyes, was among the last to enter and to leave the Park. Not less well known to most Londoners and to many provincials were two of Mr Delane's literary friends, though not both of them wrote for his paper. One of these was Thackeray, towering above all the smaller men. The other was tall Thackeray's taller friend known to his contemporaries as 'Big' Higgins, still better known to the public at large as Jacob Omnium. The two were generally to be found together. The eyes of all passengers were strained, and their tongues silenced as these two tall lumbering figures manœuvred slowly up or down the Row; not so much ridden in then as it was afterwards.

But neither the intellectual workers, nor the social butterflies attracted more attention than a middle-aged, rather over-dressed lady in a very gorgeous carriage, which might have become a Lord Mayor, and a big, heavy man, with drab-coloured, wiry hair, who sometimes sat beside her. The chariot and its occupants seemed to interest the country visitors in the Park more than did the distinguished persons already mentioned. The gentleman was George Hudson, the 'railway King,' who had not only made a fortune himself, but had been the cause of many others rolling in wealth scarcely less than his own. Within a few years he was still visible in the same enclosure, not, however, in the gaudy equipage, but as a pedestrian. The crash, in fact, had come. King Hudson had fallen on evil days. But having dragged none down in his descent, nor disclosed any secrets of the prison house, he kept friends who helped him in his adversity. The house at Knightsbridge, which is now the French Embassy, knew of course Hudson no more. Its fashionable assemblages since it became a diplomatic residence cannot have been more brilliant than those which met there when Hudson was its master. Nor, indeed, has its social splendour since been eclipsed by any of those more recent hosts whom commercial success has incorporated among the sons and daughters of fashion. Hudson's dinner table, or Mrs Hudson's reception room, were graced, habitually by the great Duke of Wellington, by the Duke of Cambridge, and occasionally by other Princes of the blood Royal. Nor, during his decline, did Hudson fail to carry himself with good humour, and even dignity. His simple, harmless, almost pathetic vanity had perhaps combined with his shrewd Yorkshire common sense to support him under his adversities. A sum which realised £600 a year had been subscribed for him, the trustees of his annuity being Sir George Elliot, and Mr Hugh Taylor. His wife and his sons were alive. But he preferred living in a solitary lodging in London. His freedom from all anxiety made this season of eclipse, he protested, the happiest time of his life. A courteous recognition from the great Lord Grey in the Park, or the kindly concession to him of the chair which he had occupied, in other years, in the smoking room of the Carlton, shed something more than a transitory gleam of comfort upon his darkened fortunes, and were recited by the old man with his north country burr to the friends with whom, to the last, he used to dine. Like another fallen star of a different system, in an earlier age, Beau Brummell, Hudson passed several years of his eclipse at a hotel in Calais, where he was visited by more friends than had ever looked in upon the great dandy of the Georgian epoch during the twilight hours of his life.

Such, then, were the chief among the more representative figures to be met with on the brightest and most varied of the social parade grounds of the capital during the earlier years of the Victorian epoch.

No single element conspicuous in the Hyde Park of the later years of the Victorian era was absent from that earlier crowd at whose composition we have glanced. The social prominence of English plutocracy whether represented by the great money brokers, whom, Anglo-Saxon or Teutonic, Piccadilly has always known, or by Yorkshire Hudson, whom it knew fitfully during the short spell of his splendour, has been, from Elizabethan or still earlier times, a feature and a force in the social economy of the town. That which, seen between the Magazine and Apsley House, would have most surprised Hyde Park loungers in the early Victorian days, had they been able to lift the curtain of the future, is not the fact of the best coaches of the Four in Hand Club being owned by men whose names have no English sound, and whose taste for horseflesh is not hereditary; but rather the vogue now attained by prevailing bicycles. Even here, perhaps, one ought rather to recognize the reintroduction of a fashion whose idea is as old as the hobby horse itself than a mode as indisputably modern as the safety wheel or the pneumatic tyre.

The Princes and Princesses who once rode their ponies between Albert and Stanhope Gates are now bearing a part in the government of Empires, but are seldom for long unrepresented in the moving and glittering throng. The 'city' in the Row is not a novelty. The Church began with Archbishop Tait to be more prominently represented than was ever known before. The most emancipated of bygone occupants of Lambeth would scarcely have looked forward to the time when a cavalcade composed of archiepiscopal children, led by a Primate himself in the van, with his Chaplain bringing up the rear, would canter to and fro along the Row. Hyde Park is not to-day visited by early water drinkers who believe in the virtues of the probably forgotten spring in Kensington Gardens hard by. But not many hours after dawn, the novelty, as to early Victorian observers it would have seemed, may be witnessed of ladies and gentlemen issuing in bands from their Tyburnian or Kensingtonian homes to gain an appetite for breakfast, and a store of fresh air for the day's confinement, by making at least once the circuit of the Park while the roads are at their emptiest, and the dewdrops still glisten on the flowers.

Something else than the extended popularity of London's most serviceable 'lung' is suggested by the contrast between Hyde Park as it is now, and as it was three or four decades since. The dandies are not the only feature in the social landscape one looks for in vain. The commanding personalities of individuals of either sex which seemed common on every social plane thirty or forty years since have largely disappeared now. The levelling influences of a democratic epoch have reduced to a uniformity of unheroic proportions those who represent in our public places the interests, the occupations, the achievements, or the society of their day. It is called a prosaic age. It is certainly, as compared with its predecessors, a lilliputian one. At the very zenith of his power, Mr Gladstone in the streets or parks of London, never fixed the attention of the crowd to the same degree as his political master, the great Sir Robert Peel. The adroit, accomplished, and singularly successful soldier, who, since the Duke of Cambridge's retirement, has been Commander-in-Chief, resembles the Duke of Wellington in stature. Neither Lord Wolseley, nor any of his contemporaries, compels as yet from street crowds the mute veneration and awe which the simple fact of his unrivalled pre-eminence as a subject secured for the Duke of Wellington whenever he set foot in Piccadilly, or turned his horse's head in the direction of the Horse Guards down Constitution Hill.

Outside the Royal Family there is no great lady who like an earlier Lady Jersey is greeted as a queen by crowds to which she can only be a name. In the same way, the average of efficiency in journalism was never so high as at present, nor the editing as well as the writing and compiling of newspapers ever more competently performed. The editor, however, of the stamp of John Thaddeus Delane does not, nor by the circumstances of the time could, any longer exist. The responsible head of a great newspaper office has necessarily become less a creator of public opinion, less even of an interpreter, which Delane signally was, of middle class English thought, than the custodian of a commercial interest, the vicegerent of a proprietor who regards the journal, first, as a great organ of public opinion; secondly, as the instrument for achieving his own patriotic purposes in his own way. While Delane was yet living, the able conductor of another great daily journal was ambitious to fill a place like Delane's in the social and political system. It was a sad mistake. In journalism, more than anywhere else, as this gentleman ought to have known, given the requisite capacity which he undoubtedly had, a man may exercise almost any power he likes on condition that he himself remains in the background, and neither in jest nor earnest magnifies his apostleship too much. The consequence was, in the particular case now spoken of, that after some years of patient forbearance on the owner's part, his solicitor waited on the editor one fine morning at his country house, and curtly handed the gentleman, who thought himself indispensable, a formal note of dismissal. Stories were told of occasional collision even between Mr Delane and the proprietary of the great newspaper. These were for the most part doubtless apocryphal. The one thing which observers knew for certain was that when the commercial master of the newspaper appeared during the evening in the same room as its literary controller, Mr Delane generally found that he had an engagement at his office. Some years after the date at which Hyde Park retrospectively has been presented, the best, if not the only, well known man of letters to be observed on horseback was A. W. Kinglake, the historian of the Crimean war. When he passed away there was left stout-hearted, short-tempered Anthony Trollope, who, up to the time of his fatal seizure, pounded his sturdy cob so many times round the enclosure between Cumberland and Albert Gates, just as a few hours earlier in his study, whether in or out of the vein, he had completed a fixed number of words of his new novel. These knights of the pen are followed (1897) by Frederic Harrison, Leslie Stephen and W. S. Lilly. The last quarter of a century in London finds us with many adequate representatives of national industry and achievement. The hero who in any department sums up the exploits and the tendencies of his age will with difficulty be found. The fact that it is the day of great successes does not prevent its being comparatively the age of small men. So long as the veteran Lord Tollemache, of Peckforton, survived to drive his team in its harness of untanned leather from Marlborough Gate to Portman Square, the peerage in its social aspect did not lack one whom Carlyle would have admitted to be in his way a hero. Since 1890, when Lord Tollemache died, Burke and Debrett contain no name whose owner is the cynosure of the holiday crowd in at all the same degree as that last survivor of those noblemen whose figures at an earlier period of this reign were as well known to the popular eye as their position or eccentricity was celebrated in popular talk.

CHAPTER II
THE NEW WEALTH

Commercial plutocracy not seen in England for the first time under Queen Victoria, but dates from Queen Elizabeth or earlier. Wealth, birth, intellect, often united in England. City traders being Lord Mayors who from 1452 onwards have founded noble houses. The chief elements in the new nineteenth century wealth considered. Gold discoveries in California 1848, in Australia 1850. Their transforming influences at home and abroad. Expert opinions of the period on the consequences and the durability of the new gold. Different views and calculations of Sir Archibald Alison, Sir Roderick Murchison, Chevalier and Cobden. A new civilization resting on gold. Australian millionaire farmers preceded millionaire gold diggers. Effects of new gold upon circulating and fixed wealth of England tested by property assessments.

'I respect the aristocracy of birth and of intellect. I do not respect the aristocracy of wealth.' The remark is attributed to the great, or second, Sir Robert Peel. It proceeds upon a confused view of the social principles indicated by the words. It comes, somewhat inappropriately, from the political successor of the William Pitt who bestowed more peerages upon the possessors of mere wealth than any Minister before his time had done. The distinction drawn by Sir Robert Peel between the different aristocracies of England involves some misconceptions of social history. In Austria there existed during the last century, there perhaps survives faintly to this day, an antagonism between the principles of birth and of wealth such as England has never known. With more than conventional fitness is the Premier of the day, whether peer or commoner, the guest on each 9th of November of the First Magistrate of London City. Within five centuries, at least fourteen noble houses have been founded by ten Lord Mayors.

In 1452 Sir Godfrey Feilding, mercer, was the Lord Mayor from whom the Earls of Denbigh descend. Five years later another trader, Sir Godfrey Boleine sat in the chair of Whittington. One of his lineage, a generation or two later, as Earl of Wiltshire, gave Henry VIII. his second wife, and England her first Protestant Queen. Some ninety years thereafter, Lord Mayor Sir John Gresham, grocer, supplied from his numerous family a Duke of Buckingham, and a Lord Braybrooke. In 1557 Sir Thomas Cooke, draper, was installed in the Mansion House. To his descendants at least two patents of nobility were granted, the peerages of Salisbury and of Fitzwilliam. In 1570 a clothworker, Sir Rowland Heyward, became chief of the City Corporation. He was the ancestor of the Marquises of Bath. Fifteen years subsequently to this date, Sir Wolston Dixie, of the Skinners Company, was at once the Sovereign of the City and the forerunner of the peers bearing the titles of Compton or of Northampton. During the earliest years of the seventeenth century there reigned to the East of Temple Bar Sir John Houblon, a grocer. His descendants were to number amongst them the Irish Viscounts who in the fulness of time gave to Queen Victoria in Lord Palmerston the most popular and powerful Premier during the first half of her reign. Within another hundred years Lord Mayor Sir Samuel Dashwood, vintner, became a progenitor of future nobles only less prolific than his sixteenth century predecessor, Sir Thomas Cooke. Those who sprang from him obtained in due course the peerages of Warwick and Brooke. When in 1711, as Tory Ministers, Harley and Bolingbroke dined at the Guildhall, they were entertained by Sir Gilbert Heathcote whose posterity was ennobled by the styles of Aveland and Donne. One of Lord Salisbury's Christian names, and his second title, that of Viscount Cranborne, perpetuate the memory of the Sir Christopher Gascoigne who was Lord Mayor of London during the first Ministry of Henry Pelham, in 1753.

These instances serve circumstantially to remind us that the titled, like the untitled aristocracy of the country has always represented, as it represents to-day, in nearly equal proportions industry and intelligence in enterprise, perhaps even more than antiquity of descent. The dramatic circumstances of his rise and of his fall; the extent to which the latest developments of science, adventure and speculation were embodied in the person and in the career of the York linendraper's son, make George Hudson, the 'railway King' specially conspicuous amongst those on whom shrewdness and opportunity conferred material success. But the type is not merely as old as the present century. It has existed as long as English civilization itself.

When Queen Victoria came to the throne, there was little in the signs of the times to betoken as near at hand the national prosperity which was firmly established before she had been seated on her throne five and twenty years. National depression followed the exhaustion of English energy and finance which had been caused by the struggle with France. Long after the heavy war taxation had ended with Waterloo, and the conqueror of Waterloo had as ruler of the State reduced army expenses to an unexpectedly low figure, the national fortunes were at an alarmingly low ebb. Sinecures had been nearly abolished. A further saving of expense had been expected by the partial or practical disbandment of the Yeomanry. But between 1815 and 1845 the series of bad years was broken only in 1822-5. Even then, English enthusiasm at the liberation of South America from Spanish rule was followed by reaction consequent upon the sinking of British millions in loans to the Spanish Republics of the New World. During the first decade of the Victorian epoch, better harvests coincided with the importation of gold in small quantities from the Ural mines. The railway enthusiasm provided fresh employment for the working classes. More even than by gold and railways was done by the fiscal reforms due to Cobden, Bright, Peel, Villiers and Gladstone to give impetus to trade, and commerce, and to make England the market of the world. Hence the origin and multiplication of English millionaires. The country was thus gladdened by fitful gleams of a long unknown prosperity. But budgets continued to be bad, and Whig finance was in chronic disrepute. During no small part of a century, English exports had remained almost stationary at £51,000,000 a year. The distress was aggravated by the cotton spinning failures of 1842-3. On the eve of these the Burnley guardians told the Home Secretary of the inadequacy of their funds for the relief of local necessities. So gloomy indeed seemed the national fortune, that the Government of the day sold the Crown rights over Epping Forest. Nor as a fact was it till the forty-fifth year of the Queen's reign that in 1882, this historic pleasure ground presented those scenes with which it is chiefly identified to-day.[3]

The first of the most striking transformations of the Victorian era took place in the eleventh year of the Queen's reign and continued during two or three years thereafter. The gold discoveries in California began in 1848. They differed from those which had preceded them elsewhere on American soil in the circumstance that the new treasures were distributed among the entire population, and were not confined to a small band of despotic aliens, as had happened under the sway of the Spanish chiefs and the Incas of Peru. In 1850-1 the same precious metal as three years earlier had been yielded to diggers on the Californian slopes and on the banks of the Sacramento River was found to exist in the alluvial plains of Ballarat in our own Australian colonies. The practical value of these new sources of wealth was variously regarded by political critics and scientific economists. The French Chevalier, and our own Cobden predicted as a result of the new gold supplies a fall in the value of money, a revolution in property, the doubling of wages and prices and the impoverishment of capitalists. Others foretold the speedy exhaustion of the new gold mines. That view was sanctioned by the expert authority of the famous geologist, Sir Roderick Murchison, who spoke of the limits of the recently discovered gold as 'Nature's Currency Restriction Act.' Sir Archibald Alison, not an incautious person, and certainly no friend to innovation, elaborately supported a contrary opinion. He engaged in a series of minute calculations for the purpose of showing that the gold supply now available could not be used up within four centuries. When the alluvial soil was drained of its precious deposits, there would, as Alison argued, remain the parent rocks, the cost of working which seemed likely to diminish and not to increase with time. Nor was this authority less sanguine as to the beneficent effects upon all classes and interests of the new gold. Commerce, he argued, would be promoted at every turn. With increasing production there would be fresh employment, a practical decrease in taxation, and generally in the payments made by the poorer classes to the rich. Before the Australian discoveries of 1850, scarcity of gold had, as Alison contended, raised the value of money, and emphasized the difference between the rich and the poor. The Currency Restriction Act had been passed in 1844. 'Nature's Grand Currency Extension Act' was the name given by the historian to the fresh sources of wealth revealed in Bendigo and Ballarat. The facts and figures were something to the following effect. The discoveries of 1850-1 had added sixteen or eighteen millions to the world's money in comparison with the eight or ten millions which in the fifteenth century and onwards had been provided by Mexico and Peru. On the other hand the economist Chevalier anticipated that, as a consequence of the new gold, money in ten years would fall by one half. 'In 1800,' so ran the argument of this economist, 'the annual addition to the gold of Christendom was barely two and a half millions. In 1848 it amounted to thirty-eight millions. In 1858 the total was a hundred and ninety millions. Hence,' he insisted, 'between 1858 and 1868 the additions to the world's available stock of the precious metal would be at least as much as the aggregate of additions during the three preceding centuries, that is four hundred millions sterling.' The stages in this induction may be thus briefly epitomized. During the three and a half centuries since the voyages of Columbus and of Cabot opened the New World to the Old, two thousand millions sterling had been added to the gold and silver of our planet. The hectolitre of wheat before A.D. 1492 cost in Paris from 2s. 6d. to 2s. 9d. Between 1848-58 it cost 16s. 8d. In other words if the usual grain test be applied, money had fallen during three and a half centuries to nearly one-sixth of its original value. It was upon calculations like these as well as upon certain other considerations that Chevalier based his argument that the fresh influx of gold would make money fall again by three-fourths of its value. This was in effect to say that to procure the same amount of subsistence as hitherto four times as much gold would be required. Cobden's anticipations were to the same effect. So general was the belief of an impeding depreciation of gold and appreciation of silver that Holland actually demonetized gold and adopted silver as its standard money. All these fears were doomed to disappointment. The hopes were more than realized. The third quarter of our present century has proved the most prosperous which modern Europe or the world has ever known.

A careful and voluminous writer on this subject, the late R. H. Patterson[4] attributes this miscalculation to the 'famous currency principle' which grew up after the great war.

The agencies that have changed the material basis underlying the structure of English society were thus fairly now in operation. They were supplemented by other circumstances all tending to produce the same result. Chief among these was the fact of the English coal supply surpassing that of other countries in its abundance and its universal distribution by land and sea. The character and the progress of the Victorian era are due in no small degree to the sagacity and shrewdness of the Prince Consort. He was now the first to recognize that the time had come when the cultivation of the artistic sense was alone needed to make the English workman the best in that world of which from the days of Chatham onwards, his country had been pre-eminently the workshop. French industry had not even yet recovered from the blow dealt to it by the revolution of the last century. That effacement of an earlier régime had differed in important particulars from all analogous movements in earlier ages. The havoc, the massacres, the proscriptions and confiscations of ancient Rome during her passage from a Republic to an Empire, had seriously affected the highest classes alone. The substitution for the French monarchy of a Robespierre first, of a Napoleon afterwards, had involved all orders in a common ruin. The Queen's husband made it the business of his life to insure the maintenance of the advantage which history itself had thus given to English industry and manufacture, and which the fresh supply of the precious metal directly favoured.

The universal attraction to Englishmen of the Australian gold fields may be summarized in a very few facts and figures. In 1852 the English emigrants to the treasure stores of the Antipodes were 369,000; a larger number, that is, than was represented by the increase of the Queen's subjects at home through the excess of births over deaths. Our population in fact stood still in order that Australia, like California, might be peopled. During the four or five years of the gold fever under the Southern Cross, we sent out 1,356,000; more, in other words, than the whole population of Scotland at the time of the Union. The annual average of English emigrants was thus a trifle over a quarter of a million. Somewhat later, the collapse of the railway mania in England and the potato famine in Ireland, swelled the average total of this annual exodus to nearly half a million.

Other results of the influx of gold during the second Victorian decade remain to be epitomized. The precious metal in the Bank of England, from less than eight millions in 1847, increased to twenty-two millions in 1853. The Bank rate during the whole decade was two per cent. The growth of trade was suddenly but steadily promoted. During 1853, twenty millions more of gold money than within any preceding twelvemonth changed hands among the public. Incidentally, it should be mentioned that a belief in the permanence of the low interest rate just mentioned caused Mr Gladstone, when Chancellor of the Exchequer in April 1853, to bring forward a scheme for the conversion of a portion of the three per cent. Consols, into Consols bearing a lower rate of interest, and that the interest on Exchequer Bills was a penny a day or one and a half per cent, per annum. The harvests of 1853-4 in England had been bad. The fresh purchases by the gold mine countries of English goods fully compensated us for the loss from this cause. The value of that custom may be judged from the figures which show the cost of life at the gold mines. In the early fifties flour rose to four times, meat to five times their usual value. An egg or a pill cost a dollar each.[5] For a miner in tolerable luck £2 were not an exceptional day's earnings. Nor between the years 1849-55 and onwards were the effects of the gold discoveries on foreign and domestic trade less noticeable. Within a single period of twelve months, the value of our exports increased by one-fourth. Most of these were required by consumers in California or in Australia as the case might be. The rise of wages owing to the rush to the gold fields amounted in 1851-2 nowhere to less than twenty per cent.; in some trades it was twenty-five per cent. In London the price of bricks was increased by fifty per cent. Liverpool, Manchester, Birmingham shared the general prosperity. Agricultural labour was not paid at a rate proportionate to its scarcity. The extent of that scarcity may be judged from Sir Morton Peto's suggestion that the Militia should be called in to complete the operations of harvesting which were interrupted by the inducements offered by contractors to navvies at wages varying between four shillings and threepence, and four shillings and sixpence a day. Thus the competition of the gold fields industry was directly instrumental, not only in increasing trade, and therefore production and wealth in the mother country, but in improving the condition of the industrial classes at home.

This rise in wages was not however a pure gain. Before the end of 1855 prices had increased by nearly one-half. The Preston strike of 1853-4 opened that campaign between industry and capital which has been paid for by the representatives of both with so serious a deduction from their profits. Before the Preston strike, the unions had been mainly political organizations; thereafter they became industrial. Meanwhile on the other side of separating oceans new Englands were being created with incredible rapidity by the new gold. Already indeed Her Majesty's subjects, without leaving their native land knew something of the Eldorado which Australia constituted even before the treasures of Ballarat and Bendigo had been unearthed. While as yet the nugget was a prize of the future, fortunes were realized by the shearing of flocks. Long before the 1851 Exhibition the Australian millionaire, returned to his native land, had become familiar to Victorian London. He did not yet often live in Grosvenor Square. He was to be found frequently in the best houses of the scarcely less palatial

Westbourne Terrace or at a later date in Rutland Gate. The gold which enriched England created Australia, whose capitals can scarcely be said to have existed before the thirteenth or fourteenth year of the present reign. Gold gave to Victoria civilization and government. It built Melbourne. The same omnipotent agency changed New South Wales from a sparsely-inhabited tract to a populous and prosperous State. The extreme youth, as national life is computed, of Australia will perhaps best be realized when it is remembered that the founder of Melbourne, John Pascoe Falkner was yet alive, and welcomed to his capital the Duke of Edinburgh on the occasion of his visit to the Antipodes in 1860; and that Henty, Falkner's associate and senior, survived at least to 1882.

In no department of industry were the immediate profits of Australian gold more appreciable than in our transoceanic mercantile marine. During the fifties European emigrants crowded every ship. Seamen's wages leapt up by a bound to £4 a month.[6] Between 1851 and 1859 the annual rate of emigrants was a hundred thousand. The gold raised during this period in Victoria fell little short of eighty nine millions. Imports rose to thirty pounds per head of the Victoria population, exports rose to fifty-six pounds per head. Previously to 1851 New South Wales could not be said to possess a foreign trade. In less than thirty years, by 1878, this commerce was reckoned annually by thirteen millions of exports, fifteen millions of imports. In New South Wales, too, the gold excitement was followed immediately by prosperity in coal fields which yielded not less than a million sterling. These are the circumstances that, rather than any domestic speculations or industries, explain the growth of the London plutocracy which has been so prominent a feature of the era now under consideration. Under Queen Elizabeth and the Cecils, fortunes made by lucky ventures in American and Indian trade were conspicuous. Under the Georges, after the victories of our great Admirals Howe, Jervis, Anson, foreign wealth was poured into England continuously long before large revenues were realized by the development of our mineral wealth. It has been already said that during some time after the Queen's accession there prevailed general distress chequered by the influx of gold from Russia and by the beginnings of railway enterprise. From the earliest fifties a change for the better set in, with what results the income tax returns will show. The impost was extended to Ireland in 1855. In that year the assessed incomes were three hundred and eight millions. Ten years later the amount was three hundred and ninety-six millions. After another decade it was five hundred and seventy-one millions. In the financial year 1882-3 the figures were £612,836,058.

CHAPTER III
TRANSFORMATION BY STEAM

All projects of increased speed in locomotion denounced when first proposed. Sir Henry Herbert, M.P., in seventeenth century, on journeys between Edinburgh and London in a fortnight. Parliament on railways. Lord Clanricarde, Colonel Sibthorp, etc. George Hudson, the railway King. Charles Guernsey, the original of Thackeray's 'de la Pluche.' Progress and sequel of the railway fever of 1846. The Queen's first railway journey. Hudson and his fall. Comparison between mines and railways as sources of national wealth. Mr W. H. Mallock's demonstration that the working classes of the United Kingdom have increased in wealth more noticeably even than the upper classes.

The truth of Mr Disraeli's humorous description, in his Edinburgh speech of 1868, of boots at the Blue Boar agreeing with the chambermaid at the rival Red Lion about the folly and iniquity of railways, appears to be rooted in the constitution of human nature. All readers are familiar with the picture of the English traveller, drawn by Mr Apperley in his famous *Quarterly* article, *The Road*. This imaginary passenger had gone to sleep in the days when public conveyances could not be counted on to perform more than some half dozen miles an hour. He awakes in the era of the lightning coaches and quicksilver mails timed to perform twice that distance within the sixty minutes. If, as archæologists say, a certain Ericthonius of Athens[7] invented some fifteen centuries B.C. the first chariot of which authentic record exists, he, too, was perhaps regarded as an enemy rather than as a benefactor by some among his amazed contemporaries. More than 3,000 years after the Attic revolutionary an English Member of Parliament, Sir Henry Herbert, said that a man who proposed to travel to and fro between Scotland and England within seven days each way would be voted fit for Bedlam.

By 1843, thirteen years, that is, after the historic steam locomotive between Manchester and Liverpool which caused the death of Mr Huskisson, the great railway systems of England existed in a form more or less complete. Eighteen hundred miles in all were open for traffic. Parliament had authorized the expenditure on them of seventy million pounds. Sixty million pounds had been so spent already. An average of three hundred thousand passengers was carried weekly. Neither by the opinion of parliament nor of the public were railways regarded with unequivocal favour, or even at all times with toleration. Colonel Sibthorp could say in the House of Commons that he considered all railways as public frauds and private robberies. Lord Fitzwilliam, Lord Lansdowne, the Duke of Wellington, Lord Clanricarde, all spoke of George Stephenson's invention in the same contemptuous tones. The *Morning Post* in February 1842 dwelt with satisfaction on the fact that 'the Queen never travels by railway;' while Prince Albert who did sometimes patronize the train between Windsor and London was obliged only too often to protest: 'Not quite so fast, Mr Conductor, if you please!' Within four months of the *Morning Post's* announcement, the *Railway Times* was able to record that Her Majesty made her first trip on the Great Western. A few months later the Royal passenger accomplished the distance between Southampton and Vauxhall in less than two hours without a hitch. Five years subsequently the Queen and Prince Consort journeyed to Cambridge for the installation of His Royal Highness as Chancellor in a train driven, as Her Majesty records, by George Hudson, the railway King. Between 1836 and 1846 the English mind was fairly reconciled to the new method of transit. The day had finally gone by when, as they had done a little previously, a firm of London solicitors could refuse the business of the Brighton line on the plea that coaches would drive off the trains in a month. From 1836 and onward the Liverpool and Manchester, the London and Birmingham, and the North Midland lines were all paying ten per cent. During 1846, the year of the railway mania, 440 railway Bills passed authorizing the construction of 8,470 miles and the raising of £180,138,901.

This was the zenith of the shortlived splendour of George Hudson, the railway King. He has been seen already in these pages, amid the Hyde Park crowd in the early forties, resting his large heavy person in his wife's chariot. The man himself had first become known on the City Board of Health in York. Afterwards he was elected Mayor of his native town. In that capacity he made the acquaintance of George Stephenson. In 1845 the son of the York linendraper, now a power in the railway world was returned to the House of Commons as Member for Sunderland. His parliamentary career is alone, if at all, remembered to-day by the frequent encounters on the floor of the House between himself and Mr Bernal Osborne. Diverting memories of these were often recalled for the benefit of his friends by Hudson's antagonist, with the generous admission of the raconteur that he had, in the ex-King, usually found his match, if not in humorous retort and thrust, yet in substantial argument. Two years after the 'King' drove the engine which took the Queen and her Consort to Cambridge, suspicions of Hudson's motive and conduct took (April 19, 1849) a definite shape. The shareholders of the Midland demanded a Committee of Inquiry. The incriminated Chairman resigned his post, and quietly accepted his permanent eclipse. It was noticed to his credit at the time, and has not since been denied, that he made no efforts at self exculpation, disclosed no names or confidential transactions, and thus refused, as unquestionably it was in his power to do, to associate persons of the highest consideration with himself in his fall. Hudson was only the type of a class whose members were invested by the railway passion of the period with brief splendour and unsubstantial prosperity. In the Upper House, Lord Clanricarde mentioned how Charles Guernsey, a broker's clerk, had subscribed fifty-two thousand pounds for shares in the London and York line. This was the undoubted original of Thackeray's 'de la Pluche.' The total of his gains appears to have amounted to thirty thousand pounds. The essential facts of the sequel with very little of fictitious amplification are given by the novelist.

A reaction, as has been seen, followed the morbid enterprise of 1846. Its results, however, have endured to the present hour. In 1845 the United Kingdom possessed only two thousand four hundred miles of iron way. The capital invested upon these was only eighty-eight millions. Before 1850, the capital had increased to two hundred and thirty millions. To-day the aggregate miles of the railways of the United Kingdom are little, if at all short, of twenty thousand. The expenditure has been six hundred and thirty millions. The gross annual income is sixty millions. In order to appreciate with approximate accuracy the part played by the steam locomotive in the creation of nineteenth century wealth in England, or to define with practical distinctness that familiar term 'the railway interest;' it is necessary to examine this matter more in detail. In 1855 the total of capital represented by the United Kingdom railways was £297,584,709. In 1894, the latest date to which the Board of Trade returns are published, the total was £985,387,855. After forty years, therefore, the railway investments of these Islands had increased by £687,803,146.

Another chief source of national wealth and industrial employment during this reign has been provided by mining enterprise. In respect of the money value of each, what are the relations which the yield of subterranean labour has borne to the enterprises of steam upon the surface of the earth? In 1855 the value of all the minerals brought to the light of day is expressed by the figures £29,579,001. The figures referring to railways for the same year were, it will be remembered, seen to be £21,507,599. This comparison between the two shows therefore that in 1855 the mines exceeded the railways in value in round numbers, by eight million pounds. The exact figures of the excess were £8,071,402. Forty years later this balance is more than redressed. In 1894 the total of mineral wealth was £80,900,453. The entire railway receipts were

£84,310,831. In other words, the surface opulence of the United Kingdom had not only made good its inferiority to the subterranean wealth, but had advanced beyond that rival, in round numbers, by three and a half million pounds. The exact figures were £3,410,378.

The interesting analysis of the resources of the different orders of the community contained in Mr W. H. Mallock's 'Classes and Masses' supplies tolerably conclusive evidence that the results of mining and railway enterprise have been distributed not very unequally between the rich and the poor, or, as Mr Mallock rather puts it, between income tax payers on £1,000 or upwards a year and those who, earning less than £150 a year, pay no income tax at all. His estimate is that the population of England contains seven hundred thousand families, equal to a total of three million souls, 'with means of subsistence, insufficient, barely sufficient, or precarious.' Although these figures represent the entire population at the Norman conquest, Mr Mallock is able to show that relatively to all inhabiting this realm the necessitous class has decreased, not increased. In the seventeenth century, one-third of the dwellers in Sheffield, then (1615) as to-day a great manufacturing centre, were dependent on charity. Thirteen years after the Queen's accession (*i.e.* 1850), out of every two hundred of our population nine were paupers. In 1882 the proportion of pauperism was only five. Between 1850 and 1897 the population has increased from twenty-eight millions to thirty-eight millions. The income-tax payers have increased from one million and a half to nearly eight millions.[8] Incomes between £150 and £1,000 have increased from three hundred thousand to nine hundred and ninety thousand. Incomes above £1,000 have increased from twenty-four thousand to sixty thousand; or, as this authority finds it more convenient to put it, the middle class has grown by six hundred and ninety thousand. The rich have been re-inforced by only thirty-six thousand. On the other hand Mr Mallock is able to dispose of the fallacy that during the present reign the very richest class have grown richer still. In 1850 the incomes of fifty thousand pounds and upwards were seventy-two thousand; in 1897 they are nearer a hundred thousand; thus while the fairly well-to-do middle classes have increased by hundreds of thousands, the professional plutocrats measure their increase only by a few simple thousands. Briefly summarized, the arithmetical argument of Mr Mallock is as follows. In 1800 the whole wealth of the country was two hundred and forty million pounds. Of that amount the workers took one hundred and eleven million pounds, leaving for the middle classes and the rich one hundred and thirty million pounds. Three quarters of a century later, or more exactly in 1881, Mr Mallock's latest date, making his argument still more applicable to 1897, the total of national wealth was one thousand three hundred millions. Of this the workers had six hundred and sixty millions. The working classes had thus, from being twenty millions behind the rich at the opening of the century, advanced twenty millions beyond the rich towards its close. From these figures, the inference is fair, and indeed irresistible, that railways like other inventions have contributed to the material prosperity of all classes equally, and have not enriched the capitalists alone.

Notwithstanding George Hudson, who has become merely a memory, or Charles Guernsey, the stockbroker's clerk who was his lowly imitator, the railway plutocracy would seem to be a phrase more full of sound than of practical meaning. If to this remark the name of Vanderbilt be objected, the true facts of the case rather confirm than disprove the present remark. 'Commodore' Vanderbilt was a rich man before he ever owned a railway share. He sold a fleet of steamers to purchase control of the New York Central Railway. Had he invested the capital realized by this preliminary transaction in any of the industries of his nation, such as the tinning of beef from a cattle ranche in California, or the curing of bacon at Chicago, he might have made the same or an even larger fortune. Railway diplomacy was only the accidental employment of Mr Vanderbilt's extraordinary genius for creative finance. The same talents exercised upon any other material, or expended in any other career could scarcely fail to have commanded same results. In another department of the industry afforded to intellect by the steam locomotive, Charles Austin made two fortunes out of railway Bills. His abilities as an advocate were probably unequalled among the generation to which he belonged. Since Austin's day lawyers of the same, or something like the same capacity have amassed wealth not inferior to Austin's out of electric patents practice, or in other branches of law which have been specially in request at the moment. While the railway fever of the forties was at its height, a little man with an intellectual head covered by a proverbially shabby hat might often of an afternoon have been seen walking down Parliament Street. He never failed to bestow a copper upon the crossing sweeper at the point where the Home Office stands to-day. Formerly the contractor usually lavished on the man a four-penny bit. But times were bad. The vail was reduced to a quarter of that amount. The donor humorously anticipated the day when he might be glad of a reversionary interest to the broom and shovel employed outside the Horse Guards. That calamity, which of course never seriously threatened, was averted. The little gentleman with the ostentatiously neglected head-gear, Thomas Brassey, was a millionaire long before he built his last railway. But his contemporary, Thomas Cubitt, made the same fortune out of building Belgravia. Railways have also often enriched the landowners through whose estates the lines have run. So high an authority as Mr Samuel Laing holds that the owners of the soil have been over compensated by the companies generally for the acquisition of their land. To this, however, the country gentlemen would reply that in countless instances they have received no more than the agricultural value for their acres.[9] Certainly the profits of this class from railways have not exceeded the gains which have accrued from the selling or leasing of other property for building purposes. The railway interest, then, as a phrase scarcely points to the existence of railway shareholders as a caste or even a separate class. Railway shares, as the statistics above quoted show, are distributed in fairly equal proportions through all classes of the community. The learned professions, especially the Church, are represented as well as the State or capital in these proprietorial bodies. In the great majority of instances, the separate sums held are small. Thus, ten years ago, the London and North Western Railway with its ninety millions of capital had about thirty thousand debenture and stock holders. Three thousand pounds scarcely represent what could be regarded as a plutocratic investment. As for the men who were the early captains of railway industry, they none of them secured more than modest competences. Vignoles, Stephenson, Brunel, Hackworth, Allport, Cawkwell, Grierson; none of these founded, none of their descendants are likely to found, territorial families. Sir Daniel Gooch, so long the chairman of the Great Western, left six hundred thousand pounds to his posterity. The greater portion of this sum was made, not in railways, but in coal and in telegraphs. Sir Edward Watkin, who is still with us, and to whose enterprise neither the mountain precipice nor the realm of air is inaccessible, has perhaps been not less prospered. It would not however be easy to multiply instances of railway opulence like these.

On the other hand Arkwright of the spinning jenny has founded two rich county families. His rival, Hargreaves, established another. The true conclusion on this subject seems to be that the wealth invested in our railways is only one, if the most conspicuous manifestation of the wealth of the community. No better summary of the facts could be found than the shrewd phrase into which George Stephenson condensed the whole subject. 'The country made the railways, and in return the railways made the country.' The prosperity of the manufacturing classes which has coincided with the Victorian era provided the money that built the railways. In return the early development of our railway system enabled us to get so far in advance of Continental nations as merchants and manufacturers that our rivals have not yet caught us up, and perhaps never will.

The future development of the English railway system may be a tempting and instructive topic for speculative experts, but is not for a general survey, such as the present. The issues between traders and framers of railway rates for the carriage of merchandise are periodically expressed in the demand for the acquisition of the iron roads, like the telegraphic wires, by the State. The mighty sections of the Anglo-Saxon race on either side of the Atlantic present the two great exceptions to the State proprietorship or State control of the public locomotives. Seeing that half the railway mileage and capital of the world belongs to the United Kingdom and to the United States, these exceptions are themselves of considerable importance. The incorporation of the railway systems of the United Kingdom into the national service would, it has been calculated, involve the doubling of the annual Budget, and an addition to the permanent Civil Service of five per cent, of our male population. If this estimate be correct, it seems likely that a Minister of the Crown will think even more than thrice before he seriously proposes the assumption of such a responsibility by himself and his colleagues.

Apart from his general obligations to the work on Railways (2 vols. Cassell & Company, 1894, by Mr John Pendleton), the writer expresses his grateful acknowledgment for valuable help in this portion of his work privately received from Mr Acworth, the great authority on modern railways throughout the world, and from Mr A. J. Wilson, the eminent writer on financial and commercial topics.

CHAPTER IV
THE ARISTOCRACY OF WEALTH AND ITS MANIFESTATIONS

Contrast between the London of the forties and the London of to-day. Gas and steam chiefly mark the century. City traders still living at Islington. The theatre not yet an institution. The parks still uncared for. Thames pollutions still recall Dickens' description of Quilp's home. The future South Kensington cabbage beds or waste ground. Absence of enormous fortunes outside commercial millionaires. Evidence of increasing national prosperity afforded by statistics of picture sales. The growth of these sales from Charles I. till to-day. The Beckford, the Horace Walpole and other sales. Gradual rise in value of great masters. Memorable sales and personages at Christie's. Gainsborough's Duchess of Devonshire episode.

The chief resemblance between the London which Queen Victoria first knew, and the capital as it was seen by her subjects on her jubilee anniversary in 1887, is the appearance of the steam locomotive at the railway termini and upon the waters of the Thames. Passing to more permanent characteristics, only the great national buildings would enable those present at Her Majesty's coronation to identify the pre-Exhibition Metropolis with the capital of to-day. Even Hyde Park, that, as has been seen, was then, as now, the recreation ground of polite London, presented an aspect very different from its appearance on the approach of the sixtieth commemoration of the commencement of the reign. Like all the other Royal enclosures, the Hyde Park of the forties or fifties was decorated by no flower beds and was in other respects habitually ill-kept. General sanitation had yet to reach its infancy. The Thames remained almost as unwholesome and repulsive a stream as at an earlier epoch the Fleet Ditch had been. Dickens' description in *The Old Curiosity Shop* of 'Quilp's' haunts was a sketch from life equally graphic and accurate of the condition of the river's shore between London Bridge and the Strand. The site of the river embankments of to-day swarmed at low water with mudlarks gathering fragments of coal and other refuse which had dropped from the wharves that lined the banks on both sides of the river. If the ladies who to-day take tea on the Terrace of the House of Commons had exposed themselves so persistently on the spot where that structure now stands, instead of catching a catarrh, they might have feared a pestilence. Even in the course of the short suburban drives made by the coaches of the Four-in-Hand Club after their meet at the Magazine, the ladies who to-day occupy the box seat would have run the risk of being shocked by the sight of corpses hanging on the gallows. Lord Grey's Reform Act had been added to the Statute Book before this relic of barbarism disappeared. The midlands were busy with preparations for the first appeal to genuine constituencies when certain electoral canvassers, merrily pursuing their work outside Leicester were horror-stricken amidst their fun by the sight of a lifeless form fashionably dressed in blue coat and gilt buttons swinging to and fro on a gallows tree by the roadway. The body was that of a young master printer, who had been hung for a particularly abominable murder. More decent times happily were near. This, which many men now living can remember, was the last gibbet that ever disgraced the Queen's highway. The city workers when they did not dwell above their offices, lived for the most part at Islington, still a country suburb, or took the bus or coach to and fro between the more rural Tottenham or Highgate and their counting room or shop. The ground which is to-day covered by the mansions, the hotels, and the flower beds of South Kensington was then either used as cabbage gardens, nursery grounds, and riding schools, or was given up to the loafers and ruffians of the streets, who chose the forenoon of Sunday as the time for settling their differences with their fists.

As a popular institution the theatre was practically unknown to the early Victorian era. The old patent houses were supported precariously. Their rivals of more recent date were on the chronic verge of bankruptcy. Night after night popular actors and actresses performed to empty benches. Pleasure seekers from the West were more likely to make up a party to see a man hanged than to make up a party for the play.

The new millionaires came in with the new gold. At this earlier date, the men who had realized great fortunes in business, who did not belong on the one hand to the wealthy territorial noblesse, or to the financial plutocracy on the other might be counted on the fingers of a single hand. The Rothschilds had been settled among us for a century. Their opulence had passed into a proverb. Other names belonging to the millionaire category were Arkwright, Strutt, Jones Lloyd, better known to the present generation as Lord Overstone, and Hope. The forerunners of that aristocracy of wealth which sways society to-day, of the Guests, the Crawshays in the iron trade, had not yet appeared. Half a century had passed since the second Pitt had declared that 'every man with forty thousand a year had a right to a peerage.' The Listers, the Holdens, and others were already prosperous manufacturers in the Bradford district. The brewing interest already knew its Basses and its Guinnesses. The peerages and the baronetcies with which these families have since been decorated were reserved for a much later stage of the reign. Even the uncrowned kings of the Australian or Californian gold mines had no subjects in London till the World's Show of 1851 had passed into history. The gradual advancement of the great retail traders typified by the name Peter Robinson, or Maple, to a corresponding dignity on a different level did not take place till our own decade. The social polish and refinement which are the attributes of the new wealth to-day, had not half a century since become dreams of fancy. Rude plenty and coarse splendour characterized the entertainments and the dwellings of the early Victorian plutocracy, as they had marked the hospitality of our Saxon or Norman ancestors. It is a commonplace of conversation to say that none can foretell where the movement which during the last half century has set in with all classes is to stop. Not only the wages of the working classes, but the payments of professional and every kind of skilled industry have increased at a rate predicted to be impossible; but every shilling buys from thirty to fifty per cent. more than formerly of the necessaries and comforts of life. The Prince Consort, as has been already said, did more than any other individual of his day to quicken English workmanship with the artistic sense. The task that waits for accomplishment now is seemingly to develop intelligence and thrift in the masses. If this work be carried to the point which may be expected from the progress made during the last half century, the conditions of the national life in England cannot fail to improve more rapidly than anywhere else in the world.

The new municipal buildings which have risen in all the great towns of the kingdom during the last four or five decades; the warehouses, offices, and shops that, if seen in Venice, would be admired for the artistic splendour of their exteriors, but which pass unnoticed on the Thames, the Mersey, and the Irwell; these are some among the outward and visible signs of the progressive prosperity of all classes of the community, since the treasures of Australia and California first were poured into England, and since the Serbonian bog of Chat Moss was turned into a safe and solid track for the steam engine. Other indications, not less conclusive and perhaps more picturesque, of the same truth are the decoration of the outskirts of every town with private villas set in landscape gardens which half a century ago would have seemed worthy of Chatsworth, and with public parks not less cared for than Royal pleasure grounds, the acquisitions of corporate enterprise, or the gifts of individual munificence. The hard facts and figures which have accumulated since in 1846 the British ports were opened to the merchandise of all nations explain in detail the transformation that has been witnessed. During the quarter of a century before the repeal of the Corn Laws, the total value of English exports, of products, of manufactures was one thousand and eighty-five millions. During the twenty-five years that followed the repeal, the value was three thousand and thirty-one millions; in other words, an increase of nearly two hundred per cent. The second quarter of a century since Free Trade, that is from 1871-1896 has raised the total value of our exports to six thousand two hundred and ninety-nine millions; and this in the face of the great and continuous fall of prices during recent years. Our import trade has expanded even in greater proportion. The total value of imports of merchandise during the years between 1871-1895 was nine thousand seven hundred and sixty-three millions. These figures do not exhaust the national profits of Free Trade. Our increased business with the great markets of the world abroad has meant a vast extension of employment among the masses at home. There is not only more work to be done. It is paid for at a higher rate than was ever known. Articles of necessity, not more than of luxury never before known in industrial households, are to-day common beneath the workman's roof. With comfort, sobriety, and thrift, which are indeed the parents of comfort, have increased too. The Chancellor of the Exchequer in his last Budget stated that within ten years the deposits of the savings banks have more than doubled. The evidence furnished by statistics of pauperism is not less significant. In the spring of 1896 poor relief was given to 739,021 as compared with 897,370 in 1857. And this although the population had grown in forty years from nineteen millions to over thirty millions. In 1857 the ratio of paupers to inhabitants was more than 47 in 1,000. In 1896 the ratio is 24 in 1,000.

The proof of national prosperity afforded by the income-tax returns was given at length in the preceding chapter. Entirely to exhaust the statistical evidence available for the propositions now advanced there may be cited the figures connected with the National Debt. This is being paid off out of the successive surpluses of annual revenue over expenditure. In 1856 after the Crimean War, the Debt stood at eight hundred and twenty-nine millions, or about £29, 12s. per head of the population. In 1895 it had been reduced to six hundred and sixty millions, or about £17, 6s. per head of the population. The amount of the Debt in March 1896 was six hundred and fifty-two millions. Thus, in the last thirteen years, the money responsibilities of the nation have been reduced by one hundred millions. Enthusiasts for Richard Cobden's memory have therefore some reason for declaring that since the measure which the genius of himself and John Bright conceived, and the statesmanlike energy of Mr Villiers promoted, was written on the Statute Book, a new England has been created. Nor has anyone seriously denied the connection during the régime of Protection between wheat at from 53s. to 112s. a quarter and the intolerable distress of the working classes in town and country expressed in ricks blazing and Riot Acts read. With the first relaxation in the Protective Tariff, some improvement began.

It continued very gradually but certainly till at last the new prosperity as shown by the figures and facts already cited was fairly established.

The prices commanded by famous pictures at the great art sales of the present and preceding periods have not uniformly attested the correctness of the popular criticism. They have, however, at all times afforded a practical criterion of the growing wealth of the country, and above all of the standard of expenditure current among the educated classes; seen in this light, the figures are not irrelevant to the present purpose. Picture sales have been a feature in the social and artistic life of England during more than two centuries. In 1649, by order of the Parliament, the collection of Charles I., the most discriminating and perhaps the greatest of Royal patrons of art, was offered to public competition. It realized a trifle less than fifty thousand pounds, probably not half of what it cost its original owner, who is said to have paid for the 'Mantua' pictures alone eighty thousand pounds. At a later sale, however, many of these paintings found purchasers at from £500 to £800 apiece. Thus, even in these early days, was the coming rise in artistic values faintly foreshadowed. But no continuous increase was yet noticeable. Not quite a century after this, Harley, Lord Oxford's celebrated collection was dispersed. The polite education of the well-to-do classes had then made considerable advances. The first of the Indian Nabobs had returned home with the spoils of the Pagoda Tree in his pocket to end his days in the coffee houses of St James's. The commercial classes were generally prosperous. Many Sir Vistos, complying with the whisper of the familiar demon 'had a taste.' The conditions of the time were therefore not unfavourable for prices conspicuously higher than had been given for the Stuart collection. Nevertheless, the interest aroused by the Oxford sale was so languid, art fanciers were so little enterprising, that the highest price recorded on this occasion was eighty-nine pounds, five shillings for the 'Jacob and Laban' of Sebastian Bourdon. The Italian masters commanded on an average only five guineas apiece. A superb specimen of Claude Lorraine encouraged no bidder beyond twenty-seven pounds, six shillings. Holbein's since famous portrait of the Duchess of Suffolk went for fifteen pounds, four shillings and sixpence. Rembrandts scarcely found purchasers at twelve guineas or even six. Pictures then supposed to be by Michael Angelo could be had for a few pounds. The highest price paid at the Oxford sale, the only one running into three figures was one hundred and seventy-five pounds, five shillings, for Van Dyck's 'Sir Kenelm Digby and family.' On the other hand, a second Van Dyck of unrecorded title went for five pounds, fifteen shillings. This was the period in which Hogarth's masterpieces were bought for prices ranging between a maximum of eighty-eight pounds and a minimum of twenty-seven pounds. This depreciation did not continue long. Soon after the Oxford sale of 1741, the paintings by which Hogarth is best known were readily purchased at a thousand pounds apiece. Even, however, after the nineteenth century had opened, no sudden rise in art values took place. In 1823, at Beckford's Fonthill sale, the principal treasures only realized an average of thirty-one pounds each, the whole collection of pictures, four hundred and twenty-four in number, produced thirteen thousand two hundred and forty-nine pounds, fifteen shillings. In the year before the great Exhibition at the King of Holland's sale, a 'Holy Family' attributed to Raphael found no bidder beyond two hundred and fifty pounds.[10] A European sensation was created by the agent of the Russian Emperor giving on this occasion, three thousand, three hundred and thirty-three pounds for a chef d'œuvre of Leonardo da Vinci. But the 'Trinity' by Rubens was not considered specially cheap at six hundred and fifty-eight pounds. Famous portraits by Dutch masters at three hundred and thirty pounds each were looked upon as extravagant. The characteristic profusion of the famous Marquis of Hertford in paying fourteen thousand pounds for some ten or twenty pictures furnished during some weeks the talk to the town. In another quarter of a century, in 1876, at the Bredel sale, the 'Enamoured Cavalier' by an artist not of the highest distinction, realized a price almost unprecedented then, but often repeated and increased since, of four thousand, three hundred pounds. That the upward movement of prices, to culminate some time later as will presently be seen in a memorable transaction of the saleroom, had fairly started twenty years ago, is evident from the details of the present retrospect. That the new development was at that date in its infancy may be inferred from the fact that at the Albert Levy sale in 1876 a landscape by Gainsborough which has since changed hands for thousands secured only a few shillings over three hundred and sixty-seven pounds. Eight years later at the Quilter sale of 1884, the enhanced value of foreign masters formed a much more conspicuous testimony to the growing affluence of the classes which supply the virtuosi of these later days. On that occasion the 'Heidelberg' of Turner was after a keen competition knocked down for not much less than two thousand pounds. The same artist's 'Zurich' in the same year went for twelve hundred and sixty pounds, nearly twice as much as it had secured only a decade earlier. Incidentally for those to whom such facts and figures are interesting on artistic, and not social, grounds, the conclusion from such an analysis as has now been attempted seems to be that since the Strawberry Hill sale and later the Bernal sale, the best works have continuously and conspicuously increased in value, but that, especially in the case of later Italian painters, Guido, etc., pictures of moderate merit have become a drug in the market. If Sir Robert Walpole was the first of modern parliamentarians, his son was equally the eighteenth century founder of the existing race of art connoisseurs. During the April and May of 1842, the collection of the toy villa whose Gothic pinnacles overlook the Thames yielded in round numbers thirty thousand pounds. After an interval of fourteen years the treasures of Ralph Bernal, whose death deprived the House of Commons of a Chairman of Committees as that of his son was afterwards to eclipse its gaiety, formed the event of the season of 1856. In the course of a thirty-one days' sale the total realized was twice that of the Walpole sale, in other words more than sixty thousand pounds.

These figures seem insignificant when contrasted with the heroic prices of our own epoch. Of these only a few and not the highest have yet been glanced at. Compare with the modest totals just mentioned the competition and the sums of money, both without precedent, expended in Christie's salerooms during the seventies and eighties of the century. The rostrum mounted by the auctioneer may be, as is said, identical with that used in the earliest days of the house a century ago. It is the only visible link with the past still remaining. The quality of the crowd of buyers is not more changed than the prices which they are prepared to give; or the national opulence which these prices indicate. In those earlier days the salerooms were in Pall Mall instead of King Street, St James's. These premises were only vacated, as many now living can remember to clear the way for the still youthful Royal Academy before it had, on its journey to Burlington House, reached the stage of Trafalgar Square. The keen Celtic face of Doyle, director of the Irish National Gallery; the strikingly handsome and Venetian profile of Sir Frederick Leighton; the delicately chiselled and thoughtful features of Woolner, more than creditable as a sculptor, far more than merely graceful as a poet; these among the company of possible buyers represented the professionally expert element. The late Sir William Gregory with his fine brow and leonine head, whose many-sided culture suggests the complete man of the Herbert of Cherbury type whom our ancestors worshipped; another Irishman on whom a picture acts as a magnet on steel, Lord Powerscourt; among Scots Lord Rosebery; the Duke of St Albans whose physiognomy in those days recalled his Stuart ancestry; the interested and intelligent presence of a representative of that exotic wealth which has encouraged English industry and art so much, Baron Ferdinand de Rothschild; these are among the best known members of the general circle. Nor should there be omitted the form of a tradesman whose position next to the auctioneer, and whose telegram and account book in hand proclaim his occupation. This is Mr Agnew, pre-eminently a creation of the new wealth of the Victorian epoch, as well as the promoter of not a few artists' prosperity. To-day the enterprising trader is to prove himself the idol of the saleroom by paying the largest sum ever known to have been given for a single painting. And that in opposition to the peer of the longest purse of the day, the late Lord Dudley. That noble connoisseur by his bid of ten thousand guineas seems at first to have secured for Park Lane Gainsborough's portrait of the Duchess of Devonshire, who won by her kiss the Westminster election for Charles Fox. Just as the hammer of fate is about to descend, the dealer intimates an advance. Amid applause, such as salutes the Derby winner on Epsom Downs, Mr Agnew[11] is declared the possessor of the incomparable canvas for the price, as yet unheard in any saleroom, of ten thousand one hundred guineas. Three years before this, in 1873, 'The Sisters,' also by Gainsborough, had brought six thousand, six hundred and fifteen pounds. Fourteen years after its first sale, in 1887, the same painting realized nine thousand, nine hundred and seventy-five pounds. Recent changes in the law of entail have undoubtedly tended to promote these unprecedented prices. The chief cause, however, is the general augmentation of wealth and the more lavish scale and ideas of expenditure that have penetrated all classes of the community.[12]

CHAPTER V
THE RICH MEN FROM THE EAST

Specific instances of the fusion with native elements of the owners of foreign wealth, especially in the case of the Jews. Growth in England from early days of Hebrew plutocracy. Different views as to number of Jew families, the names of these as preserved by Jewish writers. Westminster Abbey under Richard III. and Henry VII. completed with Jew money. Later settlements of Jews in England date from Charles II. Under George III. the prosperity of the Goldsmids foreshadows the future power of the Rothschilds. Early beginnings of the Rothschilds, on the Continent and in England. Rothschild and Waterloo; Rothschild and the Bank of England. Services of the family to the English State. Their method of using their wealth under Baron Lionel and his successors. Their example to others of their race and their work amongst their own people.

The close assimilation of the newer elements of English life to the older; the gradual but unchecked identification in pursuits, habits, culture and tastes of the aristocracy of wealth with that of birth have been already mentioned. More detailed illustration of these distinctive movements of the Victorian era are necessary to enable us to form an adequate idea of the personal and enduring influence exercised upon the society of England by those who since their national dispersion, have in all countries illustrated in themselves the chief developments and agencies of wealth. From the popular expressions sometimes employed about the Jews in England to-day, one might suppose they had become considerable among us only during the Victorian epoch. Few people, as they look at Westminster Abbey, remember that this monument of the national Christianity which the piety of Edward the Confessor began was completed under Richard III. and Henry VII. with money levied from the Jews.[13] Under Henry III. the sufferings of the chosen race in England had been severe. Thereafter, a gradual but progressive improvement in their position took place. But so late as 1633, according to a Hebrew authority named Haham, quoted in the *Anglia Judaica*, astounding though the statement sounds, there were only twelve Jewish families in this country. The distinction of re-establishing the race on British soil has been claimed for the protectorate of Cromwell. It really belongs to Charles II., and actually occurred during the first few years after the Restoration. One of the comparatively few Anglo-Jewish conversions to Christianity took place about this time. Close to the Abbey, which his ancestors' wealth had completed, in the church of St Margaret's, Westminster, an Israelite physician, Speranza Collins, abjured the faith of his fathers, and was formally received into the Anglican Communion by Dr Warmester, Dean of Westminster. By the time that the house of Brunswick was established on the throne, the fabric of Anglo-Jewish plutocracy had well nigh built itself up. The great natural philosopher Emmanuel Da Costa, whom the Italian Jews of the eighteenth century furnished to England, compiled a list by name of all his countrymen living under the sovereignty of George III. In this list there are no Rothschilds. The patronymics of most frequent occurrence are Rodrigues, and Goldsmid. This latter seems to have been the Semitic family which, under the third George, occupied the position most closely analogous to that filled by the house of Rothschild under Queen Victoria. The country houses in the Sheen and Richmond district with their deer parks and vineries owned by Abraham and Jacob Goldsmid, foreshadowed distinctly the later beauties in the same region of Gunnersbury, if not of the more distant Mentmore.

At the close of the eighteenth century, the Frankfort Rothschilds, the friends and bankers of the Prince of Hesse-Cassell, were a power in Germany only second to that of the Empire. The capital on the Main had from the days of Charlemagne been a trading centre. During the sixteenth century, its fairs caused the place to be the market of the world, and three hundred years later may have given to the Prince Consort[14] the first idea of the great Exhibition in Hyde Park. Long before Mayer Amschel Rothschild, the founder of the firm died, the prices of Frankfort were being studied as closely as those of Antwerp or Rotterdam. The third brother of Anselm Mayer, who controlled till 1855 the Frankfort branch, was evidently the first great financial genius of his family. His enterprise and judgment made him the Crœsus of Europe. They also at a critical point in his career prompted him to save from ruin more than one Paris bank reeling under the effects of North American insolvencies. At the close of the last century, the English business of the Rothschilds was transacted by the firm of Van Notten. A dispute with a Lancashire manufacturer on whom Germany and Austria depended for their cotton goods, sent Nathan Mayer Rothschild from Frankfort to England. In this way the English house came into existence, and the necessity for foreign agents outside the family ceased. The Napoleonic wars, as is well known, largely contributed in their successive incidents to the earlier fortunes of the family. Already the first Rothschild had speculated largely in the bills on the English Government given by the Duke of Wellington for the support of the British troops. Settled in London he provided the channels for the regular transmission of funds to the forces in the Peninsula. Early in 1800, he was the first man on the London Stock Exchange. His agents followed in the train of every regiment. His couriers in their specially chartered ships were on every sea. Rothschild himself, unseen by others, watched the Battle of Waterloo. He crossed the Channel in a fishing boat, and arrived in London, to find it full of rumours of the English defeat. Casually appearing on the Stock Exchange, he received the condolences of the City on his ruin. Only he himself knew what his investments were. Instead of being ruined, he had added a million to the family wealth. Such at least is the conventional account. The foregoing details are in substance taken from an entertaining volume by John Reeves on *The Rothschilds*, published by Messrs Sampson Low.

The present writer has, however, some reason to question the accuracy of the tradition of a Rothschild secretly watching the great battle. The account that Baron Lionel's friends generally gave is as follows. During the great Corsican's usurpation of the First Magistrateship in the French State, the lawful possessor of the Throne, Louis XVIII. was living in retirement in Belgium.[15] The Rothschilds, on the early morrow of the decisive battle, sent a courier to the King's villa near Ghent, to gather from the reception of the news by His Majesty how the fortune of the day had gone. The King's sitting room was on the ground floor with windows looking on the garden. In that enclosure the Rothschild emissary took up his station, so that, himself unseen, he could observe what passed on the other side of the windows. Presently a rider, fresh from his horse, still booted, spurred, and mud splashed, entered the chamber, made a low obeisance to its dethroned occupant, who, on his part, graciously extended his fingers which the messenger gently touched with his lips. Hence the outside spectator inferred Napoleon's defeat, and proceeded at once to his principals in London. As an English financier this is the Rothschild who popularized foreign stocks and loans in this country by causing the interest and dividends to be paid in London, instead of, as heretofore, abroad. Four years after Waterloo, he first identified himself closely with the English Government by undertaking a loan of twelve millions. His profit on the transaction was one hundred and fifty thousand pounds. With this sum he bought Gunnersbury, formerly the home of Amelia, aunt of George III., which had since passed into the hands of a private citizen named Copland. The Rothschilds naturally and honourably took their place among the lords of the soil in their adopted country. He who is now spoken of encountered, perhaps provoked, much opposition from rival financiers, and more than once measured swords with the Bank of England which had hesitated about technicalities of discount.

Shortly after this the New Court potentate called at the Bank bringing with him a sum of twenty-one thousand pounds in £5 notes,[16] each deposited in a separate bag. Seven hours were occupied in changing this paper into gold. For the time the general business of the establishment was arrested. The strategy succeeded completely. The next day it was announced that in future the Rothschild bills would be taken as the Banks'.

In the July of 1836 a pigeon fluttered in through the open window of the New Court counting house. The bird had travelled from Frankfort; it brought the news of the death in his native town of the great head of the firm. Many religious ceremonies of the Hebrew race have, during these last few years, been converted into great functions of modish society. The ceremonial series began when the body of the first great Rothschild known to England, in the presence of the whole Corps Diplomatique attached to the Court of St James's, was committed to the earth in the East End cemetery of his race. With that event the latter day history of the Rothschilds begins. Henceforward the business was to be conducted by Nathaniel Mayer Rothschild's four sons in England, together with their uncles abroad. Of these sons Nathaniel settled in France, Lionel, Nathan Mayer and Anthony managed the English firm. Under the régime of Baron Lionel Rothschild whom many now living remember well, the first great act of association with the English Government was in 1847 the Irish Famine Loan, supplemented as it was by munificent subscriptions for the relief of the distress which the failure of the potato crop had caused. Seven years later Baron Lionel carried out the sixteen millions loan for the English Government. The transaction for which the Lionel administration is best remembered by the present generation is the advance for the purchase of the Suez Canal shares in 1876. The announcement of that negotiation by the Prime Minister of the day in conjunction with his compatriots in the City, came as a surprise to the English people at large. It has, however, on the highest authority since transpired that when in 1874 Mr Disraeli took office, he had already decided upon acquiring for England a preponderating interest in the international waterway. Nor is it impertinent to assume that during the Sunday visits which the statesman, as Mr Disraeli and as Lord Beaconsfield, paid to the suburban home of Baron Lionel, this scheme may sometimes have been discussed. Four millions was the sum advanced by New Court, one hundred thousand pounds represented the total of the Rothschild 2½ per cent. profit.

By this time Baron Lionel had been in possession of a seat in the House of Commons some ten years, won though that seat had been only after a prolonged struggle. At the beginning of the century no Jew magistrate or sheriff existed. In 1837, Sir David Salomons became sheriff of London and Middlesex, but the true faith of a Christian test prevented him from serving. Eventually, to oblige the City, Lord Chancellor Campbell introduced a Bill removing this disability. Parliament, however, was still closed against the

Jew. Ten years later Lionel Rothschild, with Lord John Russell, was elected M.P. for London. The Jewish Parliamentary Relief Bill, supported by Mr Disraeli as well as Mr Gladstone, passed the House of Commons, to be thrown out in the Lords. In 1850 another measure shared the same fate. The sixth decade of this century had come before the first Rothschild took his place on the green leather benches. Mr Disraeli's last novel, *Endymion*, as rich as any of its predecessors in personal portraits, contains in the character of Mr Neuchatel, the banker, the most graphic pen and ink sketch of the financier now mentioned. In the grounds of Gunnersbury, statesmen of both parties, diplomatists from every Court, foreigners of every grade of distinction met each other. Here Mr Disraeli chatted amicably with Lord Palmerston, the turbulence of whose foreign policy he was fresh from denouncing in the House of Commons. Hither Louis Napoleon, when an exile in London, drove in his friend Count Alfred D'Orsay's cabriolet. Here the veteran Lord Lyndhurst instructed in habits of English thought his aptest pupil, then a showy but still obscure politician soon to become the pillar of the Tory party. It was by Baron Lionel that the Rothschild hospitalities were begun on the scale on which they have since continued. First came the marriage of Baron Lionel's eldest daughter, Leonora, to her relative, Alphonse Rothschild. Persigny, then French Ambassador in London, made a speech which the Paris Academy recognized as classical in its perfection. Mr Disraeli, always pre-eminently happy on these occasions, delighted host, hostess, and guests by a coruscation of glittering antitheses, and flashing epigrams in affectionate honour of the bride and bridegroom. The ex-Lord Chancellor, Lord Lyndhurst himself, in whose honour the Baroness Mayer had given a fête a few days earlier at Mentmore, said a few words so happy in their arrangement, so dignified in their cadence that they were subsequently set to candidates for the Newcastle medal at Eton to translate into Attic prose.

Not twenty years have passed since, on Baron Lionel's death in 1879, the fortunes of the house have been controlled by the Lord Rothschild of to-day with his brothers Alfred and Leopold as his partners. The loans for the Hungarian, Brazilian, and Chilian Governments are only a portion of the New Court enterprises since 1879. In the eyes of England and of Europe, their most important undertaking has been in relation with Egypt. In 1885, at the moment that the Western powers were at diplomatic feud with each other about the land of the Pharoahs, Egypt itself drew more and more near to complete bankruptcy. The calamity was only averted by monthly advances from the Messrs Rothschild upon no legal security, but on the strength of a private note from the late Foreign Secretary, Lord Granville. This is the testimony of Sir Michael Hicks-Beach speaking as Chancellor of the Exchequer after he had succeeded Mr Gladstone in 1885. The nine millions loan issued in that year was, of course, highly successful for its negotiators. But this good fortune had been preceded by an anxious season of protracted risk encountered with unfailing public spirit.

The Semitic capitalists of the century have been compared to a foreign garrison quartered in every European country, never completely fused with the native population, always separated from the national life, and potentially hostile to the domestic interests of the land which it occupies. In the case of the financial family whose connection with Victorian England has now been summarized this description is not borne out by the facts. Their activity as financiers and generosity as citizens during calamitous seasons like the Irish famine, are only specimens of the services rendered by the Rothschilds to their adopted country. No exceptional distress comes upon any portion of the United Kingdom without eliciting a letter of womanly sympathy from the Queen, and the opening of a subscription list in the City. At the head of this list the name of the New Court firm is tolerably sure to be seen. Members of a race whose history is like that of the Jews one of razzias, confiscations, disqualifications, patiently borne and slowly overcome, can scarcely be expected to betray no consciousness of these antecedents in their habit and speech. The bearing of the Jew, whatever pinnacle of greatness he may have climbed, is traditionally the bearing of a man on the defensive, prepared, if he sees an opening, to anticipate the necessity of resentment by showing his ability to repel offence. Those who, whether by individual experience or by ethnic tradition, have been schooled in experiences like these, are not likely to show morbid delicacy in their deportment towards others. The mart and the bourse to which the Jews have been driven are defective schools of social culture. Asiatic plutocrats are sure, therefore, wherever they may be settled, to provoke enemies in the very act of creating clients and dependents. The English Rothschilds of every generation have found opportunities of performing private not less than public kindnesses. In spite of, or rather perhaps because of this, they have wounded many susceptibilities, for there may be an insolence of neediness not less than of wealth. Fairness, however, requires the admission that the successive representatives of the great Semitic house in respect of the performance of the duties of citizenship as well as in the wise, not less than the beneficent use of wealth, have set an example to the fellow countrymen of their adoption in general, and to their financial rivals in particular. The employment of great wealth in accordance with the principles of magnificence and of taste was esteemed so highly by the cultivated Greeks of old as to receive from Aristotle a concrete illustration in his category of virtuous characters. The same tradition was preserved and exemplified in those republics of mediæval Italy that wore the closest resemblances to the older democracies of Hellas which history records. It was not unknown in England at that period when London was to the Englishman what Florence had been to the Florentine under the Medici, or, at an earlier age, what the City of the Violet Crown had been to the contemporary of Pericles. A similar sense of the public usefulness and patriotic obligations of great wealth animated the citizens of London under our own Edwards, and had previously found many modes of effective expression under Elizabeth. Those were 'the gorgeous days' in which the trader of one of the great chartered companies in the Indies or across the Atlantic, having made some exceptionally successful venture, on returning safely to his native land, and to the township which had been his cradle, was wont to testify his gratitude to Providence by embellishing the place of his birth with buildings or gardens, with galleries or terraces, many of which, as in the case of the gifts of Sir Thomas Gresham, the first of the great loan negotiators, endure to this day, not only in the college which bears his name, but in the Royal Exchange. By no family, not of English birth; by few Englishmen themselves, either under Queen Victoria or her predecessors, have the public and national responsibilities imposed by financial success, or by hereditary millions, on their possessors been recognized so frankly, or been illustrated with so happy and impressive a blend of splendour and propriety, as by the descendents of the bankers of the Princes of Hesse-Cassel who in the first days of this century issuing from their natal judengasse at Frankfort established themselves in England, and at the same time, or shortly thereafter, fixed their emporia in the great Continental capitals as well.

Whatever their natural pride in the creative power of their wealth, no one can lay it to the charge of the Rothschilds that in the use of this instrument they have lost sight of their duties to the land of their adoption. In any faithfully written chronicle of English art or sport since both were organized among us on their present plan, the name of this family must fill no small space. Their services to the breed of horses may be surmised from the popularity of Baron Lionel Rothschild's success in the race for the Derby with Favonius in 1871, as well as from the popularity which his son has since won in the same pastime. Their private houses are museums of art which have encouraged English not less than Continental talent, and which are open to every visitor who is interested in their contents. Since the Rothschilds were settled in Piccadilly and Mayfair, many others of their race have made a position in the polite life of the capital and of the country. That each of these, to mention only Murrietas, Oppenheims, Bischoffsheims, have fixed the ends and regulated the scale of their expenditure with a regard for refinement as well as pomp, and that the more prominent members of a no longer despised race have been incorporated thoroughly into the ranks of the native gentry, is due largely to the personal initiative and influence of the New Court dynasty. Nor is it merely their wealth and the influence which money has brought that have placed the Rothschilds at the head of Semitic settlers in England. Their loyalty to their nation has never been eclipsed by other interests. They have not only endowed hospitals and built synagogues. They have always exerted a pacific and unifying influence upon the various and sometimes mutually conflicting Hebraic factions; at one time they have reconciled to each other different schools of Teutonic Judaism. At another they have performed the same good office for Israelite communities outside their own Teutonic pale.

CHAPTER VI
SOCIAL CITIZENSHIP AS A MORAL GROWTH OF VICTORIAN ENGLAND

Private and individual efforts which have quickened the sense of citizenship in England and bridged the gulf between rich and poor. Historic and abiding influences of the Young England movement of 1846. How it facilitated the Factory Acts and prompted private owners to open their parks to the public. Temple Gardens and Lincoln's Inn. Effect produced by the brothers Mayhew with their *London Labour* and *London Poor* during the fifties, and also by certain articles in the *Times* and *Quarterly Review*. Lord Shaftesbury, the Poor Man's Peer. Origin of Public School and University settlements in great towns. Edward Denison and his friends before Arnold Toynbee. Individual example acting on public or corporate owners. Educate the public and actuate legislation when the time is ripe for it. Sir Erasmus Wilson's gift of Cleopatra's Needle preceded beautification of Thames Embankment.

The practical sense of citizenship by which, in the preceding chapter, the Jewish community in England has been seen to be animated is among native Englishmen themselves pre-eminently the development of the Victorian era. Its manifestation in the capital was preceded by its active display in the provinces. Few individuals of our epoch have more appreciably and definitely impressed the image of their genius on the social history of their age, than Benjamin Disraeli, first, and only, Earl of Beaconsfield. This is not the occasion on which to examine his position in, and services to, the public life of the period, as well as his place in the inner economy of the polite world. In the social movement of the industrial classes of the community, especially in their relations with their more highly placed neighbours, the work done by this remarkable man is not less conspicuous than it is seemingly enduring.[17] The political school which, at the outset of his career his genius created, that of Young England in the ninth year of the present reign, did not last long as a political organization. It was never intended to do so. Of the little coterie whose inspiring literature is contained in the trilogy of romance that is constituted by *Coningsby*, *Sibyl*, and *Tancred*, the sole survivor is the Duke of Rutland. Even he, perhaps, is better known to many readers as Lord John Manners. He was first introduced to the general public by the style of 'Lord Henry Sidney' in his friend's earliest novel. With pardonable pride in a letter incorporated by the editor of the *Quarterly Review* in an article on *Sibyl*,[18] the Duke of Rutland points back to the undoubted service which the sentiment generated by the Young Englanders rendered to Lord Shaftesbury, then Lord Ashley, and to Mr Oastler in their gradually successful efforts to pass the First Factory Act as well as generally to soften, perhaps even to sweeten the daily lot of the suffering, the defenceless, and the poor. At that time, the humane and religious fervour of Lord John Russell had not yet leavened, as it soon afterwards did, aristocratic Whiggism. Mr Gladstone's spiritualizing touch was still to be laid upon the party that he was yet to join. The scientific economists of the school of Peel, comprising as they did Cobden and Bright, were the enemies of the movement. Even the pioneer of that movement, who afterwards nobly vindicated his claim to the title of the Poor Man's Peer, was indignantly asked what he, Lord Shaftesbury, had been doing, when Lord Ashley was fighting for the Ten Hours Bill of 1844.[19]

His virtuous indignation obscured this critic's view of the fact that the peer he praised was identical with the peer he denounced.

If this were the context in which to illustrate the political permanence of the Young England agency, it would be enough to point to the perpetuation in the knights, dames, and chancellors of the Primrose League, of the sensibility to picturesque or semi-feudal effects which inspired Disraeli and his friends in their manipulation of Conservative sentiment. These qualities, at an interval of just half a century, were to reappear in Disraeli's aptest[20] pupil, Lord Randolph Churchill. As a social and unpolitical testimony to the quickening power of the new England propaganda, when its promulgation was an affair of yesterday, it may be mentioned that at the Queen's accession, as for many years thereafter, it was comparatively an unknown thing for the private parks surrounding gentlemen's houses in the provinces to be used as people's pleasure grounds. Show places on such a scale as Blenheim or Chatsworth existed then as they exist to-day. Even in the case of the former of these, in præ-*Coningsby* or ante-Victorian days, it is not likely to have occurred to a Duke of Marlborough, as it did occur to the seventh successor of John Churchill, being the eighth Duke, to engage a special train to convey several thousands of East End children from their native courts and alleys to the undulating woodlands of his Oxfordshire park. Within a few years of the appearance of *Coningsby*, Eaton was only one of the great parks which, so long as certain reasonable restrictions were observed, became not less free to town or country labourers with their wives and children than Kensington Gardens, or, as what till our age was called Battersea Fields.[21] Royal patronage had not been withheld from the movement. The memories of the present generation stop short of a time when Windsor Park, together with the gardens and terraces of the Castle, was inaccessible to excursionists by the Great Western Railway to view the natural panorama bright with all the beauties of 'blossom week,' or to hear the band on the slopes play the favourite pieces of the Queen. The capital was not yet fully abreast with this piece of social progress. Long after the gardens and the general maintenance of the public parks endowed them with fresh attractions, the private pleasure grounds of corporate owners were closed. The new philanthropic reforms were introduced here by the noble structure of the Thames Embankment. The Temple Gardens had, indeed, long been open. The flower beds and their careful tending were still to come. The Benchers of Lincoln's Inn were more exclusive. The new buildings, as they are called, flanking this enclosure, date from 1845. The Lincoln's Inn Fields' theatre had disappeared in 1848. Nearly half a century was still to elapse before the leafy paradise in the heart of this austere kingdom of Chancery law was to ring with childish voices from the courts and alleys which abut on Chancery Lane.

Within fifty years of the Queen's accession, the personal example of that Lord Shaftesbury whose name has been mentioned already was to bear rich fruit. In the *Times* newspaper during the earlier sixties, there appeared a leading article on the subject of the homeless poor of London. It was equally noticeable for the humanity which inspired it, and for its vigorous and graphic expression. Not long before this, an interest, then entirely new, had been imparted to the grim subject by an essay in the *Quarterly Review* based on the then comparatively recent volumes about London labour and the London poor by the brothers Mayhew. A host of writers have treated this subject subsequently. Many of them, conspicuously the late Thomas Archer, with a thoroughness and freshness of knowledge scarcely inferior to that with which it had been approached by the Mayhews. But in their hands the topic was absolutely new. Without hyperbole, in literal truth, the West End was then not only ignorant of how the East End lived, but with very rare individual exceptions, entirely indifferent to the mingled squalor and tragedy of that existence. Horace Mayhew survived to a vigorous and remarkably handsome old age, dying only a few years ago. His work on the deeper depths of London poverty was the one effort of his life. All his energies were thrown into it. The work when finished, if it did not exhaust him, left him so depressed by the misery which he had been investigating that he had no mind to return to the lighter departments of periodical letters wherein his career commenced, and his earlier reputation was made. A long period of social indifference and legislative lethargy as to the condition of the very poor in the capital and in other great towns now ensued. In 1865, the first editor of the *Pall Mall Gazette*, Frederick Greenwood, conceived the idea of commissioning his brother James, a well known writer on social subjects, to pass a night in the casual ward of a workhouse, rumours of abuses in the management of which were then attracting attention. About a year after this, a winter of exceptional severity afflicted the poorest portions of London, near the Docks and elsewhere, with the combined calamities of lack of labour, and as a consequence with famine, firelessness, and pestilence. Three friends, each of them then young men, all Conservatives by conviction and all under the influence of the philanthropic teaching of Disraeli's novels, were in the habit of frequently meeting with a view of maturing some scheme for the relief of that destitution at the East End, with which existing agencies of help had proved themselves impotent to deal. One of these belonged to a well known Shropshire family, Baldwyn Leighton.[22] Another, Sir Michael Hicks-Beach, has since become Chancellor of the Exchequer. The third was a son of a former Bishop of Salisbury. Edward Denison was equally quick to master the dominant facts in a social situation, and to take the action that seemed the best thereupon. Within a few days, he decided that the first step towards remedying the evils recorded morning after morning in the newspapers must be personal acquaintance with their magnitude, and their origin, as well as with the habits and homes of the distressed masses. Denison, therefore, established himself in a small house in Whitechapel, the very heart of the necessitous district.

Since then, the example thus set has been followed frequently. Denison of course was sometimes visited in his East End lodging by his West End friends. These returned, bringing with them a more vivid sense of the industrial suffering just outside the doors of the polite world than literary descriptions, however graphic, could convey to the perfunctory reader of the morning paper. Other incidents were to prove unexpectedly instrumental in deepening the interest of well-to-do Londoners in their destitute neighbours. Within a year or two of Denison's mission, the Fenian outrage at Clerkenwell Prison not only robbed many poor families of their breadwinners, but left them literally homeless. Disraeli, at that time Prime Minister, sent down his private secretary to distribute alms among the victims of the explosion. Mr Montague Corry, since Lord Rowton,[23] saw sad and strange sights during this charitable errand. His recital of these experiences was followed by liberal subscriptions to the sufferers from Pall Mall and Mayfair. From that day to this, not only has the stream of charity flowed less sluggishly; there has been also awakened a new personal and intelligent interest in the condition of the most squalid of poverty's perennial children. That feeling has not evaporated in charitable doles. Substantial funds have been organized by private or corporate munificence for improving the dwellings of the poor and for practically testifying the neighbourly solicitude of more fortunate citizens.

The demoralizing effects of public executions were exposed by Thackeray. His essay, 'Going to see a man hung' gave shape, and eventually success to the movement for the hanging of criminals within, and not outside, the prison walls. So, at an earlier day, Dickens, who of all our greatest writers was the first to interest the public in the waifs and strays in the London streets, had initiated in *Oliver Twist* a social demand for workhouse reform. The best causes are liable to abuse and caricature. There have been moments when, since the Mayhews wrote, sympathy with the lot of the London poor has seemed in danger of becoming overdone, or being degraded into a fad, a craze, a fashionable hobby, and thus of ceasing to be an actuating conviction. The modish popularity of 'slumming' as it used a few years ago to be called had of course its absurd aspects, but was, nevertheless, not an unhealthy sign. It could be compared to the froth upon the surface which concealed, and did not necessarily weaken, the stimulating and strengthening qualities below. Whether this philanthropic curiosity was displayed in town or country, the social truth of which it constituted evidence was that the commercial spirit and its harsher influences, not unfortunately uncommon among the upper classes in the early days of the new poor law, were becoming obsolete, and that the class fusion born of class sympathy to which De Tocqueville has attributed our later freedom from organic revolutions was in steady process of evolution. Edward Denison came first of all, and could only see with the eye of faith the fruits which his example was to bear in the beneficent experiment of Arnold Toynbee and in the People's Palace. So it has continued, till to-day the University and public school settlements in the East End of London and in other great cities are institutions not less deeply rooted than the parochial system itself. The kindly work is not confined to a single sex. St Margaret's House, Bethnal Green, the ladies' branch of the Oxford agency, presided over by Mrs Burrows, is as firmly established as the homes founded by Trinity or Christ Church in the same neighbourhood. Throughout the English speaking world, the same beneficent inspiration seems to have been almost simultaneously operative. One hears of analogous enterprises in the great cities of Australia and in the United States. The American movement even claims seniority over the English. Andover House, Boston, was in full working order before the cognate agencies in our own capital were complete. The devotion of Trade Unionists to their Union has been employed as a figure to illustrate the mutual loyalty to a great and good idea of those brought up in the same College or University or public school. This reciprocal enthusiasm has now been active and productive long enough to entitle it to the praise of solidity and permanence. The public and legal provisions for quickening the sense of citizenship in town and country will presently be examined in detail. That which seems important to bear in mind is that the legislature did not interpose its machinery until the private agencies, social or moral, already recapitulated, had done their work. Even the improvement in the open spaces of the capital which is so marked a feature in metropolitan progress during the last few decades, has been helped or encouraged largely by private initiative. The late Mr Matthew Arnold recognized as a graceful and original act of public service, the transport of Cleopatra's Needle from Alexandria to London at the cost of Sir Erasmus Wilson. Before the obelisk was established on the Thames Embankment the municipal authorities had prepared a home for it and converted into daintily kept pleasure grounds the little enclosures by the side of the riverain promenade.

CHAPTER VII
THE NEW ERA IN ENGLISH PARISHES

Reflection of the Estates of the Realm in the old divisions of rural life in England. Modifications in the system introduced by recent changes in local government. The English village as it now is. The public house as a place of resort largely displaced by the parish meeting room. The quickened sense of civic life shown in the speech and bearing of the villagers. The exact functions of the Parish Council, or Meeting. Relations between Parish and District Councils. Retrospect of English Poor Law system. Greater popularity of the District Councils. Other duties than of Poor Law Guardians discharged by District Councils. Clergy and Squires. How affected. District Board's composition. Its relations with magistrates, and popular feeling.

Before 1894, English parishes in rural districts possessed, as they still do, three centres of local life. The State was represented by the squire, or chief landowner, often, as may still be the case, an absentee. The Rectory, or Vicarage, with the neighbouring church was the geographical depository of spiritual power. The village inn, or public house, was the place of popular meeting, and with its adjoining skittle-alley was the source of popular amusement. Here the gossip of the neighbourhood was discussed, or the local newspaper read. London journals did not, and do not, often enter remote neighbourhoods in the provinces. The doings of the Imperial Parliament, or the Concert of the European Powers were, as they remain, of little interest to the rural tillers of the soil in comparison with the wages paid by the farmers in the district, the supervision, or the lack of it, exercised by lords of the land over the cottages of the poor. Nothing more struck the stranger who wished to acquire information as to the daily lot of the rural population, and as to opportunities for their improvement, than the prevailing ignorance or indifference about the facts of their daily life. It was not exactly Christian acquiescence in chronic want and squalor as a Divine dispensation. It was rather an unreasoning suspicion as to the motives of the enquirer, and as to the consequences to themselves of the answers given, which, if it did not seal the villagers' lips, restricted their replies to inarticulate grunts or evasive generalities.

Within the fifth decade of the present reign, all this has either changed entirely or has been appreciably modified. The public house, or inn, stands indeed where it stood. The tap is no longer the parish club room. Even the skittle-alley has lost many of its attractions. The authority of the Manor House has been divested of the superstitious sanctions with which it was once clothed. The squire and the parson are regarded as well-meaning persons with a good deal of human nature, after all, about them. As for the geographical centre of village existence, it is no longer the roof tree of the publican, but the village meeting hall. This, in the majority of cases, would never have existed but for the initiative of the clergyman. He it is who with no parliamentary sessions to attend during half the year, with no town house always ready to receive him, passes most of his time among his own people; and thus combines in his own person, very often, the two separate principles of Church and State. This village assembly room is furnished with the chief county and market town newspapers. It is without carpets or draperies, and does not consequently retain tobacco smoke. If, therefore, the villager likes a dry pipe while he reads, or chats, it may at stated hours be allowed him. Gradually, therefore, he has grown to regard the place as his betters regard the House of Commons, as the best club of which he knows. The publican may suffer, but all other members of the little community have gained.

At the present moment, the manner and the countenances of the rural company, apart from the subjects of their more than usually animated conversation, indicate a season of exceptional importance. The truth is, that an election for the village parliament is imminent. Whether the name be parish council or parish meeting, the reality is the same. That reality since Sir Henry Fowler's amendment in 1894 practically implies Home Rule for every parish in rural England. The franchise is in effect universal. Without regard to income or place of domicile every parishioner whose name occurs in the local government or parliamentary register has a vote, and is in addition entitled to attend the parish parliament. So systematic is the preservation of the separate individuality of every village, that where the number of inhabitants is below[24] 300, and the gathering is called a meeting, not a council; no association of that particular village with others is allowed to supersede the separate meeting. The executive body is thus always the parish meeting. The grouping order necessary for the amalgamation of parishes for council purposes is never given without the closest scrutiny by the County Council first, or confirmed by the Imperial authority in London afterwards. In no case is the parish meeting dispensed with. Amongst the groups we have seen discussing their affairs, one might have noticed women as well as men; for though by the decision of the Court of Appeal in the case of Drax *v.* Ffook, women can vote as occupiers and not as owners, they are, whether spinsters or wives, eligible to be parish councillors. Should the parish be without a village hall, the schoolroom is the usual place of assembly. The one spot peremptorily forbidden by the law is the public house; unless no other rendezvous be procurable for love or money. It is still too early to pronounce definitely as to the permanent effect of these institutions. The general tendency has perhaps been towards the falsification alike of the extreme hopes and fears which they first raised. Their jurisdiction includes all the functions of the old vestries and their officers, together with other novel and more drastic prerogatives. The discussions are often limited to dull details of mechanical routine, but are sometimes, as to-day, sufficiently animated. In the typical parish (a generalization from actual experience), the question of opening or closing footpaths across fields chances closely to divide parochial opinion. A little time ago, the vexed problem was the limits of a village green which had been so much diminished by encroachments as to cease almost to exist. Another issue that a little while hence will furnish material for debates not less vivacious is that of allotments for cottagers. Here as in the other cases, there is a strong faction on either side. A heavy parochial whip has been sent out by the two sets of leaders. If the matter is decided in the affirmative, and the allotment or village green extension, as the case may be, is carried, a measure of expropriation may follow, should the County Council, as superior body, sanction the scheme, and should the Local Government Board, after hearing the case of the dissidents, confirm the parochial proposals. As a check to parochial extravagance, the money to be advanced by the central authority is not to exceed one-half the value of the local rates. Inheriting the power of the vestries which they displaced, the bodies now mentioned have in their hands the appointment of overseers of the poor. 'One man, one vote'[25] is the universal principle. The employers of labour, that is the farmers, are consequently liable to be placed in the minority by their servants. Hence proceeded the assertion that the signal withdrawal of the farmers from the Liberal party, as being morally responsible for the measure, largely brought about the crushing defeat of the Gladstonians at the general election of 1895. If the farmers were animated by any such resentment towards the party which they identified with the real authorship of the Act, the feeling has already to a great extent passed away. What remains of it will no doubt evaporate as eventually sentimental grievances of this kind seldom fail in England to do. Impartial evidence, gathered at first hand, does indeed show that the increased mutual knowledge generated between farmers and their hands in the parish meeting room has resulted in an actual improvement of the relations between the two classes. All the national processes which legislative change sets in motion have worked slowly in England. It was not till the third or fourth appeal to the constituencies under Household Franchise was made that the permanent results of the peaceful revolution in 1868 could be computed with even approximate accuracy. The final consequences of the extension of the franchise to counties by the Liberals in 1884 have not yet declared themselves. It would, therefore, be premature as yet to make any definite deductions, social or political, as to the working of a system which has been operative only since 1894.

One thing more about them may, however, be said. As in the case of the farmers where, with a fair measure of conciliation and tact, the occupiers of the soil find their official intercourse with its tillers unexpectedly harmonious, so as regards the relations between the villagers and the clergyman, in the position of the latter as the spiritual, and often inevitably to a great degree the temporal, head of the community. Briefly stated, the effect of the Parish Meeting, or Parish Council, is to restore to the villagers certain of the rights which, in the old Manor Courts, they had possessed. Where the clergyman combines with the practical sense of an educated man a freedom from a suspicious antipathy to the civic activities of his flock, there is not only no jealousy of the parson's intervention in the deliberations of the parish hall; but the experience which he is likely to bring to the work is welcomed by the councillors as a valuable aid to their discussions. If, when standing for a seat on the council, the rector issues an address savouring of dictatorial self-assertion; if from his pulpit he prescribes a plan for the conduct of these elections; the reverend gentleman may find himself at the bottom of the poll. When, however, he deals with his parishioners on the assumption of their equality in all non-religious matters with himself, he disarms or prevents jealousy. He has a fair chance of being chosen by acclamation to the president's chair at the little Board.[26] Parish Councils have for the first time in the rural history of England developed a sense of responsibility among those to whom a decade ago the idea of rural citizenship, with obligations as well as rights, was unintelligible. They have, therefore, impressed the minds of those concerned in them with some sense of power. Thus far, no tendency has been displayed to use that power in a revolutionary fashion. A body which, like the average parish parliament, numbers from five to eleven, is not likely to prove a tempestuously democratic, or violently revolutionary assemblage. Finally, though, on the requisition of three members to the chairman the council may be convened at any time, its actual convention is never brought about more than thrice, and seldom more than once in a twelvemonth. Not the least good which this institution carries with it in most neighbourhoods is its creation of wider, less mean, more liberal interests in daily life, and with these interests, subjects of conversation for the village community more generous than private affairs of individual households;—what Hodge, the ditcher, does so late at night in the neighbourhood of the squire's game preserves; how much money the carpenter's wife paid for her new bonnet; or how her daughters afford so gaudy a display of Sunday finery. That the new machinery has thus far worked with less friction than might have been expected may be inferred from the statistics courteously forwarded to the present writer from the Local Government Board under date August 7th 1896. As has been said already, the Imperial authority at Whitehall acts as arbitrator in all cases of difference between the popular Parish Councils and the more exclusive County Councils as to the acquisition of land for allotments. At the time now mentioned, it was the calculation of the President of the Local Government Board that four cases had occurred of appeals by Parish Councils against the refusal of the County Council to make the allotment order; and that in fourteen cases in which orders have been made by County Councils, eight protests against them have reached the Local Government Board from persons immediately interested.

Ascending from the lowest deliberative unit in the new scheme of local self government one passes from the Parish Council to the District Council. If it can be questioned whether the average villager as yet fully appreciates the gift of power made to him by the legislature in 1894, no such doubt can exist as to those bodies that are a little higher in the deliberative scale, the District Councils. The local parliament in the parish hall may sometimes be unattended by a single cottager. The District Council, if it be not as yet popular, is at least never neglected. Seats on it were from the first objects of local ambition. This is only what might have been expected in an age, a marked feature of which is the quickened interest of all sections of the community in whatever affects the health or comfort of the labouring classes. The District Council, as its name implies, has a more than parochial dignity. Its jurisdiction is practically commensurate with the sphere of the old Rural Sanitary Authority. The relief of pauperism however, forms a first and special care of this body, the members of which are also the Guardians of the Poor. Its place of assembly is the chief small town of the neighbourhood; not indeed the County town, but generally a convenient town where there happens to be a railway station. The District Council has already contracted certain associations of local fashion. The ladies of the country side have entered warmly into its business, and often constitute a majority of its most active members. There is, of course, the complaint of impulsiveness brought against the District Councillors. Thus the domestic idea is regarded by them with more respect than it secured from their predecessors, the Boards of Guardians. Guardians were elected by the plural vote of the larger ratepayers. They had, moreover, to satisfy a property qualification in their own persons. District Councils in theory know nothing of, and in practice are affected little by, such conditions. The ex-officio magistrate, without which no Board of Guardians was complete, is systematically absent from the new District bodies. The *personnel* of the new Councils, which occupy a place midway between the Parish and the County assemblies, presents a notable contrast to that of the superseded Boards of Guardians. County magistrates are not, in virtue of that office, ordinary members of these bodies, which are almost solely elective. The dignity of the body, however, is well maintained. The chairman of the District Council becomes, in consequence of that position, a County magistrate with powers as plenary as if he were the nominee of the Lord Lieutenant. Sometimes, of course, the chairmen of the District bodies are already magistrates. That is, however, the exception. There now exist in the United Kingdom about a thousand elective magistrates, being chairmen of District Councils. By far the greater part of these are new to their legal responsibilities. A few are working men. One District Council in Northamptonshire is presided over by the master of a small railway station on the Midland line. Another has for its chairman an agricultural labourer; a third is controlled by an ex-policeman; a fourth by one who supports himself on the cultivation of sixteen acres of land. The effect of popular election is not limited to the discharge of those duties connected with pauperism and sanitation that are the primary concern of the District bodies. Assessment committees, and school attendance committees are both drawn from the District Councils. The latter of these, it is generally admitted, have done their work better since they ceased to be composed exclusively of employers of labour, and since they have become representative of industry as well. [27]

The Poor Law, which has been in force during the whole of the Victorian era, was, as scarcely needs to be said, among the earliest achievements of the Reformed Parliament. Bitter and prolonged as was the resistance to portioning out the country afresh for the relief of pauperism instead of congregating the poor of each parish in their own workhouse, the beneficent results of the change have long since been universally admitted. 'The new Bastilles' was the name first given to the unions which the Act of 1834 created, by the opponents of the Bill, with a view to excite popular feeling against it. Only the most hardened paupers, who objected on principle to industry of any kind, complained of the modicum of labour exacted from the occupants of the new workhouses. Even these shirkers have become reconciled to some sort of industry. The improvement in the habits of the whole working class was conspicuous and immediate. Thus, as in his History of the period, Mr Molesworth points out,[28] in four unions of the Midlands, there were in 1834, 954 able-bodied paupers. In June 1836 there were only 5. All the rest were in regular work. In the county of Sussex, the most inveterately pauperized in England, there were in 1834, 6,160 paupers. The Act had not been in operation two years before this total was reduced to 124. By 1836 the Act had become operative in twenty-two counties. The average of the reduction of the rates in these was 43½ per cent. The Commissioners of Enquiry, on whose report the new legislation was based, predicted that the application of their principles would restore and improve industry, would create or confirm habits of thrift, would increase the demand for labour as well as the wages of the labourer, and generally would promote the welfare of those who lived by manual toil. The Queen had not ascended her throne when the erewhile opponents of the Measure confessed that these anticipations were already fulfilled. It was not to be expected that bodies so essentially different from the old Boards of Guardians as the District Councils are would administer the Poor Law in the same spirit or on the same principles as their predecessors. Few socio-economical questions of the day have provoked controversy so bitter, or divided skilled and conscientious partizans into such mutually envenomed factions as the conditions on which relief from the rates should be granted to the necessitous poor. The uncompromising advocates of the workhouse test system, compulsory residence, that is, within the workhouse walls, maintain that in this way only can systematic pauperization be avoided, and that so alone will the not uniformly industrious poor realize the stigma of coming upon the rates. On the other hand, it may be argued that in innumerable cases timely charity from the common fund will prevent the utter break up of a needy, but not necessarily indolent home. Paupers, it may be said, who will not work, and who are, therefore, not proper objects of compassion, are never kept by any sense of pride or shame from taking up their quarters in the local union. Thus, may it not be false economy to make absolute destitution and homelessness a preliminary condition of parochial help? On these points, those who differ will never agree. What it is now relevant to point out, is that the administrative methods of the new Councillors have very generally shown a reaction from the more stringent, and less sympathetic policy of the old Boards of Guardians. Thus, the workhouse test is far less often than formerly made the condition of poor relief.

Organization in every department of activity or interest is the most conspicuous movement of the last quarter of this century. Some years must yet elapse before we know the exact point to which the legislation now reviewed has disciplined and stimulated the inhabitants of rural England. The object of the controllers of the vestries that the Parish Meetings have superseded was to keep village administration in the hands of a privileged and comparatively leisured minority. Hence it was not unusual to fix the hour for the vestry meeting at 9 a.m.; when of course the male population would be at work in the fields. Under the Act of 1894 the Parish Councillors are bound to hold their sittings in the evening after the day's work is done. From a historical point of view this legislation cannot be charged with being revolutionary. The powers which the new bodies have assumed in checking encroachments upon common land and other like offences are indeed considerable. That prerogative is not an innovation. It is rather a revival of the authority which in the old Manor Courts, presided over by the steward of the Manor lord, the freeholders could exercise. Beyond question, the most far-reaching and important change introduced into country life by the new machinery is the infusion of the elective element into the nominated magistracy. This has not yet received the attention it deserves. Under the earlier régime, as has been said, certain guardians had a seat at the Union Board because they were magistrates. Under the existing dispensation certain Justices of the Peace owe their place on the magisterial Bench to the fact of their performing the duties of District Councillors and Guardians of the Poor. The relations between the two positions are thus exactly inverted. That the tendency of this change is to soothe the suspicions once widely prevalent as to the principles on which Justices' justice was administered does not seem disputable. It has also positively increased the respect in the rural mind for the law itself as the expression of wisdom and equity. The cordiality with which the older magistrates, nominated to the Bench by the Lord Lieutenant, have generally welcomed their popularly chosen colleagues has undoubtedly strengthened this wholesome sentiment. Finally, the same career in the local polity as of old remains practically open to men serving on the Commission of Peace. Where the old J.P. Guardian was a man who did good work on the Union Board, he seldom now is debarred from doing it still. Even when he is locally unpopular, a well-earned reputation of ability or aptitude for affairs is pretty sure to bear down purely personal objections and secure his return to the District Board; a tolerably conclusive proof of the fitness of the parochial constituencies for the measure of autonomy which they have received.

CHAPTER VIII
THE NEW ERA IN ENGLISH COUNTIES

General effect of the legislation of 1888 on the English County system. Some analogy between the principles of corporation reform (1835) and County administration reform (1888). But the earlier act did not touch, as the later did, the power of magistrates in Quarter Sessions. Social circumstances, *e.g.*: the growth of an educated and leisured class of residents in country towns which have made the time ripe for the new legislation, and distributed throughout England a new class of capable local administrators. Contrast between County town life before and since the establishment of County Councils. Social pictures of county supremacy on Sessions days in the old era at hotels and shops. County self government has not destroyed the old County traditions nor deprived the old administrators of their former career. Exact functions of County Councils, and points of administrative communion between them and the old magistrates. Local idiosyncrasies of these Councils, North and South.

The legislation of 1888 has influenced the entire scheme of life in provincial England. The social prestige of the County system, centred in the extra-judicial power of the magistrates at Quarter Sessions, had not been affected prejudicially by the Corporation Reform Act with which, two years before the Queen's accession, the Whig Ministers in the newly reformed Parliament supplemented the Poor Law changes. The principle underlying the County Council Act of 1888, and before that the Corporation Act of 1835 was the same. Both marked a return to a more ancient but a less exclusive system rather than a sudden introduction of a new. Like the monarchy itself, the borough corporations were in their beginnings genuinely popular. As in the case of the Throne, so in that of the provincial polities; it was the Tudor sovereigns who narrowed and enervated the privileges of their subjects. Under the Plantagenets and throughout the Middle Ages, the corporations were elected by popular constituencies, the freemen of the town. Contracted in their scope under Henry VIII. and Elizabeth, these charters of urban freedom were, under the Stuarts, so remodelled as to transfer from the burgesses to the Crown the appointment of municipal officers. Municipal liberty having passed away first, municipal purity gradually followed. The abuses in civic life had at last equalled the corruptions which reduced parliamentary elections to a farce. Within a year of Lord Grey's Reform Act, the urban scandals became too gross to be ignored longer by a comparatively purified House of Commons. As in the case of the procedure with reference to the Poor Law, so in the business of municipal reform a Commission was appointed to investigate the corporations of the United Kingdom. The national enthusiasm for the men who had carried electoral reform against the House of Lords, against the Duke of Wellington and against the King was soon followed by a Tory reaction. In the hope of regaining for his party some of the popularity which it had lost, Lord John Russell in the summer of 1835 submitted the new measure to the House of Commons. Two millions of Englishmen were affected by the scheme. The then existing municipal bodies had been shown as little to represent the property, the intelligence, even the population of the towns as the unreformed Legislature had reflected the convictions and desires of the Kingdom. Charitable funds, bequeathed by former benefactors for the impartial relief of local want, had by the abuses of years, been diverted wholly from their original purpose. They were dispensed habitually to the political friends of the men who had for the time the upper hand in the affairs of the borough. These moneys seldom mitigated any honest distress; they were squandered in the periodical junketings of the authorities of the township, with the political partizans who were their fellow feasters. Two novelists of our time have drawn famous pictures of the same great nobleman. The original of Disraeli's 'Lord Monmouth' in *Coningsby* was the Marquis of Hertford, whose henchman, the 'Mr Rigby' of the novel, was the John Wilson Croker of real life. Thackeray's 'Marquis of Steyne' in *Vanity Fair* was the other literary likeness of the same titled original. In real life the Marquis of Hertford, as 'an honest burgess,' was a chief member of the Council of Oxford city. The Right Honourable John Wilson Croker, his lordship's steward, and his confidant in all things were the chief associates of this eminent noble in the control of the municipality of the University town. The Corporation Act of 1835 swept away these scandals, and made municipal government a fairly popular reality. Thenceforward in all corporate boroughs, the Town Council was chosen by resident inhabitants rated to the relief of the poor. Since 1835 the power of the magistrates in boroughs is exercised by the borough bench with an appeal to Quarter Sessions, that is, to the County. The measure did not a little towards re-establishing the popular privileges which had existed before the Tudor encroachments. London was not included in the Act. With that exception, all English towns on the Queen's accession had for two years been in the enjoyment of self-rule. Cobden is one of the many opponents of caste exclusiveness who have testified to the purity and efficiency of the unpaid magistracy in their functions of County administrators. These persons were of course never responsible to any constituent body. They satisfied the property qualification by the possession of £300 in land, or by the receipt of an income of £100 a year. Notwithstanding the thoroughness of the work done by them on the Quarter Sessions committees for regulating extra-judicial business, they represented no interest except that of the party enjoying political power, the supreme embodiment of which was the Lord Lieutenant of the County.

Meanwhile, there had been great changes in the composition of the residents at, or in the neighbourhood of the chief provincial towns of England. The close of the Crimean War reinforced the class now mentioned by the addition of educated, but not generally wealthy, men, who desired peacefully to spend the residue of their days in districts with which family ties made them familiar or which conveniences of sport or education rendered attractive. The absorbing powers of the capital have progressively increased during recent decades. Opulence and fashion have swollen the great public schools of the country to unmanageable dimensions. Still, to a large percentage of English parents in the upper middle class, Eton and Harrow are not the only two possible schools of the realm; life may be lived as pleasantly, and more economically, in provincial centres like Bedford, Ipswich, Bath, or Cheltenham as within the metropolitan radius. Schools, not less than hotels, have become matters of joint stock enterprise, and of federal proprietorship. The excellent places of teaching which abound in such towns as those just mentioned are pre-eminently a product of the Victorian era. Thus it has come to pass that, at innumerable spots throughout provincial England, during recent years there have settled families, not pretending to historic antiquity or distinction, but still agreeably supplementing the social resources of the County district. Many, perhaps most of these newcomers have served the Queen in peace or war, abroad as well as at home, and are thus likely to have acquired administrative experience of different sorts. These are just the people qualified to relieve their older neighbours, the local squirarchy, in their administrative work. If the machinery for establishing County Councils had been created in the era of the Corporation Reform Act, or during the first half of the present reign, it would have been premature, would at least comparatively have failed, instead of proving, as it has done, a signal success. How this institution works will best be judged by contrasting certain phases of County town life to-day and in the pre-County Council epoch. To visit such a town on a day when the magistrates were sitting at Quarter Sessions was like making an excursion into feudalism. One used to alight at the stable yard of the chief hotel to find no room for one's horse. The County's steeds had possession of the best stalls. They could not of course be displaced by, or consort with, the quadrupeds of less considerable riders. Inside the building, the same tale was retold and on every storey illustrated afresh. The apartment normally the coffee room was consecrated to the exclusive use of a select party of County justices who were still at luncheon. The drawing room on the first floor was in the occupation of the women kind of their relatives who were just about to refresh themselves after shopping with a cup of tea. The member of the general public who entered the chief shops of the place on the day devoted to County customers found himself and his patronage at a discount. The tradesman, in civil terms, profoundly regretted his inability to attend to the chance comer until he had satisfied the needs of the County justices' ladies who were expecting every moment to be called for by their lords from the Sessions House.

Socially, not less than geographically, the County continues to exist. The wives and daughters of the country gentlemen who are County J.Ps. set the fashion in their neighbourhood and are still regarded as moulded out of a clay slightly superior to that of which their neighbours consist. But as an object of fetish worship the County has in most districts disappeared. The chief linen draper in the town, as he watches the County ladies, in their dilatory fashion, toy with one fabric after another, can scarcely suppress a look of impatience on his well disciplined face. He happens to be, not less than the father and husband of these ladies, himself a member of the new County parliament. He is exercised by a fear lest the special committee of the body on which he is serving should have decided the question of certain alterations in the approach to the local capital in which he is interested, before he has had time to get to the place of meeting. Unconsciously, perhaps, his manner towards the lady relatives of his council-colleague, the squire and magistrate, has lost something of its old deference. Still, the foundations of the social system remain the same. The fusion between classes of which the County Council is the expression rather than the cause has not brought us appreciably nearer the revolution and the Red Republic than had been done by the earlier parliamentary reforms. Here, as in the case of the District bodies, the law of the survival of the fittest is unrepealed, amid the administrative changes of the hour. County magistrates who are specially qualified for County administration are elected to the new Councils in numbers sufficient to leaven these bodies. The service that they performed on the committees of the old Sessions is still discharged by them on the Boards that are of more recent growth. The venue of their exertions is changed. The opportunity of their labour remains the same. Probably the association of County gentry with country town traders widens the view of the squires, acts as an incentive to greater energy, and is actually productive of better work. Certainly, since this machinery has been in operation the intellectual resources of the chief centres of population within the jurisdiction of the County Council have been improved. New art and science museums have come into existence. The people's parks, which were already known in country towns, are better kept. New reading rooms and libraries have opened their doors.

During the rather more than half a century that elapsed between the Corporations Act of 1835, and the Local Government Act of 1888, the chief reforms effected were in the province of sanitary administration, were mainly due to the efforts of individuals, such as Mr Stansfeld in 1872, and were generally incorporated in the Public Health Act of 1875. These sanitary measures contained the principle on which the area of the United Kingdom was finally redistributed. For the purposes of County Councils, England is mapped out into sixty-one administrative counties. Each of the electoral divisions of which the County consists has a Councillor of its own. The electors are practically almost identical with the parliamentary constituencies. In the case of municipalities inside the County area, the Local Government Board decides the share of representation to which it is entitled, and allots to it on the Council one or more members, as the case may be. In addition to the councillors created by purely popular election, a certain number of aldermen, not to exceed one-fourth of the whole body are chosen by co-optation among the Councillors themselves. The term of Council office is three years. The chairman, however, who is not forbidden to receive a salary, holds his place only for one year. Like the District chairman, the County president too, without satisfying any pecuniary qualification, becomes, by virtue of his office, a County magistrate.[29] Like the Council electors, the chairman and the six co-opted aldermen are subject only to the condition of having the County vote. As in parliamentary elections so in County elections, the polling is by ballot. The incidental expenses, however, which are strictly regulated by the number of the constituency, are defrayed, not by the candidate or his friends as in parliamentary competitions, but out of a County fund. The prerogatives of magistrates in whatever appertains to the licensing of public houses, and exercised in Quarter and Special Sessions, are untouched by the new bodies. With that exception, the functions of Quarter Sessions are superseded practically by the Councils. As a consequence, the sessional attendances of the magistrates have largely fallen off; though there still exist many opportunities for joint action between the new Councils and the old Sessions. For instance, the County police is controlled by a committee whose members are selected from the old magistrates and the new Councillors. Again, when the object is to acquire fresh land for popular use; to open or endow local museums or libraries, to establish emigration funds to the Colonies or elsewhere, united action between the two bodies is usual, but not compulsory.

It has been seen already that the Local Government Board at Whitehall looks for the endorsement by the County Council of the Parish Council's proposal to acquire land for allotments and, with that purpose, to obtain loans from the State purse. Similarly, the borrowing powers for less local objects of the Councils are definitely limited. The consent of the Imperial authority is needed to enable the Council to borrow for permanent works or to issue County stock. The Council's annual Budget is closely criticized not only in debate by the Councillors themselves, but by the Local Government Board. The property rated to the County Rate which is the security for all loans is inspected periodically by Imperial officers. The accounts are examined by Imperial auditors. Meanwhile, it may be conjectured justly that the considerable remnant of country gentlemen of the old school, that is, the nominated magistrates, who have seats on the new Councils, secure a salutary continuity of administration and expenditure between the new régime and that which preceded it. There is, of course, far more of local variety and of adaptability to the needs of special neighbourhoods in the composition of the Councils than it was ever possible there should be in the *personnel* of the Quarter Session administrators. This fact would alone make it unsafe, as may be seen by one or two instances, to generalize about these bodies. If in the Midlands, in the Metropolitan shires, and in the South Western counties, power remains to a great extent in the hands of the old order, and only the tenant farmers on a large scale have influence on the Councils, the experience of the northern mining districts and of Wales is very different. Throughout the Principality, as well as on the Gloucester and Monmouth frontier, the small farmers, who are Nonconformists to a man, find themselves, for the first time in their lives, a decisive power in their neighbourhood. The same is the case in Durham. Here the colliers, also for the most part Nonconformists, containing among them many of the finest, most upright, and manly specimens of the English race, practically dominate the Council of the Northern shire.[30]

CHAPTER IX
COUNTY COUNCILS AND CLASS FUSION

Reasons why London was not included in the Corporation Reform Act of 1835. Popular character of its municipal government contrasts with Royal encroachments of various periods. Various schemes and commissions of City reform since the Queen's accession. 1853 Commission alone produced practical result in the establishment in 1855 of Metropolitan Board of Works. Relations between this Board and the City. In 1888 Board of Works superseded by London County Council. Exact relations between London County Council and the City Corporation. National and Imperial uses of Lord Mayor illustrated. Possible changes of the future. Class fusion illustrated by titled Mayors and other provincial usages.

The London County Council, which has little in common with the bodies already examined except the name, has been reserved to a chapter dealing chiefly, like the present, with the polity of the capital. For the exclusion of London from the Corporation Act of 1835, sufficient reasons, whether of principle or procedure, may be assigned. To the former category belongs the fact that the City Corporation, even during the encroachments of the Tudors and the Stuarts, had, unlike other towns, maintained its original liberties. It was, amid all its vicissitudes, not, as were the corporations described above, a self chosen, but a popularly elected, body. Secondly, the Corporation Commissioners did not think that a period within three years of Lord Grey's Reform Act, before the ground swell of the excitement, caused by that measure, had subsided, was suitable for deciding complex and far-reaching issues like those presented by the civic system grouped round Guildhall. At the same time the Commissioners expressly recorded their opinion that the magnitude of the problem ought not indefinitely to postpone an attempt at its solution and that the difference between the administrative problems of the provinces and the capital was one chiefly of degree. In their separate report of 1837 the Commissioners confined their observations on municipal London to cautious negatives. The suggestion of creating a congeries of Metropolitan municipalities had even then been made, as it has often been renewed since. This proposal was officially condemned on the ground that it would only remove an anomaly by provoking an abuse. At the same time, certain functions of local administration were specified which, within the Metropolitan area would be performed most efficiently and economically under the control of a single authority. In 1853 a special Commission enquiring into the affairs of the City Corporation, among various, but not very definite proposals, hinted that the seven parliamentary boroughs, of which London then consisted, might supply the machinery for a heptarchy of municipalities administratively associated in a central Board of Works. That body was to be composed of persons chosen by the different boroughs of the capital. No active steps were taken towards the heptarchical subdivision of the capital. But in 1855 the Metropolis Local Management Act was introduced by Sir Benjamin Hall. The result was the Metropolitan Board of Works, which remained an active power until it was superseded by or incorporated in the London County Council of 1888. All the then existing parishes and vestries of London sent members elected by the vestries to this central body. The Board of Works supplied the long desiderated unity of administration. If during its thirty-three years of rule it made many enemies, it also effected great improvements. In 1884 the Administration of Mr Gladstone produced a fresh measure of London reform. The chief feature of this was the absorption by the City of the powers of the Metropolitan Board, and the redistribution of parochial functions concentrated upon the City Corporation but now to be divided among new local bodies. This proposal proved equally unacceptable to the City which was already overburdened, and to the parochial bodies which were soon to be superseded. It had, however, advanced the question a perceptible degree; had renewed popular interest in London reform, and helped to create the public opinion which, four years later, in 1888, enabled the Cabinet of the day to include London in the Bill for establishing County Councils throughout the kingdom.

In the provinces, as has been seen, the County Councils practically have taken over the civil and administrative duties of magistrates formerly exercised at Quarter Sessions, but have in no way touched the judicial functions of these gentlemen as representatives of the Queen's justice. In the same way, the London County Council has left absolutely unimpaired the judicial power of the Lord Mayor and Aldermen organized in their various courts to execute and administer the civil and criminal law according to the historic traditions of the capital. The Common Council of London City has, therefore, to-day the powers which belong to an ordinary borough council. Outside the City limits, the London County Council with respect to drainage, sanitary arrangements generally, new streets and local improvements of all kinds, in courteous, rather than compulsory, concert with the City discharges the functions of the former Board of Works, or of a County Council in the provinces.

That this friendly association between the two Metropolitan bodies, the old and the new, should be practicable is what a knowledge of the past would lead one to expect. In civic affairs London has always been an encouragement and example to provincial townships. The magnitude of its area, the preoccupation of its inhabitants with the complex interests and exhausting activities of their daily life render London, as Cobden and others have always discovered, an impracticable headquarters for political agitation. But long before our great provincial centres had been possessed with that intense feeling of corporate life which is now the boast of Manchester or Liverpool, Birmingham, Sheffield, or Leeds, the traders who did their business under the shadow of Guildhall were united by a citizenship scarcely less stimulating and constraining than that of the little Republics of old Greece. One, and each of them, they took a patriotic pride in the material perfection to which the conveniences or comforts of their existence had been brought. Thus, as Lancashire has seen with exultation the reflection of its collective life in the great cities on the Irwell, or the Mersey, the entire Kingdom and Empire have always recognized the symbol of their unity as well as of their greatness in the prosperity or in the institutions of London City. Nor does anything more impress the mind of our foreign neighbours or our Colonial fellow-citizens than the response to appeals for help in the day of distress which issue from the Mansion House as from the heart of the English race. It is thus no exaggeration to say that the past records and contemporary services of London have proved of some moral use in promoting the success of the very latest municipal reforms. That a final stage in the evolution of London government has yet been reached no one believes, least of all the men who completed the preliminaries for the formation of the London County Council. The Commissioners of 1886-7 have themselves pointed out the anomaly of applying to London, even though it be called a County, that form of administration which is primarily intended for provincial shires necessarily identified not with commerce and trade, but with rural pursuits and interests. The City Corporation and the London County Council will both be relieved when the existing period of transition with its occasional friction and confusion is terminated. The relations between the two bodies must necessarily be mutually those of armed vigilance rather than of cordial alliance. What is known as the Unification Commission was, it must be remembered, appointed at the instance of the London County Council. The chief points of the proposal thus made was as earlier paragraphs have shown practically to merge the City in some new municipal body to the East of Temple Bar. As matters are, while the Lord Mayor and Aldermen are not County Councillors of London, the City of London has four representatives on the Council. These, however, are not the nominees of the Corporation, but are chosen by the ordinary civic constituency, the ratepayers. As a matter of fact, though by a coincidence, of the four present representatives on the Council of the City, one is an Alderman, and another a common Councilman. But they were not chosen in these capacities. As little therefore as the vestries or as the local boards is the Corporation directly represented in the London County Council, which was created by the Act of 1888. When, in addition to its hospitable and charitable functions, the services rendered by the City to the cause of national education are remembered; when it is considered that nearly all the great Guilds help by exhibitions to support poor students at the Universities, and that they also make regular and liberal contributions to the Science and Art department at South Kensington as well as to the Finsbury Institute for the technical training of mechanics and artizans, the extreme unwisdom of any scheme of London reform which shall, by wounding the pride, discourage the generosity of the historic interests now mentioned, becomes self-evident.

However cordial at the different points where they are brought into contact the relations may be between the old Corporation and the new Council, it is seemingly agreed on all sides that the true method for administering that vast and not yet finally circumscribed area inhabited by what De Quincey once called 'the nation of London,' has still to be devised. The suggestions for future reform are innumerable in quantity and Protean in character. Whether the existing areas of separate control inside or outside the City gates should be maintained; whether they could be replaced conveniently by five or ten, by six or fourteen, separate municipalities; these are the problems that, as in the past, so in the future, seem likely long to divide the minds of Metropolitan reformers. The City Corporation has already divested itself, *e.g.* in its relations with the Commissioners of Sewers, of certain functions which normally belong to a town council. Hence, it has been suggested that this process might be continued till the Lord Mayor and Aldermen practically merged themselves in the existing County Council of the capital. In that event, the administrative jurisdiction of the County Council, instead of stopping abruptly at Temple Bar, as it now does, would stretch from the Strand to the Guildhall. From thence it would radiate throughout the region generally spoken of as the City. There does not seem much likelihood of the fulfilment of this contingency. Such a scheme could not work well unless it were embraced with practical unanimity by those whom it immediately concerned. The Lord Mayor of London, and the authorities gathered round him, naturally regard with jealousy even the apparent infringement of their historic prerogatives and immemorial dignities. Nor in the interests, not of the City alone, but of the nation at large is it desirable that anything should be done which might actually impair the prestige, or even sentimentally wound the vanity of the exceedingly useful, and uniformly patriotic and generous men who are installed by annual succession in the Mansion House. The lofty attributes with which the French press and stage have invested the Lord Mayor are not entirely caricature. They indicate corresponding realities. The Lord Mayor has always been and remains to-day far more than the local head of a great municipality. In all parts of the Three Kingdoms, he, with his colleagues, controls territorial estates equal in extent, and far more than equal in revenue to a Continental Duchy. The Guildhall, with its library and museum; the Mansion House; schools and institutions like the City of London School, Ward's City of London School for Girls, the Guildhall School of Music; these are only a few of the foundations that are naturally presided over by the Lord Mayor. They all exist, not so much for the glory of the City, as for the service of the community. Possibly it might be useful to classify the complicated functions of the Sovereign of the City. It would then be seen how far the principle of devolution could be applied to his various attributes in their daily exercise. There are those who have imagined that within the empire of the Lord Mayor of the future there might be created subordinate municipalities which would act as local committees under his central control.

Few better proofs of the general intelligence and efficiency of the County Councils could be given than the wisdom with which they have discharged an educational duty of the first importance imposed upon them by a new parliamentary statute. The Customs and Excise Act of 1890 placed certain funds for the development of technical instruction at the disposal of the Councils. That duty in the opinion of the critics at Whitehall was performed so efficiently as to suggest the formation of committees from the Councils to ascertain local needs of technical training as well as practically to control, in the place of School Boards, the elementary education of the Kingdom. The Measure wherein that proposal was embodied, the Education Bill of 1896, has been withdrawn. The tribute to the capacity of the Councils remains. The educational functions with which it was suggested to charge these bodies, will without doubt, some day be performed by them.

The wholesome fusion of classes promoted in the country villages and towns by recent local government reforms has been already noticed. The same tendency has been pleasantly illustrated at other points in the social scale. The legislation of 1888 neither diminished the prestige nor trenched upon the province of the Imperial Parliament. The only point at which it can be said to have touched that body was the process connected with the acquirement of land for public purposes by Parish Councils. Here, it will be remembered; if the order, decided on by a majority of the Parish Councillors, is ratified by the County Council; if, after that, it passes the ordeal of the Local Government Board; then the Whitehall department issues its sanction for the purchase of the land in question. That order has forthwith the validity of an Act of Parliament, without having gone through the different stages incidental to legislation at Westminster.

Meanwhile, hereditary legislators have to a considerable extent practically interested themselves in, and placed their experience at the disposal of, the County Councils; just as, with regard to Parish Councils, the clergy and gentry have been seen assisting at the deliberations of their tenants or their flock. The first chairman of the County Council of London, Lord Rosebery, only abdicated that office to become Prime Minister. Among his successors were the former permanent head of the Board of Trade, Lord Farrer, the Vice-President, Sir J. Hutton and Sir Arthur Arnold. The same process of social amalgamation has been witnessed in the provinces not less signally than in the capital. The premier peer of England, the Duke of Norfolk, has been Mayor of Sheffield. Lord Derby has filled the same office at Liverpool. Lord Windsor, in succession to Lord Bute, has been Mayor of Cardiff. Lord Beauchamp has presided over the Corporation of Worcester. Lord Hothfield, one of the largest landowners in Westmorland, has been Mayor of Appleby. Lord Lonsdale has been Mayor of Whitehaven, Lord Zetland has held the same position at Richmond. Lords Dudley, Ripon, Warwick, and Crewe, have presided each of them over the Corporations of the towns from which respectively they derive their titles. If this be a reversion to an earlier usage of the aristocracy in England, the precedent had been almost forgotten before the practice was revived. The analogy that to most persons will more readily have suggested itself is rather that of the cities of mediæval Italy; when the commercial community of Genoa was presided over by a lineal descendant of the Doges; when a Doria was at the head of the municipality of Rome; when Milan and the Lombard capitals, which first instructed England in arts of luxury and in modes of splendour, were controlled by Magistrates whose pedigrees might have stretched back beyond the Empire to the classical Republic. If the civic association of the titular nobility with the new democracy of England were not popular it could not exist; and titled Mayors would cease to be returned by popular constituencies. If on the other hand the municipal compliments failed to bring with them to their recipients an opportunity of usefulness as well as a sense of honour, they would not be accepted. The plain historical truth is that the patrician landowners of England have recognized the opportunity of removing the remnant of traditional estrangement between themselves and the masses of their countrymen of which so much was heard during the years immediately following the new Poor Law of half a century since. Of that sentiment, little known except by hearsay to the present generation, the most vivid, and not the least trustworthy record is still to be found in a fiction already mentioned in these pages, Mr Disraeli's *Sibyl*. Nothing but reciprocal good can come of these relations between the classes and the masses, to apply to them the distinguishing terms used by Mr Gladstone.

An apprenticeship to the routine work of municipal affairs in view of the changed subject matter of the questions of the day is more likely to prove practically serviceable for those born into the condition of hereditary statesmen than a course of diplomatic lounging in the Courts and Chanceries of the world, or even than the grand tour which now extends from Calcutta in one direction to Chicago in another. The class fusion that is so signally the social product of the present reign has culminated in the conditions which, in the fulness of time, legislation has rather recognized than produced. Long before provincial self government was established upon the lines indicated by the Acts of 1888 and 1894, the spirit which in 1867 prompted Edward Denison to take up his dwelling in Whitechapel had been exemplified by philanthropists of both sexes in London and elsewhere. The sister of Mr Chamberlain is one of several ladies at Birmingham who systematically co-operated for purposes of house to house visiting in the poorest quarters of the town that they might practically instruct the wives and daughters of working men in the arts of domestic management, and in the possibility of keeping the humblest homes happy, healthy, comfortable and clean. Similar organizations have done a like work in Manchester, Liverpool, Sheffield, Leeds, and no doubt in all our great centres of population.[31]

CHAPTER X
THE SOCIAL FUSING AND ORGANIZING OF THE TWO NATIONS OF 'SIBYL'

Exterior of a University settlement in the East End. The scene in the street. Various functions of the University settlers within. General supervision of health arrangements; putting the law in motion to that end. Conciliation between masters and men. The higher culture for East End pupils. Coaching a Bethnal Green four. Earlier efforts in this direction. S.W. slum boys in Belgravian drawing rooms. The young lady and the ubiquitous jockey. The settlements and clubs of to-day at the East End of London foreshadowed by earlier organizations in the provinces by the agencies of the Christian socialists; the working man's colleges, etc. The inside life of settlements and clubs to-day. Schools of character to all concerned. General analogy between West End and East End clubs. Some details of the good work done for, and by, both sexes, young and old. A City missioner's testimony. Then and now in the East End. A. Toynbee; T. H. Green and this movement. Rules suggested by personal experience for the conduct of this intercourse between different classes.

In a street broad and clean, as many of those at the extreme East End of London are, but still in the heart of an unmistakably poor, often a squalid quarter, is a house which, resembling its fellows in architecture, presents even as to its exterior the appearance of being inhabited by persons of a better sort. On the pavement outside groups of men, women and boys are waiting for admission. The door is opened presently, not by a servant of either sex, but by a person, evidently a gentleman, in the prime of early and athletic manhood. The men and women are introduced into a room on the ground floor. Their host hears perhaps of a fever having broken out not a hundred yards off; of a home distrained upon for unpaid rent by an impatient landlord, or gutted of its furniture by the broker's man, of a local inspector's failure to order the demolition of dwellings unfit for human habitation, of a strike imminent near the Docks, and likely in its results to leave tens of households without clothing or food. If this be the tale poured into the ears of the young Oxford or Cambridge graduate, he at once hurries off to see whether his personal influence, strengthened as it is by some years of varied local experience, cannot move the landlord to give his tenants one more chance; or whether the tact, that is not likely to grow rusty from lack of practice, cannot promote a compromise between masters and men; or whether the knowledge of municipal law, acquired by many months of careful reading, with the help of local illustrations, cannot be so brought to bear upon the parochial officer as to induce him duly to execute the letter of the Sanitary Statute.

If none of these things have to be done the lads may be called into the chamber which serves the resident for the purpose of study and pupil-room. It is, in fact, just such another den as very likely may have been occupied by our graduate a couple of years ago when he was an Eton master and saw his private pupils at his quarters in Keate's Lane. It by no means follows that the subject of his conversation with these East End lads is primarily scholastic or strictly educational. The University resident at the East End has brought with him the taste for athletics of all kinds which he acquired on the Isis or the Cam. He devotes as much time to teaching his East End pupils cricket or oarsmanship as to awakening and satisfying their interest in learning or letters. He and his party are therefore very likely to be seen taking the omnibus or rail if the afternoon be fine, to Putney or Hammersmith, where the spectators on the bank will soon be cheering a Bethnal Green four practising starts with a Leander or a University crew.

The building of whose interior a glance has been given is probably the hired house in which two or three members of the Academic or Public School settlement live. It may be one of the many clubs for adults, for boys or girls, which to-day are scarcely less common in the purlieus of Poplar than are clubs of a different sort in St James's or Pall Mall. These institutions are among the chief instruments of civilization on which the new settlers rely. No one now doubts the service to the manners and the morals of the upper classes rendered by the joint-stock caravanserais of the West End. Three bottle men, as readers of Thackeray may see for themselves, lasted throughout the epoch of coffee houses. They very generally disappeared with the replacement of coffee houses by clubs, and with the early adjournment from the dinner table to the smoking room. A club-man in his cups was found to be a nuisance. A new public opinion was created against an old vice. Protracted potations rapidly became, as Hamlet desired, more honoured in the breach than in the observance, till a toper in St James's became as rare as a bishop in a billiard room. An analogous reform in the East End as in the West has been worked by a like agency. The fittings and the environments of the institution differ in the two regions. Their moral influence is identical in both. In this matter, too, as in so many other modes of social improvement, the Metropolis followed the lead of the provinces. East End clubs, in contradistinction to boozing-dens, existed indeed long before University settlements were known, or before Edward Denison's first visit to Whitechapel was paid; but not before at Lancaster in 1860, the Working Men's Mutual Improvement and Recreation Society had flourished for some little time. In like manner, the University settlements now spoken of, had been preceded by the organized efforts of the Rev. F. D. Maurice, Thomas Hughes, and other representatives of what was then called Christian socialism, to establish by the college for working men in Great Ormond Street a living connection between University influence and industrial well being. Even working men's colleges had existed in the country before F. D. Maurice made his London experiment. Sheffield witnessed the first of these during the early fifties. Oxford and Cambridge towns were not long behind. Thus the promoters of academic settlements were not without the benefit of the experience of their earlier predecessors as well as of the public spirited association of their contemporaries. The Working Men's Club and Institute Union had been founded in 1862 by Lord Brougham and Lord Lyttelton. Much of the machinery, as well as a nucleus, for the endeavours of the settlers of a latter day was ready to their hands before they began their work. But the idea of the combination of gymnasium with club, and of the subordination of the roughest kind of physical exercise to the ends of social culture had not been illustrated on any extensive scale before institutions like the Repton or the Oxford House clubs were controlled by men who took this way of doing honour to the name of their University or their school.

Before this, ladies living in Belgravia, revering the memory and example of Maurice, were in the habit of inviting to their drawing rooms from the alleys and by-ways in which the fashionable district abounds poor boys who could not be tempted, even with the bait of magic lanterns, to the night school. The work was found to be rather too exacting. The chivalry of street boyhood did not, as might have been foreseen, prevent the urchins from gratifying their sense of fun at her expense in the drawing room of the amateur teacher. The joke of giving, as their names, those of the famous jockeys of the hour, Fordham, Archer, Cannon, as the case may be, proved too good to be resisted. Gravity, once disturbed, could not be restored. The pupils could do nothing but laugh at each other's fun. Their would-be instructress had to acquiesce in their removal when the servant came to clear away the tea things. A public feeling in favour of order and even cleanliness has long since been generated in the boys' clubs controlled by the University settlers. First the prejudice against collars as an article of attire goes out; then a feeling in favour of washed hands sets in. In the recreation rooms upstairs boxing gloves are provided as a safety valve for the escape of the superfluous humours of Arab animalism. Then by slow degrees comes the hour when bagatelle boards may be introduced without danger of their being used for the breaking of heads, or of the bagatelle cues being employed for the perforation of the lath-and-plaster walls instead of for the propulsion of the ivory balls.

The parents are provided with the same sort of accommodation as their children. The adult clubs are chiefly of two kinds. In some, the first purpose is political. In that case the society becomes an agency for the propagation of Radical ideas, and probably an outwork of Trades-Unionism. But from many of these foundations politics, which are generally synonymous with advanced Liberalism, are excluded. In the majority, if not in all, of the non-political clubs, intoxicating drinks, though under conditions they were sanctioned by the early founders, are by common agreement, prohibited also. The popularity of these clubs with the wives of their habitués is a sufficient proof of the sobering tendency of the new resorts. In all cases, the women gain scarcely less advantage from them than the men. Each club is an organization for social entertainments and hospitalities to which members are free to bring all their women-kind.

The dominant idea of the University settlement to which these clubs are subsidiary, is to give the poorest and most densely populated working class districts the benefit of a resident gentry such as, in the clergyman or the squire, is generally commanded in rural parishes. The local separation between employer and employed; the fact that the workers do not, as they used to do, dwell to-day within sight of their masters, but are segregated into colonies of their own in another quarter of the capital, and have no access to persons better informed than themselves in the troubles and perplexities, big or small, of everyday existence, first prompted those who realized the perils of this situation, to make, as far as might be, common lot with their less fortunate fellow creatures. In New York, where these societies seem to have been known longer than in England, the phrase employed is Neighbourhood Guild. To obtain the local knowledge which can alone enable the most wise or charitable to give effective help, habitual residence under conditions and in neighbourhoods identical with the class to be benefited is absolutely necessary. The University settler becomes in fact a sort of Delphic Oracle, consulted on all embarrassing contingencies by the entire neighbourhood. To vary the simile, the enquiries made of him are not less various than the questions which the editor of a popular print undertakes to answer in his Correspondence column. The doubts and complications arising out of the law of landlord and tenant, especially out of that enigmatic being, the compound householder who so long obstructed the path of Household Franchise, require a practical knowledge of often abstruse legal points and sometimes compel resort to a professional solicitor. The precise steps necessary to put in motion the Statute for the removal of hopelessly insanitary dwellings are not likely to be within the knowledge of the dwellers by the Docks. These are only a few of the knots which for the instruction of those he has chosen for neighbours, the University settler must be prepared to untie. And this is only one of the duties which he actually performs. He not only takes part in the municipal government of his neighbourhood; he helps others to take part in it, too. Already he has himself sat on School Boards and trained grown-up pupils to fill his place.

Nor is it always necessary to speak in the masculine gender. University settlements are no more limited to a single sex than the tripos work of the Cambridge Senate House, or of the Extension lecture rooms, which enjoy the patronage of the Oxford schools. Nor is it the Universities only that are represented by these feminine settlements. The Cheltenham Ladies' College, one of the earliest, if not the first, of that kind of public schools for English girls, has already made a sensible difference in hundreds of lives in the extreme East of the town. Among the special works of which the Cheltonians have set an example is that of enabling poor mothers to procure for their children at seasons of need not merely the conventional 'day in the country,' but a sojourn of weeks, or even months, in a healthy cottage home on the seashore of Sussex or on the fragrant uplands of Kent. The machinery for accomplishing this has now been brought to a very high point of efficiency and indeed perfection. The Cheltenham ladies and their colleagues, associated under the respective matrons of the institutions, have a long list of simple honest folk within a few hours' journey of London who can be trusted to look after their little charges during their stay beneath their roof, and to send back to their homes the small boys and girls visibly better than when the children were first received by their hosts. Sometimes the Guilds of the different sexes may combine their efforts for hospitalities and entertainments, a magic lantern and lecture, it may be, or during the winter season a Christmas tree followed by supper and a dance, or to speak more correctly a general, though not uncontrolled, romp.

Most, if not all, of these East End clubs, which the University settlers aim at teaching their members to run for themselves, rather than indefinitely to leave their management to outside friends, are federated to a central association, that the late Lord Lyttelton took a prominent part in organizing. This was the body which, as has been already said, decided that stronger drinks than water should not absolutely be forbidden; but that central supervision should be exercised closely over all the establishments, and that prompt action should be taken when any breach of order, corporate or individual, was reported. The average standard of order maintained has improved, and is still improving. Generally and individually the club members have realized that their material interest lies in checking the first beginnings of misconduct, and in dealing with the offenders not only as guilty individually of a breach of order, but as violating the first principles of collective fellowship. Such a conviction indicates the progress made towards the creation of a healthy opinion upon social matters with those who, a few years ago, would have been pronounced by experts to be invulnerably proof against any sentiment of the sort. East End boys are no doubt mischievous, and even destructive creatures. So, for that matter, are all boys. If their brethren of the upper class do not break out in the same way as the urchin East Enders, that is because the march of refinement through the West End has trodden out the old race of small boys and girls, and has replaced them by little men and women whose only childhood will be reached in their dotage. The very interesting experiences recorded in the volume entitled: *The Universities and the Social Problem* [32] do indeed include some rather alarming freaks of the East End waggishness. But to the small boy in rags the process of whose reclamation from Bethnal Green barbarism to Christian civilization had only begun a few weeks since, the trick of pouring a paraffin can over a sleeping foe, and then applying a match, did not seem more of an atrocity than to a West End boy of the same age might have appeared the joke, borrowed from the pantomime stage, of placing the baby on the floor by the door for the entering nurse to tumble over, or of putting a red hot poker too close to be pleasant or even safe to the nose of an unpopular housemaid. Men like Dr Barnardo or General Booth, who both know something of Whitechapel waifs and strays, have not thought that poor children in the East End inherit an exceptional amount of original sin. Nor have they, nor others, discovered that ragged boys, nurtured on fried fish and unspeakable pudding are incapable of being disciplined into habits of obedience, truthfulness, and humanity, even though their ideas of permissible humour be not bounded by the conventional limits of gentleness and good taste. The administrators of the People's Palace, for some time after the fancy of Sir Walter Besant was translated into fact, were not always sanguine as to the feasibility of civilizing their young patrons, even through the agency of pictures or swimming baths, thick slices of bread and butter, buns, and fried haddock purchasable not much above, if not something below, cost price. To-day, though the social deportment in the pleasure grounds of Bethnal Green may lack the superficial polish, and the innate breeding, of the crowds at the Westminster Aquarium or the South Kensington Museum, a considerable advance is recorded on the part of the Harrys and the Harriets of Poplar and Whitechapel towards the carriage and conduct of the cynosures of less outlandish suburbs on Bank Holiday. There is no body of men who know unfashionable London better, or who deserve more honour for the service which they render to it than the members of the London City Mission. The work of these missioners, though undenominational, is religious rather than æsthetic. But they are shrewd observers of the social aspects of the neighbourhoods they visit. Their opinion of the practical results of the agencies that have here been described may be summed up in the words of a missioner to the present writer: 'It marks an epoch in East End civilization of which ten years ago Christian charity would itself have despaired.'

The functions exercised by the controlling authority of the Working Men's Club and Institute Union are educational as well as disciplinary. There is no reason now why any one of the affiliated societies, however impecunious it may be or however impoverished the district wherein it may exist, should be without as good a library as one of Mr Mudie's subscribers, or should not know almost as much about the history and antiquities of the British capital as the late Dean Stanley himself. The controllers of the union often make liberal advances in money for the purchase of books by the local clubs. Should these funds not be forthcoming, book boxes with wisely chosen contents circulate among the members of a Home Readers' Union. The volumes thus distributed are real literature. The subjects to which they relate are methodically mastered by the readers who themselves have selected them, and have not acted on the initiative of the more highly educated residents, Peripatetic encyclopædias like Mr Augustus Hare or Mr Percy Fitz-Gerald are ever ready to 'take walks' with them. Omniscient divines, such as Dean Bradley or Dean Farrar personally conduct them through their cathedrals into the heart of English history. Nor are the literary studies chosen merely because they are likely to help the student in his everyday work, and therefore improve his earnings. The biographies of the statesmen and soldiers of old Greece, the dramatic vicissitudes of the Republics of mediæval Italy, even the philosophy as well as the language of Dante or of Macchiavelli are taken up by men after a day's manual work with an energy that would shame an undergraduate returning from a wine party to read for his Schools. This, too, seems to be the experience of American settlements as well, of Hull House, Chicago, or of Andover House, Boston. In their capacity of schools of citizenship, as well as of education, the American settlements have felt the immediate benefit of the Oxford influence and example, incarnated not only in Arnold Toynbee, but in the late T. H. Green, professor of mental and moral philosophy, whose pupil Toynbee was; while Green in his turn had been the disciple of Benjamin Jowett. Good citizenship was the ideal ever present to the late Master of Balliol in his dealings with his pupils, just as it had been present centuries earlier to Socrates in his discourses to Plato, or in his conversations with Alcibiades. Green probably made the most valuable of recent contributions to the speculative thought and science of his University, of his country, or of his generation. He was, also, a prominent and active member of the Oxford Town Council, and of other local bodies. By their lessons in the theory and practice of citizenship, taught more publicly than it fell to the lot of their master to teach, the Oxford settlers at the East End have improved upon Green's example, with much of his zeal, and not a little of his success. More than twenty years ago the East End neighbourhoods now mentioned were first visited by the present writer, to inform himself for those portions of an earlier work, relating to that part of unfashionable London.[33] Thanks mainly to the influence and teaching of the Rev. S. A., since Canon, Barnett, great improvements in the domestic economy and material fittings of the humblest households had begun, even then to be visible. The later experiences and their social results, which have now been described, have made it possible for the writer to contrast the East End of the later eighties with that of the later nineties. The scale and the precise modes of manifestation are of course widely different, but if due allowance be made for the social disparity of Mayfair and Mile End, it is no exaggeration to say that the increased attention to the prettinesses of life shown in the boudoirs and drawing rooms of fashionable London is reflected in the parlours of those purlieus now spoken of. These though their civilization be still incomplete, have to a great extent under the agencies that have here been examined, ceased to be manifestly poverty-stricken or repulsively hideous. The discipline of character that the settlements provide for the settlers is at least as salutary as the consequences they involve for the district, whether it be in the East End, in Camberwell, or in Notting Hill, that the settlement is made. The social education for the West End club-man of his joint stock palace in Pall Mall is trivial in comparison with the training that will be administered to him by a few visits to the East End club, of which he may be made free, or of which perhaps he may himself have been a founder. The assistance of those in such a position as the University settlers is appreciated cordially by the working club-men. 'We always need, to begin with, the help of some of you gentlemen of the Oxford Settlement. Afterwards if you look in upon us from time to time, we can keep things going pretty well for ourselves.' Such is the common remark of the settler's friends. Of its practical truth there seems little doubt. The University settler and his friends in his own station are not, however, on this account to suppose that within these clubs their society is courted as a favour or regarded as a compliment. On the contrary, the atmosphere and sentiment of the place are uncompromisingly democratic. If the West Ender, by his talk or manner contributes anything of pleasure or profit to the social pool, then he is welcomed just as he would be on the same terms in the coteries of Pall Mall, or at the dining tables of Hyde Park. If, on the other hand, there be, perhaps unconsciously to himself a suspicion of condescension in his bearing, or a too visible effort after edification in his talk, then as peremptorily as he could be among his own equals at the West End, he will be voted a bore, and shunned as a prig at the East End. The roughest specimens of Whitechapel or Ratcliffe require, not less, but rather more tact for their management, than other people need. If that be forthcoming, the youths, whose element is destruction, whose ambition is to be a professional pugilist or a champion strong man, but who seldom desert one to whom their loyalty has been given, and who are the raw material with which British officers win victories on the field against the heaviest odds, are perfectly manageable. The most aggressively republican of Arabs becomes the most gentle and gracious of fellow citizens. But if either of them detect signs of patronage among their politer visitors, their backs are at once up; metaphorically their bristles stand on end like hairs upon the fretful porcupine. Familiarity they neither expect nor wish. They would even resent it. Their view of the courtesies and proprieties of friendly intercourse do not in effect differ from those held by their superiors. They are abundantly content if these ideas are practically recognized. It is with those who are removed by a single degree in the social scale above these rough diamonds, but who consider themselves altogether their superiors, that the difficulty begins. No class of servants are so troublesome as the footman tribe. No section of the body politic proves more vexatious than the intermediate order between the lower and the very lowest division of the middle class. The genuine working man in the working man's club causes none of those embarrassments which one encounters upon a level rather higher than that of the outcasts of Camberwell or Notting Hill, the waifs and strays of Whitechapel or Shoreditch. If the problem of association is practically to be solved to the satisfaction of all those concerned, there is one golden rule always to be followed. Postulating a common amount of tact and sense on the part of the University settler, or one who essays that position, let him begin by being natural, let him shun as the presage of failure any conscious effort to place his lowlier fellow creature at his ease. Above all, let him never offer his hand to shake. He himself may think the manual overture will gratify the person to whom it is made by showing that the maker 'has no false pride.' A greater mistake there could not be, as a well-born academic socialist found out when, to demonstrate his faith in the equality of all men, he shook hands with his brother's footman on receiving his shaving water. These strained amenities are an effort to him who volunteers them, and an infliction to him who receives them, a failure and a mistake, in fact, all round. The secret of Edward Denison's and of Arnold Toynbee's influence for good with their inferiors was that they not only knew these truths, but always acted on them. Hence, by their own work, and by the generation of workers whom they raised up to follow them and at whose methods we have now glanced, so much was done to span the gulf separating 'the two nations' of the English people.

CHAPTER XI
FROM AN UNTAUGHT GENERATION TO FREE SCHOOLS

State irresponsibility for national education on, and after, the Queen's accession. Summary of early movements towards educating the people. Lancaster and Bell as pioneers of educational systems. Samuel Whitbread's faint foreshadowing of W. E. Forster's Education Act. Brougham as educational pioneer. First State grant to Church and Nonconformist schools. Increased in 1839. Education Department completed on the principle of State aid to all schools, Protestant or Roman, satisfying State examiners. Mr Lowe at the Education Office and the grant stationary. National education the law of the land by the Forster Act of 1870. Free education under Lord Salisbury 1891. Elementary education now organized. External change in the English landscape. Secondary education waits. Details of progress recently made towards this.

Those processes of organization which seem in all departments of national activity the special features of English life during the last half of this century have nowhere been more visible than in the educational arrangements for the long neglected mass of the English people. Slowly, with occasional relapses, yet upon the whole with sure and steady progressiveness, there is being prepared, there now seems within measurable distance of completion, the ladder that will enable any English boy and many English girls to accomplish the ascent from the gutter to the highest teaching of the University, and so to gain a position from which merit and industry, favoured by fortune, will command the highest career open to either sex. All this has been accomplished within little more than half a century. Till 1833, the educational responsibilities of the State practically were ignored. In that year there was made for teaching purposes a grant of £20,000. The sum with annual increments was thenceforth dispensed annually by the Treasury to the National Society in Broad Sanctuary, as representing the

Church of England, and for the Nonconformists to the British and Foreign School Society. Till a twelvemonth after the passing of the first Reform Act, the most active of organizations for teaching the people had been the Church of England and the great Dissenting bodies as in the case of the School Society just named. The Roman Church on both sides of St. George's Channel never neglected its educational duties. The Sunday School system, to which, on the eve of the Queen's accession, thousands of working men and women owed practically all the teaching they had received, were started towards the close of the eighteenth century by a Gloucester printer, Robert Raikes. In the last year of William IV. there had died a Nonconformist, a member of the Society of Friends, Joseph Lancaster. To him and to the English clergyman associated with him, Andrew Bell, founder also of the Bell Classical Scholarship at Cambridge, were due the first beginnings of a scheme of instruction for the whole English people.

Two or three decades earlier than the grant of 1833, Parliament fitfully recognized its educational responsibilities. In 1807 Samuel Whitbread, the son-in-law of Earl Grey, tentatively anticipated the spirit of Mr W. E. Forster's reforms, three score and three years afterwards. By his proposal of parochial schools throughout the Kingdom, Whitbread ranks as the earliest education reformer of the nineteenth century. Within a decade, in the year 1816, Brougham took up the question, obtained a committee to enquire into the educational resources of London, and in 1820 himself brought forward an early Education scheme of the nineteenth century. The project perished amid the denominational tempest of religious rivalry which it evoked. Nothing after this was done till the date at which we have already arrived, 1833. Then, in faint forecast of the £7,000,000 now spent by the State on the teaching of its youthful subjects, a grant for that purpose of, £20,000 was for the first time made, distributed as we have seen between the Protestant Churches of the country. After an interval of six years, in 1839, Lord Melbourne's Administration excited much obloquy, and raised the 'No Popery' cry against them, by allowing a share in a grant, now increased to £30,000, to Roman Catholic schools. The House of Lords, in an address to the Queen, condemned this new policy of religious emancipation. The vote was only carried in the Commons by a majority of two (the figures being 275 for, 273 against). Together with certain other changes that endure to this day, it became law. Hitherto, the State grant had been administered by the Treasury. Now for the first time an Education Department was organized under the Lord President of the Council, and four other members of the body. The Vice-President was appointed in 1856. During Lord Palmerston's long term of office, in 1857, the Education grant rose to £451,000. It became more expressly understood that henceforth the specific duties of Education Minister were vested in the Vice-President.[34] With the steady increase of the annual grant, its province of usefulness was extended also. Subject always to the principle of State inspection, where State aid was received, the grant was no longer limited to assist the erection of new schools. Even before 1857 it had been allotted in due proportion to help schools already in existence. Portions of it were also received by training colleges for teachers. The quality of the instruction supplied in the schools had not improved in proportion to the liberality shown by the State. In 1859-60, the grant was more than a million. A Commission reported most unfavourably as to the efficiency of the schools. Hence in 1862, the then Vice-President of the Council, Robert Lowe, afterwards Lord Sherbrooke, enforced the Education reforms which he had already drafted, and initiated the policy of payment by results; in other words, the regulation of the amount of the grant in schools by the success of the scholars in the yearly examination. The teachers grumbled, but the taxpayers were relieved. The rate of increase in the grant ceased automatically. In 1870 the Education Vote amounted to one and a quarter millions instead of, as, but for Mr Lowe's drastic, if indirect, retrenchment, it would have done, to something like thrice that sum.

No fundamental change took place till the Education Act of 1870, always associated as that will be with the name of W. E. Forster. Dealt with as to its provisions, its working and its results, in elaborate detail in the author's preceding work, *England*, the Measure now rather more than a quarter of a century old will here be summarized sufficiently by reminding the reader that this legislation empowered the election of School Boards throughout the Kingdom, but maintained the system of voluntary subscriptions, and only compelled the institution of School Boards where voluntary effort had failed, and in the Time Table Conscience Clause provided a security for individual liberty. Mr Mundella's Act of 1880 made education absolutely compulsory throughout England and Wales, whereas before then the power of compulsion was left to the local authorities. In all State-aided schools, religion was to be taught either at the beginning or end of school hours, so that, without disturbance to the general curriculum individual children could be withdrawn from the sacred lesson at their parents' will, without incurring any disability on that account. These provisions met with the usual fate of legislative compromises. They deeply offended many sections. They entirely pleased none. The battle between religious and irreligious training, between what have been called the National and the Denominational systems was not decided in 1870. It has been fought over again more than once since then. It remains unsettled to this day.

During the whole of that decade, the Education Acts were supplemented with detailed legislation of a consolidating or modifying kind. No organic change took place till in 1891, the Government of Lord Salisbury adopted the first of the three Fs, long since propounded by Mr Chamberlain, and by abolishing the School pence which scarcely repaid the trouble of their collection, made elementary education as free to all children in the land, as by the law of 1870 it had practically become compulsory. The proposal to free the schools was not universally popular with the party to whose lot it fell to execute that policy. So, notwithstanding its exclusive traditions, that party had, under Mr Disraeli a quarter of a century earlier by its Household Suffrage Bill, recognized and established the English democracy. The plea on which those who had begun by resisting free schools finally accepted them was the expediency of accepting the inevitable first, and secondly the practical wisdom of obtaining credit for Conservatism by doing well and wisely that which at some future time the opposite party would have ingratiated themselves with the masses by doing badly. The results of free education were speedily visible in the increase of the children educated throughout the land. The increase of children in schools during the five years preceding the Free Education Act of 1891 had been 269,903. During the quinquennial period after the Act the increase was 421,860, or, in round numbers, just double. The first rung in the educational ladder for the benefit of all classes of the Kingdom had been fixed firmly by the Act of 1870. It was not, nor was ever, regarded by its authors as a complete Measure. It provided no regular system of higher grade schools intermediary between the most elementary teaching, and the more liberal culture of the grammar schools. The only supplement that it received from the Government under which it had become law was the Endowed Schools Act of 1874 for re-arranging the funds and remodelling the curricula in secondary endowed schools throughout the country. Private effort and local enterprise usefully came in where Mr Foster's Education Act had stopped short. In various parts of England, and especially in the great northern counties of Lancashire, Durham and York, School Boards, fortunate enough to possess controlling spirits of exceptional enlightenment, exercised their legal power to establish schools of a higher kind specially for the teaching of science or art, and generally for the tincture of the youthful mind with a more generous training. Such schools received additional grants from the Science and Art Department at South Kensington.

In this way the 1870 Act at once partially enabled the child of the poorest parents to mount through the elementary schools, to the secondary schools of the Kingdom and thence to those seats of learning at which the picked youth of the country enjoy the choicest opportunities of mental culture, or are qualified for the highest posts in after life to which English ambition can aspire. The problem now to be solved, which is in actual process of solution and of which a few years more may probably dispose, is the completion of the national ladder of learning by a more thorough organization of the agencies for advanced knowledge throughout the country, and for the passage of the pupil from schools of the lowest, to schools of the higher grade. Just as, during recent years of the present reign, successive Reform Bills have increasingly nationalized the legislative Chambers at Westminster; so the tendency and the result of the transformations undergone by the great public schools and by the Universities, that they feed, is to draw more closely together the bonds uniting these institutions with the nation as a whole, to widen their curriculum, to infuse a popular element into their governing bodies, and to make them not merely the instructors, but the representatives of the intellectual interest of the land. By remodelling the governing bodies of Eton, Winchester and Harrow, the Public Schools Act of 1868 appreciably quickened and deepened the sense of public responsibility inherent in these corporations. Nearly thirty years' experience of the Endowed Schools Act justifies the statement that the work accomplished for the grammar schools of the country is analogous to the results which the earlier legislation has yielded in the case of the more famous seats of youthful study.[35] A wholesome spirit of competition now animates the governors of these old if often still obscure endowments,[36] and daily causes fresh usefulness to be extracted from money resources, long suffered to remain idle. Later legislation, whose general aspects have already received attention in these pages, has conspired to deepen the sense of obligation, and to stimulate to efforts, most salutary for the taught, alike the governors of and the teachers in the schools.

Shortly after the Local Government Act of 1888 was passed, important functions, educational and financial, were given to the new County Councils. The grammar schools were quick to perceive a new opportunity. In 1889, thirteen representatives of the Councils, in some cases at the instance of their older colleagues, received seats on the governing bodies of the Secondary Schools. The corporations thus reformed have already begun vigorously to deal with an abuse inveterate in their smaller schools. Where the value of the endowment, from charges on the property of which it consists or from a fall in the value of land, has fluctuated the governors have been in the habit of farming out the school to the headmaster. They have, that is, assigned to him the income of the trust, and such fees as he can charge. In return, the pedagogue takes upon himself the charges of working the school, and of the teaching of a fixed number of free boys. The tendency of this arrangement is, of course, to repeat in the present day the experiences of Do-the-boys Hall under Mr Squeers in *Nicholas Nickleby*. The headmaster has upon him the burden not only of his educational work, but of the solvency of his daily business. His own stipend is too small to admit of his paying competent assistants. He becomes a pensioner on the caprice of well-to-do parents, and the instrument of their not generally very enterprising will, or of their too enlightened pleasure. The only chance for the small secondary schools thus circumstanced is their rescue by some of the more public-spirited and opulent of the governors. But this relief is forthcoming so rarely that the Commissioners generally recommend the closing of all schools existing under these conditions and the application of their endowments to purposes less obviously foredoomed to failure. Other instances of the waste of existing resources for secondary education are even more frequent and not less serious. Grammar schools of competent calibre are often geographically crowded so close together as to obstruct and paralyse their mutual efforts. Thus in South Devon there is at Chudleigh a grammar school of considerable repute. Within a radius of sixteen miles, *e.g.* at Ashburton, Totnes, and Bovey Tracey, there are similar schools capable of good work, but lacking a population of parents and children to fill their empty benches. A like experience has often occurred in the case of establishments which, not being endowed grammar schools have not come under the notice of the Commissioners. Bath, for instance, has long possessed more educational opportunities than most other cities in the West of England. The oldest of her proprietary colleges, that in the district known as 'Grosvenor,' to some extent became merged in the less ancient Sydney College. That in due time produced a successful offshoot, the Somerset College. These two latter institutions during some time were healthily stimulated by mutual competition. At last the rivalry became profitable only to the prestige and numbers of the secondary schools that, managed on the same principles, had come into existence first at Cheltenham, then afterwards on the Clifton downs, near Bristol. In 1885,[37] the Somerset and Sydney Colleges were amalgamated under a single headmastership by the title of the Bath College. This to-day is doing an excellent work. But it is the North and East of England where by the needless reduplication or ill-advised contiguity of schools of the same grade the most flagrant breaches are committed against the first laws of educational economy. Thus, in the West Riding, the grammar school of Ossett has a fair endowment but practically no scholars. Again, Walsingham in Norfolk, with less than 1,000 inhabitants, possesses a substantially endowed school, the boys attending which had decreased from 32 in 1884 to 11 in 1894. Not far off at Ipswich, Norwich, and Bury St Edmunds, are establishments of historic fame, and of present competence. As an alternative to the continued waste of such opportunities, and to promote the local completion of the educational ladder indicated in the beginning of this chapter, the Commissioners suggest that the Walsingham school should be transferred bodily to Fakenham, a prosperous and not distant town, or that the Walsingham funds should be converted into scholarships and exhibitions to be held at other places of education within the County. There are other small grammar schools which, while just paying their way, have evidently no considerable career before them. Here the spirit of commercial impatience is apt to suggest the conversion of these places of teaching into elementary schools of the better sort. But the places now spoken of often have honourable traditions, and resemble families that, through no fault of their members, have, by misfortune, come down in the world. Local patriotism dwells fondly on the creditable past of such institutions, and would be wounded by their irrecoverable degradation. Surely, therefore, these schools might have the chance of retrieving their position. That, in effect, is what the Commissioners say. Assign to the decayed grammar schools their exact place in a reorganized system of secondary education. On condition of their adapting themselves to the place thus appointed to them, assist them out of the public funds to regain full effectiveness, and, together with that, to renew their past prosperity.

Within the last few years an illustrious proof has been given that a great school is not necessarily so sensitive a plant as to depend for its life-blood and vigour on the essential qualities of the soil wherein its founders first fixed its roots. 'The Grey Friars' of Thackeray's novels, the Charter House school, which, in R. C. Jebb, now Professor of Greek in, as well as M.P. for, Cambridge University, has produced probably the first scholar of the latter half of this century, has been removed recently to the great advantage of the physical health and literary industry of its scholars from its ancient home in London city to the rural neighbourhood of Godalming town. A precedent for the same policy in less famous instances, exists. At Hewsworth, in the West Riding, Archbishop Holgate's grammar school has been closed from lack of pupils. Its endowment was merged in that of the grammar school at Barnsley, a town of some 36,000 inhabitants, midway between Sheffield and Wakefield. Within half a dozen years, the Barnsley school, thus reinforced, had achieved prosperity, and had adopted the chief recommendations for effective teaching made by the Commissioners. One thing is at least clear. If liberal education, the process, that is, of the development of the whole intellectual nature, without immediate reference to the supply of material needs, is not to become a mere tradition; if, in other words, literary culture be worth preserving as an instrument for training the mind, the cry for merging the grammar schools in agencies of specialist and technical teaching must not be adopted without consideration. The highest experts in this matter agree that the scientific and technical instruction, which is visibly a paying investment, runs in these days no risk of neglect, but that there does exist a danger of the first aims and the true methods of intellectual training being ignored. Even thus, fairly equipped as England is with the machinery for secondary teaching of the scientific sort; still better furnished as she might be with a more economical administration of existing resources, fresh provision must be made on a liberal scale before the national appliances are complete. The Commissioners have estimated in those counties to which they have paid special attention the number of boys or girls educated at secondary schools at 21,878 or 2·5 per 1,000 of the population. As might be expected, the local inequalities revealed by this analysis are very great. Thus, in Bedford, because of the great Harpur endowments of that small county, the proportion per 1,000 is 13·5. In Lancashire the population has altogether out-grown the secondary endowments available: the proportion per 1,000 is only 11. In Yorkshire it is only 2·1. In Warwickshire, notwithstanding the splendid foundations of Edward VI. at Birmingham, and the wealthy and famous schools of Warwick and Coventry the proportion remains as low as 5·2.

While these aspects of latter day education are being considered, the honourable connection of the new Local Government bodies with schools must not be ignored. Liverpool, like South Lancashire generally, is not ill supplied with agencies for secondary or technical instruction. The means of the capital and of the county would both be inadequate but for the very liberal contributions made by the County and City Councils to the schools owned by religious and secular proprietors for boys and girls. The companies thus spoken of are enabled by the Councils to carry on more than one particular school at a loss, even though the deficiency be not made good by the profit on other schools of the group. In view of the fact stated above that a great educational pioneer of this century, Joseph Lancaster, was a Quaker, it is interesting to know that the most recent Education Commission selects for special compliment the Ackworth Friends School, open to members of the Society from all parts of the world, in the West Riding of Yorkshire. The more searchingly the enquiry is made, the more distinctly there emerges the fact that private venture schools created by voluntary effort, conducted by individual enterprise, render the most effective service to secondary education. These institutions open their doors for public examination. They cannot, therefore, be unworthy of State help. Their headmasters and their chief assistants generally are University graduates, and were often trained at one of the older public schools. A fresh rung in the ladder of educational ascent will have been made when these schools, 30 per cent. of whose teachers are University graduates, receive official registration as well as whatever material assistance State recognition can confer. State organization of national teaching primary or secondary by means of official examination and by grants of money proportioned to the proficiency established by these ordeals, is, as we have seen, and as it must always be remembered, not more than half a century old, and in a national sense, scarcely therefore passed beyond its infancy. The progress indicated in the preceding remarks justifies the expectation that before very long the edifice will be crowned with a completeness worthy of the strength with which the foundations have been laid, and more than one storey of the fabric has been already reared.

Other agencies now fairly at work in this enterprise remain to be mentioned. Before the Universities had sent their resident representatives to the East End of London, and to the slums of other great cities, they had actively identified themselves with the encouragement and the testing of secondary teaching throughout the land. The Oxford and Cambridge middle class examinations began to be held during the early sixties in the chief towns of provincial England. Very soon afterwards, there were organized successively the Higher Schools Examination Board, conducted by the two Universities, and the University Extension Lectures which presently will be examined here with some detail.

But by this time the fresh appliances for elementary and secondary education, both directly or indirectly growing out of the legislation of 1870, had changed the physical, not less than the intellectual, aspect of the whole country. In the city as in the suburbs, in the provinces not less than in the metropolis, the whole landscape was thickly dotted with new piles of buildings, in all cases constructed with marked regard to convenience and health, substantial always, in some cases really handsome. These were the new Board Schools, some for the most elementary instruction of the rising generation, some for higher grade teaching, or for imparting to older children the rudiments of scientific and technical knowledge. In the former case the buildings were surrounded with gravel playgrounds, furnished with swings, parallel bars, and other gymnastic appliances, all used under the direction of an expert teacher, who alternately with the drill sergeant came on duty during play hours. The structures annexed to the actual class-rooms of more advanced pupils were furnished within as laboratories and work rooms. Here the pupils were apprenticed to the initial duties of the chemist, the gasfitter, the electrician, or of any other vocation they were destined in after life to follow. One result of this new start in the State schools was the stimulus of a competition that produced a perceptible increase of efficiency in the private schools not necessarily identified with any religious denominations. These private schools still exist; and by the greater elasticity of their system, and special opportunity of encouraging individual originality in the learners they are the salutary and indispensable adjuncts of the State institutions. The generally superannuated and often inefficient dominie, alternating between slumber over the text book from which he was supposed to teach, and unprovoked aggressions with his cane upon the knuckles or any other available part of the persons of his nearest pupils, is now replaced by a master in the prime of life and energy, who, if not a graduate in a University, has the certificate from one of the many examining bodies which attest his fitness for the place. Almost imperceptibly to-day, the elementary school matures into the secondary school. Nor is the development always indicated by a change of name, for higher grade elementary schools, to employ their official title, in which, after all his Standards have been passed, the Board School boy, between 15 and 17 years old is placed, are in effect not less of secondary schools in their way than Cheltenham or Westminster. Controlled indeed by the School Boards, they prepare their pupils for matriculation at the London or other Universities, or for entrance upon professional life. Thus, in 1894, exclusive of the capital, the English School Boards controlled no fewer than sixty establishments of this higher type. Of that number thirty-nine were organized science schools. The fabric of the buildings had been provided out of the rates. The cost of the superior teaching was defrayed by private munificence, or by the State grants conferred by the Science and Art Department which, in South Kensington began as, and still is, a portion of the Department in Whitehall. The number of boys and girls, according to the latest statistics, educated in these superior Board Schools is 4,606 boys, 2,023 girls. Outside London, the great majority of the institutions now spoken of are in the Northern, the Midland and the Eastern counties. Advantage to all concerned might be expected to accrue could these higher Board Schools be managed, if not in active concert, yet with the practical approval, and pecuniary encouragement, of the County Councils. When, therefore, by the withdrawn Bill of 1896, it was proposed to invest County Councils with educational powers, but not, save in rural districts, to displace School Boards, the new duties contemplated for those Councils were not those for which they entirely lacked preparation. In addition to all this, the great City Guilds, notably the Drapers, Grocers, and Goldsmiths provide for secondary teaching not only in London, but wherever their property lies, a machinery of proved effectiveness. The more recent Intermediate Education Act fills in Wales the interval between the schoolroom and the workroom; its precedent is sure to be followed elsewhere. The means, therefore, of technical training accessible to the very humblest classes of the community, cannot be described as inadequate. While the tendency thus is for places of secondary teaching to become training grounds for special, technical, or professional instruction, it is satisfactory that Oxford and Cambridge should hold before the eyes of the country the standard of the more general culture which is identical with real education, and should bring to the very doors of the humblest homes throughout the country the effective and inexpensive agencies for securing this teaching.

CHAPTER XII
THE LADDER OF EDUCATION

Mr Lowe's advice thirty years ago now fairly fulfilled. Individual influence co-operating with the State reforms the true secret of recent educational advance. Animating effect felt throughout the country of Benjamin Jowett's educational example at Oxford. The practical and concrete test of the helpfulness of the educational ladder to the entire community applied in detail. Instances of Board School boys, and of sons of day labourers who have risen to distinction with the help of the new educational agencies. Experiences of the Clerk of the London School Board and others. Missing rungs still to be supplied to the ladder by reorganization or slight enlargement of existing resources. Need of reorganizing the teaching profession by new local and central councils. Dangers besetting the present movement illustrated.

The theory, and, in outline, the practice, of the educational reforms reserved for the most recent years of the present reign have now been explained with as much fulness as the scheme of this work permits. It remains concretely, if of necessity briefly, to answer the question: What actually has been done? No Blue Books, or other educational statistics are necessary to convince one of the reality and magnitude of the enterprise already accomplished. 'Let us educate our masters,' was the advice of Mr Lowe when, in the House of Commons, he bewailed so brilliantly and bitterly the era of the new democracy begun by the legislation of 1867-8. The advice has been followed. A new generation has sprung up, which is demonstrably better educated and more humanized than any of its predecessors. The diminution of pauperism and crime; the gradual disappearance from London and from other great towns of the uncontrollably rough element among the street observers of public holidays; the growing competition among the industrial classes of museums or picture galleries with drinking bars on Sundays and on popular feasts; these are the more superficial signs of the progress already made and still going forward. Intelligent foreigners,[38] the very men who are said to anticipate the judgments of posterity, declare that within the last twenty years the physiognomical type of the London street loungers and loafers has visibly improved; that the look of the vulture which was habitual on faces pinched by hunger, and puffy or pallid with debauchery, is no longer the dominating expression of feature; that the rapacious arabs of the pavement who were formerly ready to devour the new comer outside Charing Cross or Victoria railway stations, where they have not disappeared, have become orderly, intelligent, and not altogether the reverse of polite. It requires perhaps an Englishman to appreciate at their true worth, the more delicate gradations of this improvement as it is illustrated elsewhere. Go into the pit or gallery of a London theatre, on the Surrey side or in Hoxton. In look, in manner, and in the kind of conversation between the acts, the play-goers have changed. If there were ever any danger of an orange or ginger-beer bottle descending from the gallery to the pit, the peril is now obsolete. Should the situation be Shoreditch or the City Road, the strains of the orchestra intermittently may be accompanied by voices joining in the chorus with original variations. But the melodies, however irregular, only express an honest holiday enthusiasm. Schools elementary, whether of the first or second grade, secondary, technical or scientific, explain much of this new improvement in the facial characteristics and at all public places in the general deportment of the humblest of Her Majesty's subjects. But they do not account for the entire change. Something like twenty years ago, when a work named *England* was in preparation its author by personal inspection of the localities mentioned, ascertained that the latest reports on the truck system as in some parts of Staffordshire it continued to exist, and of the agricultural gangs in more northern counties, faithfully depicted the social condition of great masses of the mining and rural population. The same local examination to-day presents a cheering contrast to the writer's earlier and depressing experiences. In every town and village of the United Kingdom it is now easier than was ever known before for the very poorest to live in a cleanly, a godly, sometimes even in a comfortable fashion. All the necessaries, most of the superfluities, of existence are to-day unprecedentedly cheap. Wages have risen all round, till a pound a week has become the normal pay of unskilled adult labour in the town, and about twelve shillings in the country. Some conspicuous evils in our industrial system have indeed yet to be removed. The fines and deductions[39] to which, often without just cause, the earnings of factory hands are subjected, have been denounced with just severity, though in moderate language, on platforms and in print, by Sir Charles Dilke. On this side of the Millennium finality in social legislation will prove, it is to be feared, not less difficult than in political matters Lord John Russell found, to his disappointment, was the case. The advance of civilization itself creates new social conditions which call in their turn for periodical legislation. Till the resources of all classes are equalized, there must be some who cannot protect themselves, on whose behalf the legislature must interpose.

That is only to say that England is not Paradise. Meanwhile, socially as well as educationally, the progress made is so great that two decades since the most sanguine prophets would have pronounced it to be impossible. The Staffordshire miner, the roughest perhaps of his class, would no longer be represented, even by *Punch*, as proposing to 'heave half a brick' at a new comer for the offence of having a strange face. As for setting the bull-pup at the parson's little boy, the suggestion is less likely to come, if at all, from the collier than from the mischievous undergraduate, the son of the collier's employer who is home for his College vacation, and indulges a pretty canine fancy. The eighth Duke of Devonshire is not a social leveller. But on a public occasion he had the frankness to define the difference between the Sunday crowds in Hyde Park round the Reformers' Tree, and the week day crowds in the Ladies' Mile as being that the former were not nearly as well dressed as the latter. That implied compliment to the manners of a metropolitan mob at once showed the discernment of him from whose lips it fell, and emphasizes the truth of the views expressed in the present context. Even the carnival of Lord Mayor's Day has felt the touch of those humanities that are said in the Latin grammar example to soften manners and not permit them to be brutal. The London crowd which, as Mr Disraeli knew, was the most emotional in the world, is to-day the best conducted, and incomparably the least drunken. As for its occasional rowdiness: what are these little outbursts in comparison with the horseplay of the prosperous gentlemen in glossy, silk hats, with high white collars, and deep wristbands, who, having placed a new rose in their button hole, drive high-stepping cobs to their suburban railway station every morning and who, if a stranger strays into their Stock Exchange deal with that unfortunate person as an Epsom mob treats a welsher. Continuation schools, lectures, universally accessible for adults who wish to carry on their education beyond the limit of their school days, the discipline of collective sight-seeing in museums and galleries; the habits formed at free libraries; these are the agencies that share with the teaching which the State provides the distinction of rearing a new generation, not merely veneered by a superficial decorum, but wholesomely controlled by a public opinion of its own quite as real as that which dominates Belgravia or Pall Mall.

Before considering the provisions necessary to complete the educational ladder, it will be well from specific instances to see what the facilities already established have done towards promoting the ascent from the Board School to the University. The following instances now published for the first time, are supplied by the courtesy of the Clerk of the London School Board. In 1879 a boy whose first learning was gained at a primary London Board School, obtained on entering a secondary school the Carpenters' Foundation Scholarship, together with the Conquest gold medal. Shortly afterwards he became captain of the City of London School. Proceeding thence to Cambridge, he won a Foundation Scholarship at Trinity; eventually was placed in the first class of the Classical Tripos, became next a Fellow of Trinity; and subsequently held a high position in the Board of Trade. Another lad of equally humble birth in 1880 got a mathematical scholarship at Queen's College, Cambridge, was among the Senior Optimes in the Tripos and in 1886 was appointed a mathematical master at one of the great public schools. In 1881, another Board School boy, having received the Greek and Latin certificate from the Universities Examining Board won a classical scholarship at St John's, Oxford, and afterwards a First Class in Classical Moderations. A little later he was placed fourth in the First Class of Civil Service candidates. He has since developed into a useful official of the Local Government Board. Another boy of like antecedents won a scholarship at St John's College, Cambridge; subsequently came out first class in one division, second class in another division, of the Theological Tripos; carried off the Jeremie Septuagint prize, open to the whole University, and afterwards became a successful parish clergyman. Other distinctions won by candidates of the same category are a scholarship at the City of London School; in 1883 a first place in the competition for vacancies in the India Office; in another case, and with the other sex, in 1885, the fifth place in the London Matriculation test, the Gilchrist and Reid scholarships, and later First Class Academic Honours for English. This instance is the more memorable because it is the earliest distinction of the sort won by a Board School girl. Since then the same young woman has become an assistant teacher at the Ladies' College in Jersey. This example has often been repeated since. Three or four of the prize winners at Girton College during the later eighties were London Board School girls. The well-known senior curate of St Saviour's, Everton, Liverpool, a High Honours Cambridge graduate, had been a Board School boy. His colleague had been enabled by a Fishmongers' scholarship to enter at Sidney Sussex College at Cambridge. In the summer of 1880, F. J. Wild was the first London Board School boy who went to Balliol. Nine years afterwards, this lad entered the Indian Civil Service, and became Assistant Magistrate and Deputy Collector in the North-West Provinces. 'Bachelor of Science, Bedford College, first division, 1891;' 'Recommended by Wesleyan Conference for training in their theological institutes and for the Home ministry;' 'Teacher at Diocesan Training College;' these are comparatively common entries in the catalogue of Board School honours for this decade. In or since 1893, there have been some half dozen cases of Board School boys taking College and University Honours at Oxford as well as good places in the Indian Civil Service competition. The experience of the London Board Schools is not unlike that of similar institutions in the provinces. A decennial calendar after the Oxford precedent of distinctions academic or professional won by Board School pupils is a volume which it would really be worth while to prepare, and materials for which are accumulating on all sides. Pending the completion of the ladder for ascent in the normal way from the Board School to the University, private encouragement supplies many of the missing rungs. Thus, the vicar of a Herefordshire village noticed the quickness of his gardener's son; helped him to enter the Hereford County School. From this the lad got a scholarship to Malvern College. Afterwards, one of the first Board School boys who won that honour, he carried off the entrance blue ribbon of a Balliol scholarship. In due course the gardener's boy took a first class in Classical Moderations, and a first class also in Classical Greats.

Typical instances have now been cited sufficient in number and variety to show that, as seems to be the general opinion of the last Education Commission, notwithstanding incompletenesses and imperfections here and there, enough has already been done to enable every clever boy in whatever station he is born by his own industry and volition to secure the same opportunities of cultivating his gifts as the nobleman's son who wins the Newcastle medal at Eton. The personal effort and initiative of the late Master of Balliol, Benjamin Jowett, did more perhaps than has been done by any other individual to promote this work. Under him the College of Wycliffe not only maintained the prestige which it had acquired in the days of Dr Jenkyns, and which was greatly increased by the successor of Jenkyns, Robert Scott, but became at once the patron and the pattern of minor places of education throughout the country. Provided they showed ability and industry, the day labourer's and the artizan's son were welcomed from the provincial grammar school as warmly at Balliol as the Sixth Form boy from Harrow or Eton. The connection between secondary schools of all grades in the provinces and the University on the Isis had already been promoted by the agency of local examinations; it was rendered more intimate by the Socratic interest which Jowett took in the intellectual welfare of the rawest lad from the country if only he showed the slightest sign of mental promise. Jowett's stimulating sense of citizenship was felt during his life in the remotest corners of the country. Its animating influences have survived his death; they still operate as an inspiring force wherever the domains of municipal and educational life converge. This good man and patriotic citizen did not live to witness the active assumption of educational responsibilities by the County and Borough Councils from which, not vainly, he hoped great things. An educational system in thorough touch with Oxford and Cambridge on the one hand and on the other hand with primary village schools; this was the ideal that Jowett, Lake and Stanley advocated to the earlier School Enquiry Commissions. Jowett lived long enough to see in the case of several great provincial grammar schools, notably that of Bradford, his ambition fulfilled.

In many, if not in most districts, the new provincial Councils have now added as many rungs to the educational ladder as could fairly be expected. The wants which still await fulfilment are definite. They ought not to prove very difficult to supply. Local endowments supplemented by a moderate amount of State help, will, if wisely directed, provide the larger facilities still needed for the promotion of higher grade elementary school pupils to grammar schools. In order that there may be no further waste either of the money or of the machinery for national education, a drastic scheme of reorganization seems to be a cardinal necessity. Secondary education is a phrase too mechanically interpreted as a synonym for technical or scientific education. If the Statutes be interpreted literally, the County Councils are empowered only to levy a rate for a higher school grant when the teaching which that grant defrays is to enable a boy or girl to learn the elements of some remunerative handicraft, and is thus expressly sanctioned by the Technical Education Act of 1890. If the Councils have gone beyond this, and pecuniarily ministered to the needs of a more generous culture, they have acted, so to speak, at their own peril, or that action has been rendered possible by the private liberality of their more opulent members. In addition to this need of a new definition of the ambiguous epithet and substantive employed so often in the foregoing text, a new educational authority which can officially survey every department of the entire field of teaching has become indispensable. Centralized at Whitehall this authority will to some extent inevitably be. Its operation, however, must be highly elastic. The conditions of its control must be adaptable to the infinitely varying conditions, social, geographical, material, sentimental, of the United Kingdom. The most recent enquiries show that there is much less dissipation of educational energy by the mutual overlapping of schools than might be expected. The single instance of this sort to which attention has been directed by the last Commission is that of Bolton, where there exists an unprofitable competition between the grammar school and the Church Institute Boys' School. Elsewhere, however, as at Leeds and other great towns of the North, Mechanics' Institute Schools, Higher Grade Board Schools, trench respectively on each other's province, though each of them, by slightly varying its curriculum, does good work and is in great local demand. The explanation of the latter fact is the universality of the appetite for higher teaching created in the large centres of the English population. The most frequent, and with proper care the most easily remediable form of overlapping occurs when the higher divisions of a lower grade school retain pupils already ripe for a higher grade school. What are the exact limits to be placed respectively to the provinces of elementary schools of both grades? and what to the grammar schools on the one hand, or the University schools on the other with which the rudimentary institutions ought closely and cordially to co-operate? these are problems with which, in the fifty-ninth year of Her Majesty's reign, there does not exist any single authority competent to deal. The confusion between the jurisdiction of the educational bodies now in being is comparable with that which existed in the relations of the various administrative authorities and areas in the case of local government before these functions were comparatively simplified by the legislation of 1874 and of 1888. The Education Department in London has no concern with secondary schools save so far as some of these are inextricably intermingled in their operations with the finance or the teaching of primary schools. The Charity Commission wherein the Endowed Schools Commission is now merged, can only take cognizance of the agencies for higher teaching for a special purpose and from a single point of view. This loose and very partially effective machinery of control has since 1890 received a new element of complexity from the educational power vested with such happy results as it has been in the County Councils. The educational branch of the Privy Council office in London has long attracted to it young men of industry and talents from the Universities as well as of considerable administrative ability developed at a later date by official experience.

Meanwhile the profession of the teacher becomes more highly organized each year. The value of its material interests is constantly increasing. It still remains without any direct representation in the official world comparable with that which is secured to the civil and military services by the Council of the Secretary of State for India. The headmasters' annual conference has during the last few years supplied a useful medium for the interchange of opinions and experiences between the recognized chiefs of their vocation. The College of Preceptors has its occasional meetings. Certificated assistant teachers have formed themselves into a loosely coherent body of their own. None of these can, except in an indirect way, place their practical experience at the disposal of the central authority whose consent is necessary for any organic change in the teaching subjects of schools that receive a public endowment. In the case of schools whose speciality is a sound commercial education, proofs of late have multiplied that the object of this training may often be more faithfully accomplished, to say nothing of the intellectual gain to the learner if the boy who is going to stand behind a counter, and may sometimes be called upon to write a business letter for his employer, is instructed in something beyond the arts of summing and penmanship. Many boys of the humblest birth show a remarkable aptitude for applied logic and political economy when the elements of physical science fail entirely to attract their minds. The educational council which might be auxiliary to the Vice-President of the Council will perhaps number amongst its members men who, from their own practical knowledge, can give sound advice in cases where the teacher ought to be entrusted with the power of adapting the education, not merely in a general way to the vocation that is hereafter to engage the learner, but to the idiosyncrasies of the pupil as well. The stipends of assistants in secondary schools are often unwisely and wastefully low. Men and women who work so hard as these persons do are entitled to the assurance that their emoluments will be regulated by the consideration that comes of knowledge as well as the severer equities of commerce.

The first thing, therefore, as all who on this matter speak from experience agree, is to establish local councils for educational purposes which by the prevention of confusion and overlapping between schools of different grades, will directly promote the economy of educational force not less than of expenditure. As for the central authority which the interests alike of teachers, of taught, of children and parents, of the State, and of its subjects demand, substantial unanimity as to the composition of that body exists among those who are most qualified to give an opinion. Generally it is suggested that the new Council might be shaped after the model of the Indian Council. To come to particulars, there would be, in the first instance, a certain number of Crown nominees; secondly, the Universities, perhaps the great public schools or other public educational bodies, would be asked to select representatives of their own. Another element in the new central authority would be experienced members of the teaching professions. These might be chosen partly by the headmasters in conference, but to some extent by the assistant teachers employed in every variety of public schools from the highest to the lowest. It would seem on the whole advisable to select the teachers' members by the direct vote of the class immediately concerned. The machinery for doing so would not be difficult. Voting papers, as in the case of London University in the choice of appointments to the Senate, or of professional representatives on the Medical Council, would be employed. In this way, every registered teacher would have a voice in regulating the details and rewards of his profession to the great increase, as cannot be doubted, of its *esprit de corps*. In the case of elections to the local authority for preventing waste and confusion between local schools an analogous method might be employed. The registered teachers, that is, would in each neighbourhood choose their proportion of the members of the local educational body.

Signs are sometimes visible of a reaction from the enthusiasm for educational progress that has engaged the national energies during the last half century. There is a danger, one is told, of educating boys or girls beyond their capacities, and above their station. The increased competition for the positions of governess and clerk, means misery and ruin to many of the candidates who would be more suitably, comfortably, and far more remuneratively employed in domestic service, or in manual labour according to their sex. The virtues of humility and respect for superiors are said to be crushed out in the scramble for knowledge that may enable its possessors to better themselves. Servant maids, one is told, no longer confine their demands to permission to wear a fringe, but stipulate for a pianoforte in the basement, or a bicycle with which to take their airing on their Sundays out. That upon the humbler levels of the community the progress from ignorance to education should be accompanied by real or apparent disturbances of the personal relations between classes was to have been expected. Seasons of transition such as the present always generate a certain amount of personal friction or of social displacement. Those just being emancipated from the illiteracy or semi-barbarism which have been the traditions of centuries have not yet overcome the agitating strangeness of their new and improved condition. Those above them in the social scale have not yet been able to decide whether to conciliate their educated inferiors as possible friends, or to stand on their guard against them as actual enemies. As the situation becomes more familiar, it will prove less strained. Common sense as a supplement to their zeal, seems the chief want of the educational reformers, official or private, of the day. The tendency is to postpone the development of intelligence to the acquisition of knowledge. The masters whom we are now educating are not in the habit of using their minds for the mere pleasure of intellectual exertion. Hence they often give an impression of being far less intelligent than they really are. The correct use of common words in the mother tongue ought orally, not out of any lesson book, to be taught all boys and girls. The difficulty experienced by the persons now spoken of in clearly answering a simple question is often insurmountable. The tendency is, not to digest the query as a whole, but to catch some word used in it and then to make a remark suggested by the association of the sound of the syllables, and so practically to evade the question put. The cheap diffusion of newspapers and magazines confirms rather than corrects these failures to concentrate the mind in the casual talk of everyday life. It is not beneath the dignity of the State educator to deal with the defect.[40]

CHAPTER XIII
THE GREAT PUBLIC SCHOOLS AS MIRRORS OF THE AGE

Social importance of Eton, Harrow, and other great schools, as representing the social evolution of the epoch. The conventional mistake that the new wealth has been injurious to the social tone or scholarly studies of public schools. In the case of Eton the historic details and educational statistics prove the falseness of the statement. Progress of the school shown by success in the new as well as old examinations during the incriminated period of the last forty years. New social elements have increased the value but not the expense of Eton. The fourteenth Earl of Derby as a typical Eton product.

The whole region of public elementary and secondary education, whose improvement is so conspicuous an incident in the recent domestic or social annals of the time, has now been indicated at sufficient length and minutely enough to convey an accurate notion of the facts. One may, therefore, pass to those educational levels which stand a little higher, and up to which recent reforms of popular education are, as has been seen, gradually assisting the progress of Board School children. The sociological feature of the present reign has already been described in these pages as a process less of revolution, than of evolution; of the natural incorporation of new elements into an old fabric, of the harmonious assimilation on the part of a polity that is the growth of centuries, of the ideas and types that are the products of to-day. These processes can nowhere be witnessed more crucially in operation than at those little worlds, the great public schools such as Eton and Harrow, which, as they have ever been, are the faithful microcosms of the great worlds that lie beyond them. Many of the accounts of Eton which periodically find their way into print seem inspirations from Baron Munchausen. The school that during centuries has been the special training ground for the country gentlemen of England, which was once to such an extent the nursery of future lords spiritual and temporal as to enable Dr Keate to include among his titles to respect the fact of his having flogged in their youth the whole Bench of Bishops,[41] is conventionally represented as corrupted at its heart by the predominating influence of the sons of the 'new rich' on its classic soil. The parent who wishes his son to be at the school where his sire, and his sires before him, had been, is disgusted by reading romantic accounts of the bank balances in Windsor town kept for their boys by the plutocrats, Saxon or Semitic, of the City. It may, therefore, be said authoritatively that thus far research has failed to bring to light a single instance of the new rich Etonian who possesses during his school days a banking account of his own. Now, not less than formerly, the lad who returns to his tutor's or his dame's with a £5 note in his pocket is looked upon by his comrades as in luck.

Forty years ago, when a Public School Commission was making its enquiry, the cry of the commercial Crœsus swamping the country squire was first raised. The most practical proof of its hollowness is that the expenses of Eton, if still prohibitive to many parents, have not increased of recent years. What has rather happened is that the school outlay has been remodelled. The charges are to-day inclusive. If comparatively fresh items figure in the school accounts, the incidental outlay on casual subscriptions and a long catalogue of extras is now superseded. The real cost of Eton and of other schools like it is what the individual boy chooses, or what his friends allow. The expensive habits of the Etonian are more a domestic, than a scholastic, growth. No advocate of the *nouveau riche* theory has ever asserted that the scale of living in the clubs of Pall Mall has become insufferably profuse since gentlemen enriched by commerce, prone, like Mr Mantalini, to despise details of petty cash, have been made free of these establishments. There is not, nor has there ever been, the slightest danger of the Etonian or Harrovian of the old aristocratic order being corrupted by plutocratic schoolfellows. The son of Sir Gorgius Midas in real life proves to be a quiet, sensible lad, with a just and shrewd sense of the value of money, and perhaps less likely to waste his father's substance in the 'sock shops' under the shadow of Windsor Castle than his form comrade, the son of the squire whom Sir Gorgius could buy up half a dozen times over. At other places than the great public schools of England, a studious boy may find himself more in the way of amassing knowledge. Nowhere will he learn so many lessons useful for the daily conduct of life, which books do not impart. Nowhere will he have such opportunities for the acquisition, the development and the display of practical common sense. So far back as the later fifties of this century, an Eton master, the late Mr Durnford, the respected father of him who still represents the same family on the Eton staff, alluding to the decline in the manufacture of Longs and Shorts in pious Henry's shades, could say: 'Latin verses are with us things of the past.' There is, however, no reason, as the list of Eton honours at Oxford or Cambridge will show, for imputing to Eton any decline in the essentials of classical scholarship. Since the new wealth is supposed to have contaminated the standard of plain living and high thinking among the old gentry, in 1851, the famous son of a famous father, a name venerable in the Law Courts and on the Thames, J. W. Chitty, an old Etonian, won at Oxford a first class Vinerian Scholarship, followed by a Fellowship at Exeter. About the same time R. G. W. Herbert the late Permanent Head of the Colonial Office carried off, as a scholar of Balliol, the Hertford and the Ireland, and a Fellowship at All Souls. The late Lord Carnarvon was not so infected by the plutocratic idleness of Eton as to miss when at Christ Church the highest honours of the Classical Schools.

Three years later when according to the conventional view the 'rich vulgarians,' as the Mrs Major Pompley of *My Novel* calls them, must have entirely crowded out the sons of squires as well as the humanities themselves, another country gentleman's son, the late Edward Herbert who died at Marathon in 1870, had as his brother scholar at Balliol, also from Eton, another son of a Western squire, Edmond Warre, to-day Headmaster of his old school. In the same year the son of a 'squarson' to employ Sidney Smith's useful term, also an Etonian, Henry Barter of Merton, the evil associations of plutocracy notwithstanding, won the highest mathematical together with second class classical honours at Oxford, and was only just beaten by the present Bishop of Hereford, for the University Scholarship in mathematics. This list of instances belongs to the era (the fifties) when the corruptions of the new wealth were most rampant at Eton, seems to refute the mechanical charge; that list may be closed with the name of a country gentleman's son, since then Chancellor of the Exchequer, Michael Hicks-Beach, who, Eton and Christ Church notwithstanding, took a first class in the Modern History schools in 1858. About the same time the member of a Liverpool mercantile family, the son of a great statesman, W. H. Gladstone, had not at Eton so unlearned all he had been taught elsewhere as to be prevented from winning a studentship at Christ Church. His contemporary at Eton, A. C. Swinburne, the poet, won at Oxford the Taylor scholarship for modern languages about the same time. The catalogue might be extended indefinitely. The representative names likely to convey the fullest idea to the general reader have now been mentioned. A further selection of patronymics would confuse rather than instruct or interest. It will be enough to say that in or since the sixties down to 1896, of the highest honours in the Schools or in the Colleges at Oxford 400 were obtained by the sons of country gentlemen who, notwithstanding the new wealth had like their fathers before them been sent to Eton and who were not apparently quite demoralized by that ordeal. At Cambridge the total of Academic distinctions won by Etonians of the same grade as at Oxford, is as might have been expected higher, and amounts in round numbers to 550. A competent judge in these matters, speaking with no personal prejudice in favour of the school of Henry VI.[42] or of its Cambridge sister King's College, but with much experience of classical examinations, J. Y. Sargent, told the present writer not long ago, that Eton was the one school in England whose boys could write tolerable Greek prose.

Any social change that may have come over the place since the introduction of the new wealth into the country would seem to be very different in fact from that described by fiction. The presence of a large number of boys whose parents derive their income from no hereditary acres and whose domestic associations are therefore different from those of the country gentleman's son has indeed produced an effect, but one which is the very opposite of its current misrepresentation. Before the Victorian era opened, well-to-do commercial fathers were, as readers of *Coningsby* will remember, in the habit of sending their sons to the seat of education most in vogue with the titled and untitled patricians of the realm. Such influence as these have had has proved notoriously healthful to the whole school community. The newcomers have with scarcely an exception been trained from childhood to an adequate appreciation of the value of money and are the last boys in the world to be permitted to squander it for mere show. Before their advent to the place, Eton might have been charged with narrowness or partiality in the composition of its life; congenial enough as the training ground of peers, opulent commoners, diplomatists, and other destined dignitaries of State or Church, but less salutary for lads who had their own way to make in the world, and who while doing so, must expect to come into collision with the men of the City, the office, and the shop. The genius of every great English school is essentially democratic. Boys are valued by their fellows not for what they have, but for what in themselves they are; not for the antiquity of their family descent, nor for the depth of their father's purse. The boy who dazzled his mates with the glitter of sovereigns fresh from the Mint would be suppressed as promptly by the public opinion of the place as the toady or the parasite. To-day no English lad is so little likely idly to waste his parents' cash as the young Etonian.

There is no school which so far as social discipline is concerned better enables its boys to dispense with the University and yet lose so little by not going there, or which turns out its boys such ready-made little men of the world as the foundation of Henry VI. That this is to-day the special attribute of Eton, possessed by it in common perhaps with Harrow, is due to the circumstance of its having become representative of the entire life, commercial, not less than squirearchical or patrician, urban not less than rural, of the whole country. The truth is that the *nouveau riche*, as he is represented by the popular imagination, is the product of romance, or the creation of the stage. The antagonism between the socially emancipated of yesterday and the descendants of houses which had become considerable before constitutional government in England was known is imaginary and in direct contradiction of the experiences of daily life. The son of the new man of one generation as to his tastes, his prejudices, his politics, his pursuits, the performance of his duties, the choice of his pleasures, becomes, in the next, socially indistinguishable from the scion of the oldest nobility. On all points he has unconsciously, as is the way with the imitative race of boys, modelled himself after the pattern of those country gentlemen, divines, civilians, soldiers, and sailors, who are for the most part the reverse of plutocratic, and whose sons have been brought up at home under conditions which would make them physically intolerant of the bad taste that may be defined as a missing of the due proportion of relative things. The Lancashire trader's son who at school finds himself next in form to the boy of ancient family is quick to imbibe the social traditions and intuitions with which the atmosphere is charged. He has been sent to school to make acquaintances perhaps as well as to learn; but certainly not to dazzle his schoolfellows by the glitter of his father's gold. If the Manchester lad possesses more pocket money than some of those in his 'house,' he is pretty certain also to set them a wise example in the careful spending of it. The truth is that with the whole system of public examinations and with literary competitions narrowing the entrance to all kinds of professional life, the genius of the place at the great public schools has undergone the same modifications as at the Universities. The schoolboy who has obtained his exeat for a few days as he bounds off to the station to catch his train, may be thought to have left all care behind him. Enjoyment, however, is very probably not the reason of his visit to his friends in London.

Sandhurst or Woolwich examinations, competitions for the home or foreign service at Burlington House are quite as likely to be the object in view as the visit to the dentist by day or to the theatre by night. This early acquaintance with the responsibilities of life exerts a sobering influence on the most constitutionally volatile of Eton or Harrow striplings. The lad whose path of pleasure is darkened by the shadow of the ubiquitous examiner loses prematurely the juvenile appetite for veal and ham pies, jam tarts, ginger beer, even for cocoanut paste. When there are not examinations at a distance, the ingenuity of Oxford and Cambridge provides the machinery for them hard by the Playing Fields on the Thames or Byron's Tree at Harrow on the Hill. 'Posing' in some form goes on all the year round. It has become in effect obligatory on the public school boy to obtain before going up to the University the certificate which frees him from the Littlego examination, or which if he enters on other careers, secures him an analogous dispensation.

The higher certificates in the University examinations are not easy to obtain. They uniformly indicate a high standard of proficiency. The success of Eton in these ordeals has been steadily progressive during the last twenty years. From 39 in 1875 the Eton candidates had risen to 88 in 1896. The total of certificates and distinctions won by these, an aggregate of 1,413 candidates, was, during this period of twenty years, 1,516. Meanwhile the number of Eton boys who, without passing through an intermediary stage at the professional crammers, take good places direct from their school in the Indian and Home Civil Service competitions has increased during the last few years by something like 10 per cent. The Eton 'Army' class is also doing well. The number of boys proceeding to Sandhurst and even to Woolwich straight from school as others proceed straight to the University increases annually. These statistics go some way towards disproving the conventional reproach made largely by ignorance against the most representative of English public schools of being socially and economically demoralized, or intellectually sunk in indolence by the malignant influences of the new wealth. If there were any truth in such an accusation, the maintenance of the traditional standard of scholarly excellence in exceptional cases would not be combined, as to-day it is, with the visibly demonstrated improvement in the work of the rank and file of the boys. The truth is, that at all our great schools, Eton like the rest, the new elements among the boys have tended to produce a wholesome change in the public opinion of the place distinctly favourable to a higher average of school industry. The ideal Etonian of history is, and seems likely long to continue, the fourteenth Earl of Derby, translator of the *Iliad*, and perhaps the most brilliant parliamentary debater of the century. 'He saps like Gladstone, and he fights like Spring.' So runs Lord Lytton's spirited and familiar line concerning this most typical of Eton worthies. No one would have welcomed more warmly than he the statistical evidence here given that under its latest Headmaster, the study of the new ologies, and the manual mechanics practised in the Eton workshops which Dr. Warre has established have not ousted the older humanities from their place, and that, the new wealth notwithstanding, it has ceased to be a reproach against any boy at the old school that he is a sap.[43]

CHAPTER XIV
THE NEW OXFORD AND CAMBRIDGE

Changes in the social life of Oxford and Cambridge visible on the surface since 1860. Social differences between Oxford and Cambridge as places of residence. General results of the unattached student system established in 1868. The idea of the University as distinct from the colleges, socially prominent in earlier days, has acquired new prominence since. The admission of non-collegiate students. Vicissitudes in the popularity of the Union as a social club and as a debating society. Its earlier distinction repeated in later years. The unattached students' scheme in its practical details and working. Academic successes of students, especially in Theology. The Extension Lectures scheme, personal details and general results.

Under the new and quickening influences imported into the second half of the present century, the changes in the conditions of social life are more visible at the two great Universities than at the public schools. The public school boy has been seen hastening to the railway station that he may catch the train which is to convey him from the place of industry, not to the old holiday fields, but to a fresh seat of studious exertion. In like manner, a fair proportion of Oxford and Cambridge graduates now pass the greater portion of their lives in hurrying to catch trains from their academic termini to scenes of provincial activity. The commercial traveller of the old order as Dickens described him was not more incessantly on the road than the Oxford or Cambridge Extension lecturer. He, like the movement he represents, is the product of the age that has given us Bradshaw. Oxford and Cambridge have in fact been brought to the doors of those who cannot themselves go to Cambridge or Oxford. Nor is the new element, among those who have taken their degree, the only change that has been witnessed in the *personnel* of the place. Enough has been written about the domestic revolution which has transformed what till the later sixties, had continued a cloister into a flourishing provincial centre of family life; about the nursemaids with perambulators in the parks, the children trundling their hoops along Addison's Walk, or playing ball under the statelier avenue which fringes the Christ Church meadows. In reality this feature in the social polity of Oxford, however interesting or striking, has never marked so visible a contrast to the preceding epoch as it may have done at Cambridge. The capital on the Isis has always been a considerable county town. From a time to the contrary of which memory does not run, Oxford has had extra-academical attractions of its own for persons without any interest in its studies. It has always been a hunting, steeplechasing, and generally a sporting centre. Its neighbourhood is probably more picturesque than that of its sister on the Cam. Like other midland counties, its environments have never been without more manor houses and country gentlemen's residences than is the case with the academic section of East Anglia. As far back, therefore, as the later fifties certainly, and it may be much further, social Oxford possessed an existence not less distinct from, or independent of, academic Oxford, than Windsor, Harrow on the Hill, Rugby, Cheltenham, or Marlborough possess a social machinery of their own apart from the schools which are a feature in their respective neighbourhoods.

What will really strike the eye of one revisiting Oxford after a long interval is less the signs of the latest developments of domestic life than the appearance of greater youthfulness in the undergraduates. Where this juvenility is real, and not the illusion of the spectator's own advancing years, it is largely to be explained by the order of students new since 1868. Not without much opposition or till after long resistance, the Oxford statutes in that year relaxed the most exclusive condition written on their page by the disciplinarian severity of Archbishop Laud. A return to the mediæval usage was sanctioned. Once more it became possible, after a lapse of three centuries, for young men to go to the University without going to college. The Vice-Chancellor matriculated students furnished with credentials of respectability, and with enough of learning to satisfy the masters of the schools. Provided, in other words, they had a fair prospect of passing Responsions, which do not constitute one of the public examinations, but mark the survival of the old entrance ordeal prescribed in the days when the University was everything and the Colleges comparatively nothing. If he were not legally of age, the formal consent to his life in lodgings of his parents or guardians was further required from the non-ascript undergraduate, as well as a general testimonial to the probability of his deriving educational benefit from his new opportunities. Littlego might be excused by the delegates in the case of students not intending to proceed to their degree, but only to study systematically some special subject. In the place, however, of the 'Smalls' testamur, or its equivalent, the special student was tested closely as to his aptitudes for the subject of study he professed.

The total yearly cost, all entrance fees included, of the non-collegiate youth would average between £50 and £60, instead of thrice that sum, not perhaps an exaggerated estimate, for his collegiate brother. £10 covers handsomely all the initial outlay. The period of residence required for the degree is twelve terms. These must be kept in what is called 'full term' which is rather later than the almanac term, and also in a duly licensed lodging house. In exceptional cases these conditions may be dispensed with. In no case will the undergraduate who has no porter's lodge to pass before he 'knocks in' at night find more liberty than the intramural student. His landlord or landlady in the town may perhaps promise not to communicate some irregularity to the authorities. But so surely as the unattached commits the smallest breach of academic discipline, sooner or later it will reach the official ear; he will find himself a marked man.

Men who are now middle aged, or even elderly, looking back to their college days will recollect that there prevailed an invisible system of surveillance, and even espionage, much more close and real than it was at all pleasant in the days of one's youth to admit. That supervision has now become more subtle, ubiquitous and unavoidable, till at last the unattached freshman realizes that wherever he may be, he lives and moves in a whispering gallery, as much as if he were a famous figure, in the heart of London society and of the London season.

The practical success of this innovation was immediate. It has been tolerably complete. Within thirty years of its introduction, that is on the 1st of January 1896, the University books showed the existence of 480 graduate or undergraduate non-collegiates. Of these 245 were at the date mentioned *in statu pupillari*. The authorities to which these students are immediately subject are the Vice-Chancellor, the two Proctors, a Censor who stands in the relation of College tutor to the whole body; two other tutors associated with him who give advice on all subjects, and seven delegates, being members of Convocation. The Censor is the head of the whole unattached system; to him intending students should apply for all practical information. The teaching available for the University alumni now mentioned is at least as effective and wide as any of the colleges can offer.

At the instance of Mr Jowett, a great friend of the scheme, other colleges than Balliol soon opened their lecture rooms to non-collegiate guests. The Honour tutors especially allocated to the unattached, include distinguished Fellows of Balliol, Christ Church, Lincoln, Magdalen, University College, Wadham and Worcester, as well as famous theologians from Keble, or a non-collegiate M.A. not less accomplished than the present Professor of Modern History, Mr York Powell of Christ Church. The extent to which the young men thus provided for have profited by their opportunities, may be judged from the following epitome of examinational statistics. Two first classes in Classical Moderations, 2 also in Mathematical; 13 seconds in Classical Moderations; 39 third classes in the same examination; 7 Mathematical thirds in Moderations; these represent the distinctions gained in the older Honour Schools by the students who as an institution have not yet completed their third decade. Although thus far they do not seem to have done very brilliantly in the Philosophy and History Schools, they have won a first class in Jurisprudence, 2 in Modern History, 12 in Theology, 3 in Natural Science, one in Oriental Studies, as well as some dozen places in these studies below the coveted level of *classis prima*. The Bachelor of Civil Law examination is known to be one of the hardest on the Isis. In this the unattached may be credited with one first class, one second, as well as one third and one fourth. During the period now spoken of, several University prizes have been carried off by the new comers. Thus a non-collegiate candidate has won the Denyer and Johnson scholarship in Theology four times, the Pusey and Ellerton scholarship (Hebrew) the same number, as also the Senior and Junior Kennicott (also Hebrew). The Davis scholarship in Chinese was for the fifth time won a few years ago by an unattached, and for the second time the Taylorian scholarship in Modern Languages. Among older and better known distinctions open to all comers, the Arnold Historical essay has been won by an unattached; the Chancellor's English essay, and the Ellerton essay have been won twice. While it will thus be seen that the new students have acquitted themselves specially well in Theology, they have in twenty-four cases gained open scholarships, and in three cases open Fellowships. The Bowden Sanskrit, the Burdett-Coutts scholarships also figure among their list of honours. In the Pass schools 310, a proportion of 72 per cent., have satisfied the examiners. As an instance of their being on their entrance up to the scholastic level of the average public school boy, 30 or 40 unattached have elected to pass Responsions before matriculation and have done so without any difficulty.

The general conduct of the new undergraduates, who, some prophets had predicted, would demoralize the University by their rowdy example, has been with scarcely an exception, exemplary. Only one disciplinary case, to employ the euphemism of the last official report, seems to have occurred. With the enterprising alacrity which to their own credit, to the good of their colleges, to the benefit of the whole University, the representatives of the different societies on the Isis display in attracting special talent to the foundations in which they are respectively interested, some absorption of the unattached into the colleges was inevitable. It has, however, been less than one might have expected. The average of these migrations does not vary much, and seems to proceed at the rate of between 20 and 25 per year. Nor, apparently, does there exist any dissatisfaction among the non-collegiates with their own position in the City of Colleges. Thus when they migrate to a college, the attraction is generally found to be the exceptional facilities for instruction in a special study, *e.g.* Natural Science or History, afforded by the foundation in question. As, by implication, has been already stated, Mr J. A. Froude's successor in the Chair of Modern History was, throughout the greater portion of his career, a non-collegiate. Together with the present Recorder of Londonderry, Professor York Powell was one of the first batch of unattached students in 1868. Superior conveniences for the studies respectively to their taste, rather than economy, were the motives which sent the future Professor and the future Irish lawyer, Mr T. G. Overend, to the University and not to college. Mr Powell took his degree as a member of Christ Church; Judge Overend was unattached to the last. Both obtained high Honours in the Schools. The after success of each began directly they left the University. Having been called to the Irish Bar in 1874, Mr Overend was in 1885 the leader of his circuit as well as a Queen's Counsel. His health alone caused him to give up his practice and take a County Court judgeship.

Thus far the unattached graduates in residence never at any given time seem to have exceeded 50. Their rivalry with the colleges is, therefore, in point of numbers not very formidable. Nor do they seem appreciably to have affected the social or intellectual life of the place. Like the great public schools the two Universities are to the present generation what they were to its predecessors. Athletic accomplishments have declined as little as general scholarship. The pastimes, however, are conducted far more economically than was once the case. Instances of young men being hampered during their professional struggles by the evil legacy of University debts have decreased so steadily as to justify the hope of their ultimate and entire disappearance. Thus the Oxford undergraduate as Leech used to depict him, or as Thackeray in *Pendennis* drew the typical pupil of both Universities; throwing away his father's money at the end of the term in London in exaggerated tips to hotel waiters and cabmen, is to-day as much of an anachronism as the Etonian in his teens who has not learnt that if care is taken of the shillings, the pounds will take care of themselves. In one particular, though perhaps accidentally, the non-collegiate undergraduate as an institution has coincided an interesting modification of the social conditions of Oxford life. Early in the present century, the conception of an academic as distinct from and independent of a collegiate polity was more present to the undergraduate of that epoch than it was to his successors half a century or so later. This fact is one among the explanations of the popularity of the University Union Debating Club during the student days of Mr Gladstone as well as of the comparative disfavour into which it had fallen during the student days of, for example, Lord Randolph Churchill. There appear, however, periodically to take place reactions in favour of the nursery ground of future orators. Mr Asquith, already of Cabinet rank, to whom probabilities, as well as Lord Rosebery's words, point as a coming leader of the House of Commons, belonged to a slightly older generation than Churchill. Before he took his degree in 1863, he had established the same sort of reputation for himself in the Union as had been won two or three generations earlier by Mr Gladstone, and as seventeen years afterwards was to be won in the same arena by Mr G. N. Curzon, in 1897 Foreign Under Secretary.

During the later sixties, there came into existence, as further developments of what was practically a collegiate example, social clubs for undergraduates. These, in effect, though not in theory, were generally recruited from a few colleges. Such societies have doubtless not lost their earlier popularity. They have witnessed a fresh access of favour to the University Union Club. They have perhaps helped themselves to contribute to it by causing the Union, in the supply of creature comforts, to compete with the collegiate lounges. A room for the reading of novels had been regarded as a dangerous innovation at the Union before 1865. It was not till after that year that a smoking room was sanctioned, or the refreshments of tea or coffee supplied. That in the future as in the past the chief work of the Universities will be done through the agency of the colleges is no doubt not less true than that at Eton, like Harrow, the tutorial system will co-exist with the most liberal and sweeping innovations which may be introduced. The colleges depend for their success on the same conditions as the non-collegiate delegacies. In prosperous seasons when trade is good and money plenty, there will be few vacant rooms either inside the college walls or outside in the licensed lodging houses. When times are bad, the list diminishes. Thus in the October term of 1896, 621 freshmen entered the colleges as compared with 734 in the preceding twelvemonths; Christ Church had only increased by 11; Worcester doubled its numbers; at the same time Magdalen, always a popular college with the public, had fallen from 53 to 40, Balliol from 49 to 36, Lincoln from 24 to 17. As for the non-collegiates, there was not only no increase but an actual diminution; the figures here were less by 11 than in the preceding twelvemonth.

The great contrast which in comparing it with its normal condition two or three decades ago would be noticed by the Oxonian who revisits Oxford to-day is the change from an habitually stationary to a visibly locomotive population on the part of those who formerly seldom left their college rooms. Down the chief streets of the towns on the Isis and the Cam respectively, even at the very height of term time, there is a constant succession of cabs conveying young men in the prime of life to the railway termini. These are the fellows and tutors of the different colleges whose predecessors seldom or never used to leave their University during term, save when college business took them for a few hours to their lawyers in Lincoln's Inn, or to the college estate bailiffs and stewards in the country. Such are not the missions that explain this increase of railway bound traffic when as yet no vacation is in sight. Those now spoken of as hurrying off to some provincial spot are well known in their University and a few hours hence will be warmly welcomed at their provincial destinations as Extension Lecturers on subjects of popular interest. What has happened is this. Certain enlightened inhabitants of both sexes in some district of manufacturing Lancashire or in agricultural Devon have been struck with the state of ignorance in which their school course has left many young men and women. At the same time they have noticed indications of a wish with those of maturer years to make up for early neglect by later application to branches of study of all kinds. Books alone have failed to supply the want. Intelligent and profitable reading is a scientific habit properly to be acquired only by those who have been drilled into it and who have already some general acquaintance with the topics treated in the written page.

The County Council, as we have repeatedly seen, discharges already some of the functions and dispenses some of the funds of an Educational Department. Very possibly private munificence accompanies if it does not prompt this corporate enterprise. The next step is to communicate with the University Extension Lecture agency at whichever University, Oxford, Cambridge, London, or Victoria, according to the preference displayed. After the expenses have been guaranteed, the lecturer appears. To enable his hearers intelligently to grasp his plan of discourse, the discourse itself is prefaced by the distributions of a synopsis, which is in its way a work of literary art, whose readers, without any other help than its perusal may gather something more than a mere foretaste of the ground to be covered, or of the instruction to be conveyed. Such a syllabus as that of the Oxford lectures by Mr Shaw or Mr Marriott on different periods of English or French history, like the Reformation of 1529, the Revolution of 1689, or the age of Louis XIV. at once assists the working men for whom they were planned, and serves as a model for the taking of notes. Each lecture of every course of twelve is followed by a class during which the lecturer is in the Scotch term heckled by his audience. Essays are set, looked over, and returned to the writers with marginal corrections. At the end of each course an examination of both sexes is held, and certificates of merit are granted. The sons and daughters of the local gentry, day labourers in factory, field, office, or shop figure in nearly equal numbers among the students, the women being slightly the more numerous, and acquit themselves equally well in the examinations.

The system has only attained to its present completeness within the last few years. The idea of it had occurred to Oxford reformers so far back as 1850 when residents and non-residents alike were asking how the educational machinery on the Isis or the Cam could be made more available for all classes of their fellow subjects. The Oxford Hebdomadal Board was addressed on the subject, the names of Lord Ashley, Mr Gladstone, Lord Sandon being among the signatories.

The great Dr Pusey, whose mind was as truly liberal as his Churchmanship was high, had been struck recently by the number of great Anglican divines who were the sons of small tradesmen. It was for Oxford to revive the example of the ancient monks of Durham, and to devise means for bringing the University within the reach of the poorest in the land. Another member of Christ Church whose pointed features, dark complexion, saturnine habit and rare scholarship will be recalled by many readers of these lines, Mr Osborne Gordon, joined with Professor Hussey in impressing by almost daily protests this popular duty on his too exclusive Alma Mater. At this time religious tests existed in all their historic severity. There was no matriculation without signing the Thirty-Nine Articles of the Common Prayer Book, and no degree till after a like process with reference to the Three Articles of the Thirty-Sixth Canon.

These facts account for the then dominant Liberalism of educated opinion inside and outside the University. Had tests ceased to exist when they were abolished in Ireland, as both Canning and Sir Robert Peel at one time or another had suggested, it is scarcely speculation to say that the demand which in 1868 brought about the unattached system and, after another decade or so, the Extension Lecture system, might not have organized itself with such drastic results. The non-collegiates might have come into existence while as yet the Great Western Railway approached the Cherwell no nearer than Didcot. The Extension Lecture machinery was not less dependent upon the propulsive power of steam than the iron engine of Stephenson itself. To-day Bradshaw's Guide is as indispensable a part of the lecturer's equipment as his manuscript notes. Here, as at other points in our secondary education, more organization and more endowments are required. There should be more inducements to young and competent graduates who have the knack of imparting their own knowledge to large or small classes to take up this work as a career, not as an occasional auxiliary to other occupations. The Extension centres also need to be supplemented more largely with local colleges such as that for which Reading is indebted to Oxford and Exeter to Cambridge.

CHAPTER XV
FROM THE OLD SOCIAL ORDER TO THE NEW

> The concrete personal result of the civic, social, and educational processes already described is now to be examined. The personal contrast between the new generation of young men and women of the middle class, most likely to strike an Englishman returned to London after long absence. Sex emancipation. The typical physique of both sexes has been visibly modified, amongst other agencies by bicycle practice. The stately maiden or matron of the period was unknown to John Leech; has been drawn faithfully by Du Maurier. Some social ideals are unchanged, but older middle class ideals have passed out of date.

In the foregoing chapters a general view has been given of the social conditions under which, modified it may be by the influences of his historic past, the character of the average middle class Englishman of the Victorian epoch is formed. What is the personal result, the concrete individual product of these forces? The epithet 'middle class' is employed in deference to traditional wont, but is in great measure misleading because the tendency of the age, the uniformity of the social and educational discipline through which most Englishmen pass tends increasingly to obliterate distinctions of conventional grade, and in tastes, pursuits, prejudices, to assimilate all to a single type. 'They look upon you as we do upon a December fall of snow; as a seasonable, unaccountable, uncomfortable work of God, sent for some good purpose, to be revealed hereafter.' The restlessness which in the British visitor puzzled the Mussulman when *Eothen* was written as a national quality has of late increased among us.[44]

From those who represent Royalty to those who represent manual labour for daily bread, an impatient restlessness is socially a note of the period which has perfected steam locomotion by sea or land, and by the electric telegraph has almost annihilated time. The cheap press, with its ubiquitous correspondents and historians of all contemporary ranks and occurrences in the body politic, has transformed the severely domesticated Briton of both sexes, of all ages, who belonged to a bygone generation, into an eager, actively enquiring, socially omniscient citizen of the world, ever on the lookout for new excitements, habitually demanding social pleasure in fresh forms. The insularity of the national character has to some extent disappeared in the tide of new ideas, and novel modes of life that from Continental sources are perpetually overflowing into our land. The Universities, as shown in a preceding chapter, have been brought to the door of the labourer at his bench, to the shop assistant at his counter, to the clerk at his desk. If this does not always imply an universal access of real education, no one who knows the England of to-day can doubt that it never fails to mean the multiplication of all kinds of knowledge, or to generate the social aspirations, and the thirst for that kind of self-improvement, real or imaginary, which is accompanied by a growing demand for social existence of an animated kind, for a daily life less insular in its organization and less restricted to the domestic hearth. Some prejudices, as was natural among a conservative people, were on its first introduction excited against the new order of things.

Late in the seventies of our century the social craze of what was called 'rinkomania' set in. Any available buildings were laid down with floors more or less lubricated, on which the sons and daughters of the various sections of the great middle class, shod with a peculiar adaptation of wheels, slipped about, and called it skating. These resorts were no doubt admirably conducted. Acquaintances made at them were probably blameless. They often perhaps ended in blissful and desirable marriage. But not without a shock to her sense of maternal propriety did the English matron of old-fashioned ideas see, or hear of, her daughter being twirled round in the arms of some youth just introduced, or perhaps without even the preliminary of that easy form. The young woman could cite plausible precedent for the process. The most fond and nervous of mothers suffered her fears to be allayed. No evil, and it may be hoped some good, to mind and body, came perhaps from these experiences.

It was, nevertheless, an innovation on the usage of generations to which bygone ancestors and ancestresses would not readily have reconciled themselves. In plain words it signified the revolt of the sons and daughters of the middle class against their exclusion from modes of social enjoyment that to their contemporaries slightly above them in the social scale had long been allowed. They had read of the subscription balls planned by the astute Scot, John Almack, at Willis's Rooms, in the last quarter of the eighteenth century. More recently they had seen accounts of subscription dances in what were then aristocratic watering places like Scarborough, or of the more cosmopolitan revels where chaperons were largely dispensed with by their well-born charges at Baden-Baden and Homburg. What claim did the accident of birth constitute to a monopoly of the more stirring and less exclusive forms of pleasure? Thus it came to pass that the pastime which followed the generally patrician Almacks at the interval of a century from being a romp of children became the mildly gymnastic function of youths and maidens of maturer years.

The next stage in this progress is marked by the popularity of the lawn-tennis ground. The private gardens of urban or suburban villadom were soon too small for the wielders of the racquet. The common enclosure of the crescent, the square, or the 'Gardens,' was coveted one day by the players. It was possessed the next. After this, the transition to lawn-tennis subscription clubs, with public grounds, and championship matches open to all comers was easy and natural. The parlour of home soon dwindled into an insignificant spot to the overgrown boys and girls engaged in 'All England' tournaments of their own.

Meanwhile, the gentlemen and ladies who called themselves society, and to whom a portion of the newspaper press was set apart, were indulging more enterprising tastes still, in a manner duly recorded by their daily and weekly journals. The rage for 'making up a party' for everything; researches into the London slums, or visits to the French play, came in; superstitious veneration for the ceremonial etiquette of a past day went out. The mere expedition to the theatre was scarcely stirring enough without the preliminary dinner or the subsequent supper at the modish restaurants which cause certain quarters of London metaphorically to abut on the Boulevard des Italiens or on the Palais Royal. They who now from afar imitated this glittering example had not, it is true, like their betters, any 'smart' sets of their own.

That was no reason why the favourites of fortune should have all the fun to themselves. The daughters of the professional class and of those below them in the social scale were as well educated, as intelligent, as personally presentable, as those whom a partial chance had made conventionally their superiors. Why should the persons born with the proverbial gold spoon in their mouths alone be emancipated? Friskiness was an attribute not confined to the born inheritors of that which called itself society.

Thus the laws of middle class orthodoxy were subjected to a process of general relaxation like to what, rightly or wrongly, was fancied to have taken place in more exalted circles. Clubs for private theatricals followed the subscription dances, in suburban town halls. Bayswater wanderers or South Kensington shooting stars reproduced some theatrical favourite from the repertory of the Prince of Wales's or the Gaiety on the amateur boards of Westbourne Grove, Brompton, or Chelsea. In all things the accredited exemplars of the latest and most cosmopolitan mode were followed by the younger generation of the classes that conventionally were still regarded as strongholds of the ethical severity which Puritan ancestors handed down. The development was of course inevitable. In the long run it will not be found to have done any harm. But incidentally it has involved a considerable modification of the old ideas and habits of many hundreds among Her Majesty's subjects whose special attribute was once supposed to be, in Froissart's phrase, 'to take their pleasures sadly.' Lord's Cricket Ground on an Eton and Harrow match day; the Hyde Park Magazine as the meeting point of the Four-in-Hand Club; any one of some half-dozen eating houses bordering on Bond Street, frequented under a Gallic title by the home-staying Briton; these have ceased to be the appanage of Belgravia or Mayfair alone; the crowd which resorts to them is quite as representative of the newest interests as of the oldest acres.

In theory and in practice 'society' considers itself, and to some extent is still, a close corporation. It is bordered by a fringe not always easily to be distinguished from the holy fabric itself. Its doings are more and more moved by influences originating outside its own limits. If this were not so Lord Beaconsfield would not have been able truthfully to say in his last novel *Endymion* that London which during the earlier days of the Queen's reign was a very dull place had now become a most amusing one. No one knew the capital better or during his later years had tasted of its lighter pleasures more discriminatingly than the critic who made this remark.

As the English race owes much of its vitality and vigour to the variety of the elements, Anglo-Saxon, Danish, French, of which it is a fusion, so English society would long since have been disintegrated by its own power of boredom and its own monotony of texture unless it had extensively recruited itself by alien elements as diverse and as invigorating as those with which the House of Lords, eagle-like, periodically and wisely renews its youth. The personal preferences, prejudices, predilections, of the old and unreformed social polity remain. The tradition of an aristocracy is unbroken though the system has undergone additions so organic.

In many places the Victorian squire and lord of the manor is not in the present year a direct or indirect descendant of those who at the Queen's Accession were settled on the estate he holds, and who inhabited the house wherein he dwelt. The idea of such a change of tenure or of an alienation of family rents to a race of strangers would have shocked the ancestor and might even thrill his mouldering remains in the family vault with horror. As a fact, however, the passage from the old to the new régime has involved no revolution nor even much abruptness in development. The truth is, the estate was so heavily dipped, whether by mortgages or dower charges; the margin left for irregular expenditure was so narrow, as to leave the property in a chronic instability of equilibrium; a longer succession of bad seasons than usual, one or two farms unexpectedly without tenants; these experiences would not be felt by the territorial magnate, nor by a landlord who had other sources of income than his acres. Such incidents are quite enough to reduce the small squire to practical indigence. His children have to be educated, though his farms may be unlet; his sons' bills must be paid; his daughters portioned off in marriage. Instead, therefore, of sitting at the head of his table in the old Hall at his 'rent dinner,' the squire, one of a long race of squires, has transported his family to economical quarters in Bath or Clifton, Brighton or Boulogne, where living is tolerably cheap, opportunities of education are plentiful, and society of a sort is forthcoming. Or if since Lord Cairns' Settled Estates Act modifications of entail have removed the earlier difficulties in the way of land transfer, the family connection with the property may have ceased altogether; the estate may have passed into the hands of some lawyer, banker or trader belonging to the county town; of some manufacturing plutocrat from the further North; of some mill owner whose successful ventures have made him a millionaire. But the life lived at the Hall or Court, or Manor, whichever it may be, under its new proprietors violates few of the old traditions.

The squire of to-day, who was the banker, solicitor, or brewer of yesterday, reproduces very successfully the existence of the more ancient predecessors whom events have caused him to expropriate. His son is at the same school, at the same college, or in the same regiment as the son of his predecessor; his daughters are not less fond than the daughters of his predecessor of riding to the meet, or of driving in state to the county ball. He himself is more diligent in the business of quarter sessions, transferred to County Council, than the squire before him was; his wife is not likely to neglect the duties of the parish Lady Bountiful; her poultry yard may be decimated by Reynard; her husband refuses on that account to connive at the enormity of shooting a fox. Rather will he take a pride in being able to boast that when there is a meet on his property, the coverts are never drawn blank. In due time he may accede to the mastership of the subscription pack which more liberally than his predecessor he supports. The last squire was a judge of horses and cattle at the County Show; the new squire will doubtless in due course fill that position; meanwhile, though he may have been born in a warehouse and bred at a desk, his taste for shorthorn breeding is worthy of an exclusively territorial lineage; he himself plays as well as dresses the part to perfection, and might be matched for tramping across stubble or plough and bringing down partridges against the least commercial of the squirearchy.

This is only typical of what during many years has been taking place among all classes. A discreetly generous administration of the Poor Law operates in the long run as an insurance payment against revolution. The fusion of classes not less than the organization of professions or enterprise is the keynote of our epoch. The process has, without an exception, been one of levelling up, not down. The classes called indifferently higher, or older, have proved to possess an unexpected aptitude for communicating the tastes, the pursuits, the habits, the very instincts, which have descended to them from their forefathers, to the newcomers that the distribution of wealth, the opportunities of industry, the innumerable vicissitudes of life, have incorporated gradually into themselves. Thus it has come to pass that society in England, in itself the most miscellaneous of all conceivable composites, is saturated throughout and cemented as to its different parts by a real homogeneity. The method of attainment has varied, will continue to vary infinitely; the ideal standard remains uniform. In most country districts, the notable exceptions being the mining regions of the North, or the aggressively Nonconformist portions of Wales, the old J.Ps. where their qualities entitle them to do so, have as a preceding chapter has shown held their own against their new colleagues on the County Councils. The achievement finds its exact counterpart in the broader and more purely social processes just described.

That which has been called the restless, the aspiring, self-assertive, inquisitive spirit of the age is not confined in its manifestations to any section of the community, urban or rural, territorial or commercial, of gentle or ungentle birth. It has been accompanied by a distinct change in the figure and in the general appearance of the English youth of both sexes. Suppose an Englishman who had left his country at an early period of the present reign, and who, having made his fortune in the Colonies, had returned to pass the residue of his days in his native land. What are the changes that would most impress his mind? It cannot be doubted that foremost among these would be the visible obliteration of the conventional distinction between the aristocracies of birth and money, the oligarchies of manufacture and of land. As from the window of his club, from his seat in the hotel coffee-room, from his position at the theatre, the opera, or from his chair in Hyde Park, he watched the representatives of the new order which during a few decades had sprung up in the old country, he would be aware of an improved expression of countenance upon the faces of the quietly and well dressed young men, of figures taller, better set up, and better carried, among the young women as well.

The ideal of English womanhood as represented in the sketches of George du Maurier is a faithful generalization from actual life, historically accurate in all its essential details. Even the lofty stature since the bicycle began to develop certain muscles and parts of the human frame, is now seen to be no figment of the artist's imagination. The feminine forms which, towering majestically above the thrones of wheelwork, look down upon the dwarfed passenger or equestrian, are to-day perceived to have been presented on no exaggerated scale in the pages of *Punch*. English women have always had a beauty and a durability of attractiveness unique throughout the world. It is only of late years that to these qualities, consequently on improvements on their physical regimen, the maids and matrons of Britain have added a certain Junonian majesty of proportion that John Leech could not depict simply because in his day it did not exist, but that is portrayed with the fidelity of historic truth by the pencil of John Leech's successor. This latter development has been an unmixed good. The transition from the eventless purely domesticated existence to the locomotive, semi-public, generally unsettling, and exciting life in the case of the future wives and mothers of middle class Englishmen, has had its transient disadvantages. It was not indeed to be expected, nor was it possible, that the change from samplers and school rooms to skating rinks, lawn tennis tournaments, bicycle grounds, and suppers after the play at restaurants, could be accomplished with perfect smoothness, or that the bread-and-butter miss described by Byron should without any jar to the nerves of her compatriots develop into the girl of the period, though on a less aggressive scale than she was once sketched by a popular novelist in a famous article. The most circumspect of chaperons, the most drastic of duennas cannot ensure her charges against sometimes making ineligible acquaintance on these public pleasure grounds. The records of the Law Courts show that the dancing youths of subscription ballrooms, in the suburbs, are not invariably conducive to the domestic happiness of middle class homes. The development was to be expected. The percentage of friction or scandal was inevitable. As Brummel's valet said of his master's crumpled neckcloths: 'These are our failures;' in other words, they are the social miscarriages incidental to the strangeness of the new order. As the class now spoken of becomes more habituated to the cosmopolitan modes which it has assumed, the rôle will doubtless be played without any misadventures.

Nothing less than a progress from insularity to cosmopolitanism is the social enterprise in which the upper classes led the way, and in which those who are always ready to imitate their example have followed them. The fashion is not yet fully acclimatised. For that reason carping critics, unjustly perhaps, have suggested that English families who take their holiday at Boulogne-sur-Mer would do well not to carry with them on their return to their suburban homes in England the social usages which flourish in the Assembly Rooms of an Anglicized French watering-place.

CHAPTER XVI
'THE PLAY'S THE THING'

Summary of the agencies and incidents preparing the way for the revival of the theatre as a popular institution, Macready and his purifying influences inside the theatre. Charles Kean at the Princess's. Usefulness of Rugby and Eton associations to each of these respectively. Miss Faucit (Lady Martin); her last appearance at Drury Lane; her enduring influence on the profession. Mrs Boucicault, Miss Kate Terry, Mrs P. H. Lee, Miss Ellen Terry and others. Henry Irving; his first London hit at the St James's, afterwards at the Lyceum under Bateman. His success characterized. T. W. Robertson's plays. Other circumstances of the time favourable to the new popularity of the play.

At the different seaside resorts fringing the greater part of southern England from Beachy Head to Penzance, by the new sort of life organized at Eastbourne, Hastings, and innumerable other places, one is reminded very practically that only twenty miles of intervening sea separate the French from the English coast. The British climate may be less favourable than that on the other side of the Straits for the open air existence of the French littoral. The more praiseworthy, therefore, and not the less persistent are the efforts of visitors and residents on the unsunny side of the Channel to acclimatize themselves to the *al fresco* habits of Boulogne, Dieppe, Trouville, or Biarritz.

Brighton has not yet very visibly changed its régime since the days when George IV. lived at the Pavilion. Its newer rival, Eastbourne, has taken advantage of a local conformation, and especially of a paved sea front to present the stranger with various little reproductions of what is most characteristic in the social exterior of French holiday life during the bathing season. It is not only one or two families, mutually intimate, which meet and pass together the greater portion of the day on the esplanade that lies in the shadow of Beachy Head. The whole place practically turns out, settles itself down for a day's occupation, if the weather be fine enough, on the causeway above the pebbled shore. The ladies produce knitting instruments or appliances for domestic needlework. The men have their newspapers or books. The circle exactly after the French fashion is formed, big enough in compass to admit all the polite population of the place. When the luncheon hour approaches, there is a move not from off the sea front, but to some of the covered shelters that stud at intervals the esplanade. Improvised tables are covered with white cloths. The company, that the French stranger at a glance recognizes as belonging to the order of *bourgeoisie*, proves itself long to have outgrown the dislike to public meals common to most English men and women at the period of the Queen's accession. At night the boarding houses, hotels, or private dwellings that in a long line rise just above the sea terrace seem practically to amalgamate themselves into a single dancing hall.

Other instances, more picturesque, or at least more suggestive, of the naturalization of continental examples, at English holiday resorts may be given. Eastbourne is indebted for the full development of its natural attractions and for the addition of its beauties of art to the Duke of Devonshire. Amongst other buildings with which the place has been enriched is a town hall of graceful proportions and artistic aspect. This building is crowned by a clock tower so exquisitely shaped and standing out in such classic profile against the dark South Downs in the background as to justify the local vaunt that had it been in Florence sightseers from all parts of the world would have flocked to see it; and guide books would long since have commemorated the glories of, a new Campanile added to the historic list of fair structures. While the Eastbourne clock tower is awaiting the architectural canonization it deserves, the town itself has still more closely approached to southern exemplars by starting a carnival of its own.[45] The slovenly and bedraggled mummeries into which the Italian saturnalia have degenerated have not prevented the enterprising authorities of the Sussex watering place from mimicking the battles of flowers and confetti that are still supposed to relieve the approach of Lent in the City of the Popes, but which as a fact have during late years only formed another feature in Roman vulgarity. One advantage over its more Southern original the Sussex shore imitation possesses. Real confetti are not employed. Pellets of tissue paper are missiles at once less costly and less dangerous than sugar plums. In other respects the continental type has been reproduced rather too faithfully. Whether on the Corso, the King's Road, Brighton, the Esplanade or Terminus Road, Eastbourne, the whole pageant, as to the costume, the humours, and the hand artillery of the mummers, resembles equally the scenes on the return from the Derby by road to be witnessed between Clapham Common and Hyde Park Corner.

It was, perhaps, the foreign imitations in the social scheme of English life increasingly visible during his later years to Matthew Arnold which inspired that close observer with the advice to his countrymen to organize the theatre. To some extent, indeed, the counsel had long been anticipated. The organization of the stage into a wholesome agency of popular amusement and teaching began with Macready, the earliest of that line of considerable actors who have served their generation during the Victorian epoch. But the prejudice against the play prevailing among other than the austerer classes long survived the work of this great reformer of the English stage. The company which fills a theatre to-day in respect of ethics and behaviour is not inferior to the fashionable occupants of an opera box on a subscription night.

It was not always so. When between 1827, the year of his first, and 1851 the year of his last, appearance at Drury Lane, Macready was the head of the theatrical world, he found some difficulty in eliminating certain objectionable elements from the auditorium of Drury Lane. He persisted with his work. At last the moral atmosphere of a London playhouse was admittedly as unexceptionable as that of Exeter Hall. Macready himself who was born in 1793, and lived till 1873, had been educated at Rugby, as Charles Kean who followed him, had reached the Sixth Form at Eton. Macready, too, was in his day almost as much a favourite with the clergy of the Established Church as, since his *The Sign of the Cross*, Mr Wilson Barrett has become in ours. If the Etonian Keate inspired respect by the consciousness of his having birched future generations of statesmen, the Etonian Macready reflected the prestige of respectability upon his profession from the fact that during his retirement at Sherborne in Dorsetshire, most of the Anglican clergy noticeable for their elocution had received lessons from him in the art of reading.

Charles Kean's acting life covered the period between 1820 and 1868. Like Macready, he was a favourite in the provinces before he made his mark on the London boards. With him there began, or was fairly established, the improvement of stage, scenery, costume, and in all incidental accessories that has been brought to so high a point of perfection by the genius, industry, and well-judged lavishness of Henry Irving. Byron's enthusiasm still glows in the words of his famous eulogy on the acting of Charles Kean's father, Edmund Kean, who seems to have been perhaps the most powerful and moving artist that the English stage has known. The energy, passion and fire of the Keans marked a reaction from, and were to some extent a protest against the stately and frigid classicism of the school of Kemble. They thus appropriately coincided in point of time with that romantic movement in English poetry which in his satire Byron ridiculed, but which in his practice he did so much to promote. The epoch, during which these attributes were displayed by Kean and his followers, roughly may be said to have synchronized with the season of the influence on the thought and diction of English poetry exercised through the publication of the *Reliques* of Thomas Percy, who, towards the end of the last, and early in the present, century, was successively Dean of Carlisle and Bishop of Dromore. This book probably did more than any other single volume ever issued from the press, to quicken and complete the revolt of English taste against the formal models of the age of Pope. From the personal life, character and wide social acceptance both of Macready first and of Charles Kean afterwards, the English drama directly, as well as indirectly, was a gainer. In those days the social fusion was not nearly so complete as it has since become; but Macready and the younger Kean had both been popular in their school days. In after life Rugby and Eton respectively rallied round them. The amalgamating agency of the Garrick Club, practically so familiar at rather a later day, was not then an operative force. But of the Athenæum and similar institutions Macready and in his turn Kean must have been free; their private acquaintances and visiting lists were as large and as representative as those of their successors during the present decade of the Queen's reign.

It is not, however, under a dynasty of high tragedians that the full development, as a social and intellectual force, of the Victorian drama was to be attained. Long after the theatre became respectable, it remained dull. The audience seldom dwindled to the point of invisibility which a little time before was in some theatres habitual, and not infrequent in all. Before the period now spoken of, Lord Lytton, of whose place in letters more will be said elsewhere, had gone some way towards repeating the dual successes in Parliament and at the playhouse achieved by Sheridan in an earlier day. *Money* was produced in 1840. Exactly a quarter of a century afterwards a dramatic hit not less palpable and destined to have results more considerable was made by an author till then little known on the London stage. The year in which *Society* was played at the Prince of Wales's, till then the Queen's Theatre, in a street off the Tottenham Court Road, will be remembered by the theatre-goer as that in which Henry J. Byron's last burlesque was produced on the same boards and in which one of the actors in that extravaganza, *Don Giovanni*, Mr John Hare, took, for the first and only time in his life, a woman's part on the stage, wearing the petticoats of Zerlina, the simple peasant girl. The real significance of this occasion lay in its marking a new era in the fortunes of the nineteenth century drama. The germ of Anthony Trollope's novels of domestic life, may be seen in Bulwer-Lytton's fictions of *The Caxtons* school. The part performed by the author of *Society* and its dramatic sequels for the English play resembled the performances of Anthony Trollope with regard to the English novel. Like Bulwer, Robertson fashioned his dialogue on the model of Sheridan. The writer of *Money* laboured to reproduce the antithetic polish of his original. The author of *Society* and the series that followed it was attracted rather by the caustic repartee in which the author of *The School for Scandal* excelled. The change thus introduced at a theatre of which till then few had ever heard, was the substitution of the realities of contemporary life in drawing room, club, shooting field or camp for the threadbare traditions, stilted sentiment, and fustian talk of conventional melodrama. Whether the original were, or were not, too trivial for reproduction, it is at least human nature to which the mirror was now for the first time during recent years held up. The contrast between Robertson and most of his immediate predecessors who were nearly his contemporaries was not less marked than that between those masterpieces of the Laura Matilda school, which delighted Mrs Wititterly, and the works of Miss Edgeworth, or that between the *Great Cyrus* and the author of *Waverley*. The *dramatis personæ* of Robertson were the men and women, the youths and maidens, the old bucks and young officers, the pretty servant girls, their ogling followers, the dapper apprentices, the seasoned topers whom the English public had long known from Leech's drawings in the 'London Charivari,' but who had not often been met with recently on the London stage. Now, for the first time within the experience of many, the theatre became the fashion; the stalls at the Prince of Wales's first, and at other houses soon afterwards, were peopled by occupants as modish as the Italian Opera when Piccolomini sang in *Traviata*. Even then, however, the first night of a new drama, though at the most popular playhouse fell very short of reproducing the personal distinctions of a première at the Comédie Francaise or the Palais Royal. That was to follow in due time. Early in the sixties an impressario, with judgment sharpened by American experience, became the lessee of the same theatre, the Lyceum, which twenty years earlier had been managed by Charles Mathews and Madame Vestris. The first great feature in Mr Bateman's management was the powerful and picturesque acting of his accomplished daughter in *Leah* first and in some Shakespearian parts afterwards. About the same time an actor with whose name in coming years the Lyceum was to be more widely associated had given the public specimens of an art surprisingly vigorous and picturesque. Henry Irving first played before a London audience in 1859. In 1866 he had the good fortune to be cast with Miss Herbert (Mrs Crabbe) in one of those character parts in which he has had few equals, the worthless, persecuting husband in *Hunted Down*. This was in the theatre that witnessed the first triumphs of the great singer Braham, that more recently had been filled from pit to gallery by the laughter loving admirers of Mr and Mrs Frank Mathews,[46] or by the appreciative few who realized the charm of the more subtle impersonations of Alfred Wigan. The place, therefore, was of good omen for the rising star. The most accomplished dramatic critic whom in England the century has produced, George Henry Lewes, and the lady who bore his name, but is best known to the public as George Eliot, author of *Adam Bede*, both witnessed the début. 'Ten or fifteen years hence,' said the gentleman, 'that young man will be where Kean once was, at the head of the English stage.' 'In my opinion,' faintly murmured the lady, 'he is there already.'

Meanwhile, the popular taste of English playgoers had been educated by the impersonations of Miss Faucit as well as by her own literary expositions of Shakespeare's characters, and by the written discourses of her future husband, Sir Theodore Martin on cognate subjects. The daughter of an actress, Lady Martin received her first education for the stage from an actor, one of a race of actors, Percival Farren, of the Haymarket Theatre. This is the family which at the end of the eighteenth century gave a Countess, acknowledged on Mrs Abington's retirement to be the first actress of her day, to the Derby peerage. Its living representative, the gifted and exemplary William Farren, more than recalls to the present generation the genius of his predecessors. Soon after her arrival in London, Miss Faucit joined Macready's company, and her 'Juliet' became a classical performance. Probably the last occasion that this lady was seen on the London stage is her performance of 'Rosalind' in *As You Like It* at Drury Lane during the sixties. As a proof that Lady Martin has exercised an abiding influence on her profession for good it is enough to mention the names of Mrs P. H. Lee, as 'Juliet,' of Mrs Boucicault, the graceful and accomplished wife of a popular husband, Miss Kate Terry (Mrs Arthur Lewis), peerless in romantic melodrama, under the lesseeship of Benjamin Webster at the Adelphi. Some bright particular star from the days of Sir Walter Scott downwards has never failed any generation of the Terry family; Henry Irving's inexhaustible co-adjutress has only illustrated anew the ancestral tradition. Artists whether of the pen or pencil, practically experienced in all the publics of Europe, have been unanimous in testifying that there is none with whom conscientious toil and excellence are so sure ultimately to yield the reward of fame and profit as the public of England.

The theatre with us was firmly established as an honourable and lucrative institution directly men of intellectual power and of competent education began to throw their energies into it as they might have done into the law, the legislature or any other of the liberal professions. Samuel Phelps was born some ten years later than Macready; he was trained in Macready's company; under him Sadler's Wells became once more the prosperous school of classical drama. Some years junior to Phelps, Walter Montgomery laboured in the same line. Both of those men unconsciously were preparing the way for Henry Irving; they were each endowed with high gifts of mind as well as with shrewd common sense. Their detractors of course were not wanting. Neither Montgomery nor Phelps, on the score of public appreciation, had more reason to complain than Henry Irving himself. If, therefore, the reason is asked for the revived popularity of the play in all grades of English life, the answer must be not so much the exceptional brilliance of individual successes as the qualifications of industry not less than aptitude which a succession of actors has brought to the vocation. Sir Henry Irving, as a stage artist may have his mannerisms or defects. Whatever career he might have embraced, he would have made his mark in it, because, besides being a great actor, he is a remarkably clever and far-seeing man. He is therefore in this way historically true to the best associations of his art.

Public speakers at theatrical fund dinners are apt to cite as novel instances of the drama's popularity the proportion of young actors who have been educated at Eton or taken a degree at Oxford. So far from this being a novelty, it is rather, as the illustrations mentioned above show, the reversion to an older order. Henry Irving's knighthood only implied the just recognition of qualities that in another walk of life would have earlier elicited for their possessor a like distinction from the State.

In accounting for the approximation as to popularity of a London to a Paris première which to-day so much impresses the foreign visitor, other circumstances must be remembered. During the last decade or two, especially since the collapse of the second French Empire, the English capital has been, to an entirely new extent, the pleasure ground of the world, and at all seasons of the year contains a large floating population of strangers, Anglo-American or European, as well as of British subjects visiting for a few days from other parts of the Kingdom, the capital on the Thames. These birds of passage seldom possess a large social acquaintance in the capital; the men among them do not always belong to clubs; the ladies are too busy shopping to invite, or to make, calls; the theatre is thus for a constantly increasing proportion of those who sleep within the bills of mortality the easiest and the most attractive form of pleasure. Hence as might be expected, the far more amusing repertory of the Victorian theatre at the end of this century than at any previous epoch. With a Pinero, or a Grundy, to mention only two typical names; with pieces so diverting as *Charley's Aunt*, or *Bootles' Baby*, to mention only one or two representative plays, the Englishman whose chief pastime the play has become finds laughter moving relaxation as effectually, more economically, and to himself a great deal more intelligibly within the roar of his own Strand, than by travelling to a Paris boulevard. The integral part now occupied by the play in the life of the most respectable portion of the middle class is shown by the spacious theatres that have lately risen in such decorous suburbs of the metropolis as Brixton.

Its utility as an agency of mental improvement and moral teaching is suggested by the surprising success of the new religious drama that beginning perhaps with the *Judah* of H. A. Jones, has reached its climax of well deserved success in *The Sign of the Cross* of Wilson Barrett. The suburban theatres have not as yet provided a great field for original talent in the playwright; as might be expected, their patrons seem to prefer pieces that have already received the stamp of public approval. While musical comedies indicate an increasingly popular compromise between Drury Lane and the *Alhambra,* the romantic drama has once more proved to be not less attractive than when three decades since *The Corsican Brothers* first filled the Princess's with enthusiastic audiences. This perhaps at the present moment is the latest of all the successful revivals on the English stage. The plays respectively founded on novels, *The Prisoner of Zenda,* and *Under the Red Robe,* are not only above the average as to merit, but show that the popularity of the cup-and-saucer drama of Albery and Robertson is consistent with a vigorous affection for the melodrama which in Bulwer's *Lady of Lyons,* and in Boucicault's *Colleen Bawn* once absorbed the enthusiasm of the pit.

CHAPTER XVII
THE STRANGER WITHIN OUR GATES AND OUR OWN TEEMING MILLIONS

Technical reasons rendering an exact comparison of foreigners settled in England at different dates impracticable. Approximate results yielded by the analysis of official figures, and their lessons. Danger of German competition with English clerks exaggerated. Actual occupations followed by foreigners. Allegations concerning alien pauperism tested. Proportion of foreign to English pauperism in London. Percentage and nationalities of foreigners in great towns of England and their occupations. Theories about population, especially Malthus. The Malthusian doctrine examined by the light of English experience. Objections to it summarized. The truth and the details of English population since 1793. Views of Dr Price and others as to decrease refuted by Cobbett. Figures and facts of increase. How the non-pressure on means of subsistence can be explained. New industries.

In the preceding chapter it was mentioned that one of the elements in the increased popularity and prosperity of the theatre as an English institution is the growing addition of foreigners to our native population. This will be a convenient place at which not only to analyse the composition of the foreign influx to our shores, but generally to examine the rate and the results of the increase of our population. Official data for the numerical estimate of the strangers within our gates is not forthcoming with the certainty and completeness that might be desired. The reason given by the parliamentary report[47] is intelligible enough; and is to the following effect. The English census takes cognizance of birthplaces, not of nationalities. British subjects who have been born abroad are indeed asked to state the fact, but frequently fail to do so. When the return reaches the Registrar General, the confusion is frequently such as to render it doubtful whether the foreign birthplace implies a foreign nationality as well. This uncertainty was not removed, but was rather increased, when the Enumerating Officer exercised his ingenuity in deducing the national identity from the surname. For instance few patronymics are more distinctively German than Müller. None is more likely to be written by an English clerk as the indubitably British Miller. The result has been at different times an understatement of residents in England who are foreigners both by nationality and birth, and an overstatement of the foreign-born British subjects. The operation of the principle adopted in the last census is exactly opposite to this; it tends to overrate foreign subjects domiciled in England and to underrate English subjects who were born beyond seas. The general consequence is that as the Report already mentioned reminds one, the foreign residents returns for 1891 are not minutely comparable with those for previous censuses. It will be enough to restrict ourselves on this point to the returns of the last three censuses 1871, 1881, 1891, a period of twenty years. Of persons being foreigners both by birth and nationality residing at these epochs in England and Wales, there were in 1871, 100,638; in 1881 there were 117,999; in 1891 there were 198,113. The process indicated by these figures seems to have been at varying rates going forward through a long series of years.

For the two decades between 1871 and 1891, the growth of foreigners among us was 98 per cent. It will, therefore, probably not be a serious miscalculation to estimate the total of strangers within our gates as having doubled itself during the more recent years of the Queen's reign. This estimate derives fresh probability from the fact that between 1881 and 1891 the increase of foreigners domiciled in England outstripped by nearly six-fold the augmentation during the previous decade. The greater part of foreigners in England and Wales are with us for business purposes, or are sailors on board ships trading with England. As, therefore, might be expected, most of them are to be found in the great industrial centres, or at the large seaports. Thus, of a total of 198,113, 95,053, or nearly one-half were enumerated in London; 15,536 in the suburban counties of Surrey, Kent, Middlesex, Essex. Lancashire contained 25,109 with an overflow of 2,254 into the suburban parts of Cheshire. In Yorkshire there were 15,755; in the mining counties of Durham, Glamorganshire, Northumberland, though not engaged in mining but in shipping coals, there were 14,908. The foreign miners, it may be said, actually at work in England are very few. The town in which the total proportion of foreigners to the population has always been highest is of course London (the strictly metropolitan area); the London foreign population is 23 to 1,000. In the suburban districts of West Ham, Willesden and Tottenham the proportion is 10 to 1,000. In the provinces, next to London come Cardiff with 21 per 4,000, South Shields and Manchester each with 18 per 1,000, Leeds and Grimsby each with 16, Liverpool and Hull each with 14; Newport and Swansea each with 12; the other towns where a proportion of 10 per 1,000 is reached are Sunderland, Hastings and Brighton. Of the 198,000 odd foreigners now under consideration, 1,804 are Asiatics coming from China, Persia, Arabia or elsewhere; 1,062 are from Egypt or some other part of Africa; 26,226 are Americans; out of these 19,740 belong to the United States, the subjects of the Stripes and Stars enumerated as domiciled among us in 1881 were 17,767, an increase of 11·1 per cent, during the decade. The number of English living abroad is of course immeasurably greater than that of foreigners living in England. Thus in the case of the United States alone, in 1891 there were settled 1,008,220 English people; this was an increase of 35·2 per cent. over those enumerated in 1881.

The complaint that foreign competition in England itself is crowding native industry out of the market recurs periodically; it renders of special importance to Englishmen the estimate of the European foreigners who have, during the period now under review, immigrated to our shores. The total of those composing this category, men, women and children, has been 168,814; as for the reasons already explained one is cautioned to remember, this is an outside calculation owing to the inclusion in it of many who though British subjects, omitted to set this forth in their schedules. Of the 168,814 European foreigners, 101,255 were males. From this total may be deducted 7,421 as boys under 15, and 3,039 as men of upwards of 65; the sailors, in number 15,035 should not appear in the estimate. When all deductions under these headings of industrial ineffectives have been made there is left an aggregate of 75,760 effective competitors with native industry on English soil, whom during these decades their respective countries have equipped and sent forth against us.

With our own population of 37 millions steadily increasing, the numerical rivalry seems less alarming than might have been imagined. As a matter of fact that rivalry strictly speaking may be larger than the provisional estimate now given would show. It sometimes happens within the experience of local registrars that to avoid English jealousy and so to have a better chance of obtaining work, industrial aliens Anglicize their own patronymics, change them for purely English names, or give English towns and counties as their places of birth; for the most part these deceptions are detected by the enumerator. In St George's in the East, however, in Spitalfields, in Mile End Old Town and elsewhere some registrars seem to think the fraud often passes undiscovered; but others, with equal experience, disavow any reason for the suspicion of such a practice within their areas.

As in the case of our Scotch and Irish colonies, so, too, with our settlers from the European continent the men largely outnumber the women. Whereas in the general population there are 106 women to every 100 of men, and 35 per cent. of the people are under 15 years of age; among the

European foreigners there are only 67 women to every 100 men; only 8·8 per cent. of the whole are under 15. In the case of Swedes, Norwegians, Danes, chiefly of course, sailors, there are four men to every woman, and sometimes as many as seven or eight. That in the case of Belgians, French and Swiss permanently settled in England, the men are outnumbered by the women is of course to be explained by the demands made for the former in the capacity of governesses, milliners, and serving maids. The figures relating to the sex of the strangers within our gates, as might be expected, fluctuate. Especially notable is the difference between the statistics for 1881 and for 1891; in the former year children under 15 formed 6·4 per cent. of all foreigners; in 1891 the percentage had risen to more than 8.

The inference to be drawn from this statistical contrast suggests a new kind of immigration and probably implies that with a view to permanent settlement in England the foreigner was transporting his household gods bodily to our shores. Much has of late been heard about the crowding of pauper aliens into England. Some of the figures just examined may have involved cases of outdoor relief. Of this there is no evidence. But that a very serious addition was in this way made to the pauperism within English workhouses does not appear to be true. The exact figures and facts on this point may perhaps as well be given; of the 36,871 foreign Europeans living at the time of the last census in the East End of London, only 105 had seen the inside of an English union; out of the other (English) 668,243 inhabitants of these parts of the town 13·5 per 1,000 were pauper inmates; in other words, the proportion of foreign to native pauperism in those districts where foreigners chiefly congregate was less than one-fourth of the proportion of paupers in the remaining population. Of these foreigners inside English unions 51 were Germans; 16 were French; 14 were Russians or Poles; 5 were Swiss; of the remainder no more than 4 came from any single foreign State.

'Made in Germany' is a phrase round which there has centred lately much controversy, political, economical, social and personal. This will have prepared the reader to hear that on an analysis of the nationality of our foreign residents, Germany heads the list with 50,599; Poles and Russians come next with 45,074; then the French with 20,797; afterwards follow in the order indicated with numbers fluctuating between 10,000 and 5,000 Austrians or Hungarians, Dutch, Norwegians, Swiss; no other nationality contributed more than 5,000; the Russian and Polish names, which, after the Germans, constitute the majority are so unmistakable as to render a comparison between their numbers in 1881 and in 1891 tolerably safe. This, for reasons already stated, is not so in the case of foreigners with less distinctive patronymics. In 1881 the Poles or Russians enumerated were 14,468; in 1891 they were 54,074; the increase in ten years had thus been some 212 per cent. Germans, in number 50,599, constitute nearly one-third of our whole foreign population. Of that moiety, 1,981 are teachers;

1,198 musicians; 5,358 domestic servants in private families or inns; 659 are professional cooks. To pass to a higher social category, 1,207 Germans are established in business as brokers and merchants; 1,966 as clerks; 393 are commercial travellers; 2,833 are sea-faring men; 282 are jewellers or goldsmiths; 889 are watchmakers; 794 cabinetmakers; 1,309 are butchers; 2,340 are bakers; 276 are sugar refiners; only 592 are classed as general labourers; 5,042 are occupied in ministering to the needs, luxuries, or vanities of the person from the making of coats to the dressing of hair, or the preparation of feathers for Court head dresses.

From these figures two facts of some interest emerge. The business clerks who are complained of as interfering so disastrously with the clerical labour market of Englishmen do not represent the largest contingent of Teutonic industry among us. Numerically the most serious competition of German with English industry is in the case of domestic servants. German tailors are second in order of importance; the clerks come after, not only these, but other occupations. Next to Germany, Scandinavia, Belgium and Spain seem to supply the most numerous competitors with the industry of the British middle classes.

The growth of the purely English population, not complicated by any foreign elements accompanied, as it has been, with a steady increase of national prosperity is enough to supply instructive material to the philosophical enquirer into the facts and figures of English progress during the Victorian epoch. Before looking into these by the light of the once accepted theory of population it will be as well clearly to state what these doctrines are, as well as to summarize the criticisms to which, on the face of them, they are open. The doctrine of Malthus was first put forward by him at the end of the last century. During the first years of the present, while the reverend philosopher was professor of history and political economy at Haileybury, few subjects excited so much interest or controversy among writers on political philosophy or comparative statistics. The doctrine, as it was originally propounded by its author, is that population tends to increase in geometrical ratio, that subsistence only increases in numerical ratio. It followed, therefore, that unless the population be periodically thinned by the external influences of pestilence or war, the poorest classes chronically must be at starvation point, and that unless the multiplication of the race be checked by prudential restraints, within a given time the point will be reached at which the population on this planet is altogether in excess of the means for its support. On the threshold of the discussion which this proposition elicited, the obvious remark was that it asserted not an actuality but a possibility. Hence, unless, instead of a tendency, a proved experience could be asserted; unless, in other words, in the place of a tendency to increase existing, a historical increase could be established, the commentators on Malthus maintained that the danger which he foresaw was too remote to be reckoned with. The following is the line taken by the critics of the Malthusian theory. It was declared to rest upon a series of hypotheses which as a matter of fact were never fulfilled. Granted that if the progression foreseen by Malthus took place, the calamity apprehended must ensue; it was maintained, as a matter of fact, that the abundant safeguards existing in practice were ignored by the alarmist *doctrinaires*. Supposing each marriageable pair upon the earth to marry first, and to produce afterwards as many children as a normally healthy couple may expect, not only subsistence, but standing room in this world would fail them. Experience, however, shows the fulfilment of any such forecast to be a moral impossibility. In daily practice there are apart from difficulty of subsistence many checks which avail to keep increase of population within reasonable bounds.

Thus, statistics show that more than half the human beings born die from accidents or ailments before reaching marriageable age. Of those who actually reach that age, an uncertain, but considerable proportion fail to find mates; the men perhaps because they are over fastidious or selfish; the women possibly because they lack attractions of dower or person. With many more the course of true love runs crooked; the desired partner not being attainable, a solitary life is led. In other cases, the fear of not being able to maintain a conventional position acts as a deterrent. Then there is the considerable percentage of cases where legitimate opportunities of marriage are denied. Thus Colonial frontier men in solitary wilds have few opportunities of courtship or matrimony. Soldiers constantly changing their station; or sailors with a brevet wife in every port, are not usually marrying men, or the founders of numerous families. Of those who marry, many have no children, some have only one; others have sickly children who die. On the assumption that everyone in the world married, each pair must have two children to keep up the population.

Hence the critics of the Malthusian theory have calculated that, striking out of their count those who cannot or will not marry, and those who, marrying, are childless; merely to maintain the population without increasing it, every married couple ought to produce a family of six. Though according to the Malthusians themselves this sufficiently liberal allowance of progeny might be reached without any calamitous consequences, practical acquaintance with the contingencies of domestic life shows that this quantum will not often be reached. If in any part of the world there existed conditions favourable to marriage and to fecundity, it was in Australia, shortly after the earliest gold discoveries, but when many immense fortunes had been made in farming; here there was work for all, wages were high, living cheap, cultivable, but uncultivated land abounded; finally there were no catastrophic checks from earthquake, pestilence or famine to the multiplication of human beings; if, therefore, the Malthusian doctrine could anywhere be verified, surely it would be here. Notwithstanding all these inducements to marriage and the propagation of the species, the actual rate of population increase was 2 per cent. a year.

Hence it may perhaps be inferred that this represents the normal rate. That falls far short of the geometrical rate which the Malthusians would have us expect. The physiological truth, as expounded by experts in these matters would seem to be that in proportion as subsistence is more abundant and of a better kind, life more regular and artificial, fertility decreases. Scientific physicists point as proof of this statement to the fact that wild animals when domesticated or in good condition are less prolific than in their normally savage and poor state. So it is with women in the western wilds of Ireland, or in the Scotch Highlands. As their food and clothing are scarce and coarse, their maternity increases. The inference from the facts now cited clearly is that whatever the terms of the Malthusian proposition may mean, their significance does not warrant the conclusions that ardent Malthusians have at all times drawn from them.

But it has been asserted that famine and plague are the Divinely appointed checks to the growth of population; thus showing some external restraint upon the multiplication of the race to be necessary to prevent population outstripping subsistence. The most familiar proofs offered of such an assertion are the periodical famines in India, especially that in the province of Orissa, and the Irish famine from the potato failure in 1846. On these proofs the following remarks suggest themselves. In the case of Orissa, numbers had nothing to do with the famine or consequent mortality; the people died because the heat of the sun untempered by rain literally scorched the food supply out of existence; if there had been only as many hundreds as there were millions, the same calamitous result, though on a numerically smaller scale, would have ensued; a province of Central India was decimated because the food did not exist. The famine therefore was real.

In the case of Ireland, no famine at the close of the first decade of the Queen's reign existed in the same sense that it had done in Orissa; the potato crop alone failed; corn, dairy produce, food products generally were plentiful; corn in fact was being exported from Ireland while the Irish themselves were perishing from starvation. The calamity therefore was less the stoppage of supplies by Providence as a check on population than a pecuniary failure. Nor was it a visitation as regards which man could plead exemption from responsibility. The potato rot did not come upon the Irish peasantry in a day or in a week. The disease had appeared in Eastern Europe so early as 1844 and 1843; it was scientifically certain that eventually it would reach Ireland. When, after due warning it attacked the plots of miserable soil reclaimed by peasant industry from hillside and bog, the destruction of the staple of native food wrought by it was gradual. Weeks and months were required to complete the process of rotting. Nothing was done. The people died not from the unkindness of nature, but from the neglect of man. Had the prudential restraints of the Malthusians limited the numbers to half the actual total, the agrarian policy which was responsible for the diet of potatoes instead of corn would have resulted in the same poverty and, therefore, in the same death.[48]

One is not here concerned with the abstract truth of the theory of population enounced by Malthus, but with its applicability to, or its instructiveness in the case of, the England of Queen Victoria. What then are the facts of population here to be dealt with? The multiplication of the inhabitants of this country is known never to have been so rapid as during the century which opens with the French Revolution in 1793, and which witnesses at its close the sixtieth anniversary of Her Majesty's accession. Earlier periods of augmentation may therefore be omitted. A hundred years ago, Dr Price, maintaining population actually to have decreased, spoke of its decline as a great danger. Cobbett and other more accurate observers, or less incautious generalizers, in opposition to Dr Price, established circumstantially the fact of an increase; but the possibility of a contrary view being taken is as suggestive as it now seems remarkable.

Mr Thorold Rogers has been guided by his study of prices to the conclusion that the standard of comfort in living began to rise among us from the Reformation of the sixteenth century progressively onwards; and that even during the eighteenth century the masses were enjoying a golden age. Between 1750 and 1800;—the period during which the factory system began to be known, and the problems of population and production were both closely discussed,—no fear of population getting ahead of subsistence suggested itself. Similarly during the Corn Law agitation 1840-6, the increase of production from English soil, notwithstanding the economico-agrarian law of diminishing return was proved to have outgrown the population. Later and more detailed statistics show that since 1831 population with us has increased 30 per cent., capital 100 per cent., purchasing power 600 per cent. During the last half century the average price of corn has been falling. Our demand for foreign corn has increased and is increasing. This evidence fortified by the income-tax returns, forbids the notion that during the last two centuries population in England has outstripped the means of its support. The conclusion is therefore irresistible that the natural tendencies to increase of inhabitants, whatever the occult possibilities may be, practically are counteracted by motives invisible and undefinable, perhaps, but not less potent. As a writer in *Macmillan's Magazine* [49] points out, population generally increases up to the relative limit set by the power of procuring subsistence at any given time and place. The absolute limit as is shrewdly remarked, could only be reached when the highest skill and organization have extracted the last possible morsel of food from the earth; that experience has not yet been reached. So far from population always getting ahead of subsistence, its increase is by no means invariably as rapid as the development of the food supply. Both between 1560 and 1760; again between 1830 and 1880, this seems to have been the case in England.

During many years, as each decennial census has appeared, timid sociologists may well have felt misgivings whether England could continue to support her ever multiplying millions. The fears of science have not been verified by the facts of experience; thus exactly a quarter of a century since the census return of 1871 seemed to leave no escape from the conclusion, that population had already all but overtaken the means of subsistence, or that unless our numbers were at once arrested, it must in a very short time do so. Since 1871 we have added 7 millions to our population, the equivalent, that is, of 1,200,000 families and the same number of working men. Instead of the pressure on subsistence being greater, or the average condition of our people being worse, the exact opposite has occurred. In comparison with the state of things two decades since, the masses among us are to-day better housed, better clothed, better shod, better fed, better educated. There is, as in an earlier chapter was shown, a steady decrease of pauperism; the number of those who with their dependents of all kinds live on the result of their investments, is growing constantly. Whether it be due to the reduction in the cost of conveyance, to the opening up of fresh fields of supply, or to the appreciation of gold, the fall in prices of the chief articles of consumption, corn, sugar, tea, cotton, timber, is a visible and a great benefit to the country.

The fact that the increase between 1881 and 1891 fell short by about a quarter of a million of that which signalized the preceding ten years has been demonstrated by statistical experts of scientific authority not to indicate pressure on means of subsistence, but to be explicable by the stationariness of the population in many rural districts as well perhaps as by the disinclination, reflected from French and American precedent, of Englishwomen indefinitely to fulfil the functions of maternity.

During the period now spoken of, with the exception of mining, the great staple industries of the United Kingdom have none of them increased, while agriculture has decreased. It may, therefore, well seem problematical how the 1,200,000 fresh heads of families have found a livelihood for themselves and their belongings.

The explanation can only be that several new, as they are often nameless industries have during this time come into existence. Birmingham, the home of small industrial enterprises and in a less degree Sheffield, would of themselves explain the mystery. And here specific mention of a personal experience seems necessary. When the present writer by local observation was first acquiring material for such writing as that of which this book consists, he visited among other places Sheffield, under the obliging personal conduct of its then, and happily its present, Member, Mr A. J. Mundella. Close to one of the largest factories in that capital of cutlery and furnaces is a small establishment owned by a single proprietor who from that source of income alone, has realized a considerable fortune. This gentleman contracts for the purchase of all the refuse, the waste paper, the gilt or tin foil and other unconsidered trifles included which accumulate in the rubbish heaps of other premises. On their reaching his place of business, they are placed in a furnace; all the impurities are burnt out of them. There remains a nondescript residuum of charred and apparently worthless substances. Some of these, however, contain particles of gold dust; these are placed into a crucible; eventually there is often left a deposit of the precious metal which the jewellers are ready to buy. The gold watch chain worn by the Sheffield industrialist now spoken of, was of several carats, and was manufactured entirely out of the yield of this refuse. The incident is worth mentioning as a concrete suggestion drawn from real life of the protean methods of industrial money-making that are constantly being discovered by the ingenious and unabashed industry which in Virgil's phrase, conquers all things.[50]

CHAPTER XVIII THE HOUSE OF COMMONS AS A LANDMARK OF POLITICAL PROGRESS UNDER QUEEN VICTORIA

> Comparative novelty of constitutional government as understood to-day, and of real parliamentary representation during the first years of the Queen's reign. Dissatisfaction with, and defects in, Lord Grey's Reform Act. The new Chamber for the Commons nearly contemporary with the reformed House. Retrospect of different places in which the Commons have sat. Growth of social conveniences at Westminster. Recent changes that after half a century would most strike the visitor to Westminster. The ladies in Parliament. Discomforts of their earlier parliamentary position as compared with its luxuries and ascendancy to-day. Changes in the House itself. The day of the youthful M.P. Modifications in the procedure of the House of Commons. Obstruction. Its origin and prevention. Influence of the House to-day.

Constitutional Government and a popular legislature, did on Her Majesty's accession, both exist in England. Neither of them was more than four or five years old. Each therefore had arrived only at the experimental stage. The Reform Bill of '32 had scarcely begun to be operative when its imperfections made themselves felt. For the first time indeed in English history popular constituencies had been organized by that Measure. But while all householders rated at £10 and upwards had a voice in the national Government, various old historic franchises had been abolished. At Preston, for example, the suffrage had previously been in practice universal; so that there, and at Windsor like Preston, the Reform Act had a disfranchising effect.[51] All sections of the middle class were enfranchised by the Measure of 1832.

With some show of reason it was complained that, while numbers were now supreme, opinions and interests were, as in the case of pocket boroughs, better able to make themselves felt under the nominally exclusive régime which had been swept away. The new constitution was not the only parliamentary novelty that signalized the opening of the Victorian epoch. In addition to a new parliament returned by fresh constituencies there had recently risen at Westminster a new Palace containing of course a House of Commons comparatively fresh from the workmen's hands. The old structure had been burnt down in 1834. The pile of buildings designed by Barry as its architect which is now so familiar a feature in the London landscape did not assume its present proportions in all their completeness till the reign had entered upon its second decade. During the six years between 1834-40 the Houses sat in a temporary building which had been run up with miraculous rapidity. As nearly as possible ten years after Her Majesty received the early visit of her Chancellor at Kensington Palace, more exactly on April 13, 1847, the Peers took possession of their new Chamber.

Three years later, May 30, 1850, the Commons met for the first time beneath the roof that shelters them to-day. Since the People's Representatives and the Barons were constituted into separate Assemblies, the building which the famous Clock Tower surmounts is in fact the fourth meeting place that has been assigned to the Commons of England. It was not till 1547, the first year of Edward VI. that the chapel of St Stephen in Westminster Palace was prepared for the Commons. Before that date they had assembled in the Chapter House.

The Speaker's Chair was then the former seat of the Abbot. Beneath this roof were passed the Statute of Provisors 1350, the Statute of Præmunire, the Act of Supremacy, and the Act of Submission. Until St Stephen's became the synonym for the Popular House, party government can hardly be said to have been, even rudimentarily, established. Government by groups, the rule in the French Chamber theoretically held to be so mischievous in England, but in whose direction we seem to be making further progress each year, was practically the rule in the pre-St Stephen's period. Nor would it be easy to exaggerate the influence favourable to a hard and fast dichotomy into parties exercised by the structural arrangements of the secularized shrine.

What are the points of contrast in the economy of the Commons' House of Parliament and its precincts to-day which would most strike the shadowy observer revisiting the place by the glimpses of the moon after half a century's absence.

The accommodations of comfort, study or pleasure that now make the House of Commons not perhaps the best but a really good club, are only the fulfilment of undertakings which our imaginary spectator would remember as having been begun when he was last there. Neither would he be much surprised by the increase in the occupants of the Strangers' Gallery; nor in the greater conveniences enjoyed by the reporters. Long before the necessity for Barry's new building had arisen these improvements in the internal fittings of any House of Commons were anticipated. When in 1847 the Hereditary legislators were about to settle in their new home, they were much exercised by the conditions under which, and the exact places where, their wives and daughters should view the progress of their debates. The first suggestion of appropriating to the peeresses the gallery that runs above the Ministerial Bench elicited from the late Lord Redesdale the blunt remark: 'It will make the place like a casino.' To-day the bright toilettes lit up by the sun pouring through the multi-coloured glass, and blending with the bright tints of the decorated walls form nearly the most picturesque feature in the afternoon of a London season.

Amazement, approbatory or the reverse, at this spectacle is the beginning of surprises which the spectral visitor would find in store. Descending into the hall which separates the two Houses, he would meet a commoner acting as a squire of dames, escorting detachments of ladies to points whence they could best see the House of Commons celebrities of the hour. Looking through the swing door of the Representative Chamber, the parliamentary Rip Van Winkle would for the first time in his experience note the flutter of muslins and silks through the grating that bars the compartment just above the reporters' benches, and that is known to-day by the name of the Ladies' Cage. In 1834 this was a novelty as yet undreamed of. The germs of it may perhaps first be detected during the opening year of the present century.

In 1800 the admission of the Irish Members after the Act of Union involved structural alterations in the Chamber. Among other things a chandelier was fixed in the centre of the ceiling. At the same time a round hole was cut for the escape of the hot air. The top of the orifice was protected by a balustrade. From above this chandelier ladies were permitted surreptitiously to peep over. In that extremely uncomfortable and rather perilous position they saw what they could of the speakers and heard murmurs of the debate. The first subsequent novelty was the introduction of a few chairs. The temporary structure for the Commons after the 1834 fire was in the old House of Lords formerly known as the Court of Requests, occupying as it did much, if not all, of the site of Edward the Confessor's palace. The Lords themselves at that time met in the present St Stephen's where the Commons meet to-day. Nor was it till after the first Reform Bill that the domiciles of the two Assemblies were exchanged.

In the building which served the Commons between 1836-40, no provision was made for ladies. By the report of the select committee of 1836 this fresh accommodation was suggested. On the 3d of May in that, or in the following year, the House ordered[52] that a place should be provided where, with less discomfort, and more dignity than from the lamp balustrade, ladies could listen to the speeches, and catch an occasional glimpse of those who delivered them. In the temporary structure the exact spot thus allocated to them seems to have been behind the Speaker's chair, if not actually beneath the floor. Experts at least have discovered no alternative situation as possible. The Ladies' Gallery of to-day as it exists just above the Reporters' box is divided into three parts. The western third is reserved for Mrs Speaker. It is called by that lady's name. Here she receives as her guests personal friends or semi-official personages of her own sex. The two eastern thirds of the compartment now spoken of are at the disposal of Members for their wives and friends. There is a ballot for the Ladies' Gallery a week in advance. Certain representatives of the people have been favoured, as the result of consummate dexterity or rare luck, with singularly uniform success in this ordeal. During the earlier period to which reference has been made, there are believed to have been instances in which ladies clandestinely found a place not only in the balustrade above but in the ventilating chamber beneath the floor. Thus, when they did not flutter as angels above, they burrowed like moles below. Nor, as we have seen, was it till Barry's plan had become an architectural fact that the wives and daughters of the people's elect were delivered from these two predicaments.

To-day a lady visiting the House of Commons during debate has her 5 o'clock tea as comfortably as in her own drawing room. If the weather be sultry, or the debate tedious, she can refresh herself during the interval between tea and dinner with strawberries and ice as luxuriously as at Gunter's in Berkeley Square. During the more monastic period of the modern House of Commons, there occurred a short interval in which a very few ladies on the floor of the House itself on the same side as the Treasury Bench were stationed on chairs so placed that their occupants could hear without being seen. One day a sudden witticism of an orator upset the gravity of the listening stateswomen, and scandalized the Speaker. That laugh proved fatal. Henceforth Members were forbidden expressly by the House to secrete ladies in any part of the Chamber, either above or under the floor. To-day in the interior of the Chamber itself ladies are not more visible than formerly. The proposal to remove the grille that converts their gallery into a cage is still made periodically; but with as yet no great appearance of success.

Outside but still beneath the parliamentary roof, or within the parliamentary precinct, the sex that is no longer 'suppressed,' pervades the place at all hours. The Members' dining room, where male strangers can be invited, is not yet open to guests of our new *ecclesiazusæ*. All other parts of the premises are already pervaded by them. In the basement a room has been discovered in which the fair guests of Members can be entertained when the debate is over by a supper which may well repair the omission of a dinner. The river frontage of the Westminster Palace during some years has been surrendered at discretion to the politicians of the petticoat. Lord Redesdale foresaw the coming resemblance of the interior of the Peers' Chamber to a music and dancing saloon. Even his alarmist imagination never pictured at the height of the London season an assembly of ladies upon the Terrace just outside the Chamber, enjoying as the guests of the elected of the democracy ices, strawberries and cream, all the other modish adjuncts of 5 o'clock tea. This they have done since 1888. More recently there have been added waitresses attractively dressed in a black and white uniform. Some years ago Mr John Bright, a special habitué of the tea room, arranged a subscription for a wedding present to the young person who presided over the cups and saucers, when on her marriage she retired into private life. Even that statesman would not perhaps have undertaken his graceful and chivalrous task in the case of a whole regiment of tea room nymphs.

The lady M.P. has still to come into existence. Her sex controls votes and vicariously receives them. In New Zealand and other Colonies the same sex records votes directly as well as influences votes indirectly. If, as other precedents might suggest, the mother country is advancing towards the Colonial usage, is there any abiding reason why to their parliamentary influence already established beyond doubt, the mothers and daughters of England should not add the responsibility to public opinion which a parliamentary seat would bring and which they now escape?

The personal changes in the composition of the House of Commons are only less striking than the innovations in its social life. Years have passed since Mr Disraeli's oft reiterated remark that the future of English politics was to the English youth. In a sense different perhaps from that which the phrase was first intended to bear, this consummation seems in gradual process of fulfilment. In 1837 a chief amusement of visitors to the House of Commons was to count the number of bald heads in the Assembly. Those phenomena, as the legitimate results of age, are very nearly unknown to-day. During the first three decades of the Queen's reign the average age of a Member was between 50 and 60. Now it is probably not much more than 40. Often it happens that senators are so fresh from school as to be unable to forget their schoolboy phraseology, and to address the Speaker in the exact terms they used but the other day to the master of their Form. Thus, 'If you please, Sir, Mr Speaker, Sir!' is the opening often heard of late years from a boyish senator who rises to address the House in response to the eye of its President. In other respects, the typical M.P. has changed not less conspicuously. Men of the social and political quality who followed the lead of Sir Robert Peel first, and of Mr Disraeli afterwards, who could be taken for nothing else than the country gentlemen that they were, have been replaced by men whose antecedents and whose interests are not less manifestly commercial.

Long after the abolition of the Corn Laws the description of the Conservative party given in the Life of Lord George Bentinck continued to be true. A glance sufficed to show that these 'men of metal and of acres' were the products of their native soil. Specimens of this class lingered at times pretty plentifully after Household Franchise was added to the Statute Book. The tall erect figure of Mr Newdegate, broadened, but not bent, by age, still retaining much of the elasticity of youth; the less rugged and angular, but physically not less well developed, presence of Sir Rainald, afterwards Lord, Knightley; these were specimens of Members not uncommon within the memory of the present generation. To the same order, in spite of a very different appearance, belonged the parliamentary Cato of those days, Mr J. W. Henley, the veteran Member for Oxfordshire. If the wisdom of the House, its occasional intolerance, and its hereditary good sense, were ever incarnate in an individual, they resided surely beneath the compact sturdy figure with the countenance, seamed and gnarled as of an ancient oak, of that remarkable man. Before Quarter Sessions had given place to County Councils, Mr Henley and others of his class ceased to be known in their places.

These were the men, contemporaries of Disraeli and Northcote, brought up in the same parliamentary, often in the same social, school as them. These, too, were they who for his mastery of parliamentary law, his excellence of parliamentary manner, and his maintenance of historic standards in parliamentary debate, could almost tolerate the Liberalism of Mr Gladstone. With a pang they anticipated the day when his withdrawal would rob the Assembly of the last surviving monument of the eloquence and bearing which used to be the familiar attributes in the first assembly of gentlemen in the world. Already debating of the old stately order had begun to go out of fashion. Thirty years after the Queen's accession, in the Reform discussions of 1867, Mr Lowe had made one of the latest and happiest hits ever secured by a familiar phrase from Virgil. In 1881, after the death of Lord Beaconsfield, Mr Gladstone pointed a reference of the same kind with not less felicity when he applied to his rival on returning from Berlin the words by which the Latin poet indicated the commanding presence of Marcellus among the winners of the *spolia opima*.

With these exceptions, there is no recent record of signally successful quotation in the House of Commons from classical authors. Not indeed for want of classical scholars. Professor Jebb, Sir G. O. Trevelyan, Sir M. W. Ridley, are at least the equals in this respect of their seniors.[53] The simple reason is that Latin and Greek quotation which were once held to be, as Mr Disraeli said of invective, an ornament of debate, have passed into the heritage of outworn words and faces. To-day if honourable gentlemen illustrate their meaning by a metaphor or clench an argument by an epigram, they go for their *tropes* and ideas, not to the library, but to the laboratory. Thus one of them not long since was heard to compare the mind of an opponent to a series of condensing chambers. The masters of the grand style in parliamentary oratory, as it may be called, cannot be said to have passed away while David Plunket, Lord Rathmore, lives. But the business of the House of Commons is done in Committee. A Committee of the House of Commons is like a committee of any other gentlemen professedly met together to transact the greatest amount of work in the shortest space of time. Telling arrangement of ideas, clearness of thought, conciseness of phrase, dexterous support of special views by figures and facts; these are the qualities bred in the parliamentary atmosphere to-day. In such categories are the ideals consciously aimed at to be found. No competent person seriously supposes the average of intellectual power in Parliament to have declined. Mr Gladstone and other experts have testified that it has increased, and that the 1893 Parliament contained more men of first rate capacity than any within modern memory.

The interest taken by the nations in the doings of the House of Commons has not permanently abated, nor is likely to do so, seeing that its attraction resides less in the letter of its debates than in the circumstance of its being a continuous commentary on the social as well as political history of the day, a concentration, epitome, and amalgam of the human nature of the period. The vicissitudes of human affairs, the sudden growth, the not less sudden rupture, of human friendships; the involuntary perjuries of political allies surely as laughable in the sight of Jove as the perjuries of lovers; the sworn confidants and colleagues in one Administration transformed into the mortal antagonists of the next; these are the episodes of everyday life reflected upon the stage of the Theatre Royal St Stephen's. Can they then, fail to be more full of dramatic charm than the entertainments provided in any other playhouse of the realm? The parallel between the theatrical and parliamentary stage might be made still closer. As on the former, so on the latter there are certain stock parts always sure to be enacted, whatever the title of the play, or the nature of the discussion.

The Mr Henley already named, pre-eminently representative as he was of the hard good sense and rugged honesty of the Tory squire, was not a novelty in the Chamber. He had his forerunner in the 'down-right' Shippon, as Pope calls him, of a Georgian House of Commons. He it was who, as a Jacobite opposed to Sir Robert Walpole yet said of himself and his adversary, 'He is for King George; I am for King James. We differ on most things; but Robin and I are the two most honest men in Parliament.' The theatrical and parliamentary analogy might be illustrated much further. One or two more instances will suffice. The stage character whose chief function is to keep the audience smiling and to enliven dulness by a laugh has his exact analogue in the parliamentary humorist, whose very rising is the signal for a burst of anticipatory merriment. In the nineteenth century the name of that humorist has been, during its first half, Sir Charles Wetherell. He relieved the severity of the 1831-2 Reform Bill discussions by convulsing his hearers with laughter at the farcical absurdity of his sallies, or by the ludicrous incongruity of the metaphors with which he pointed his invective.

Half a century later the name of the performer is changed. The function discharged is identical. In the place of a Wetherell there sits now a Bernal Osborne, now a Patrick Boyle Smollett, now a William Gregory, and again a Wilfried Lawson, or a Labouchere. In any case the wag is indispensable to the proceedings of the House. In every new Parliament he makes his appearance, if not quite so early, yet with the same regularity as the Queen's Speech, or the Debate on the Address.

Other rôles are equally familiar, and with the same undeviating regularity are forthcoming. High or Low Church, dry or Evangelical, the different champions of the Church, each in their own era and from their own point of view, come forward to defend the national Establishment. These are the gentlemen whom in once addressing a deputation of them Mr Disraeli characteristically styled 'the children of the Church.' Of this section, during the earlier decades of the reign, Sir Robert Inglis was a chief. Round him were grouped a little band in which Mr Spooner, and thereafter the intrepid Mr Newdegate, and poor Mr Whalley, with his jaded, hunted look, had a place. The burly presence of Sir John Mowbray, the less robust, but wiry figure of Mr Talbot, both Members for Oxford University, belong to a later date. When these may have disappeared, successors are already visible to take their place. The stalwart form and patriarchal beard of Sir John Kennaway, the less athletic and more sensitive figure of Mr Stanley Leighton are even to-day powers in that ecclesiastical faction. The two sons of Lord Salisbury, Lord Cranborne and Lord Hugh Cecil belong to another generation, but to the same category of ecclesiastical defenders.

During the Queen's earlier years, Chartism, that is to-day only a name, was an active force. Most of the points of the Charter itself have quietly become law. The Septennial Act has not indeed been repealed; but practically the term of parliamentary life has been shortened. The ballot has quietly superseded the hustings. Payment of Members is seriously discussed. Election expenses have been much reduced. By the Redistribution Bill of 1884, an appreciable step towards equal electoral districts has been taken. The Georgian House of Commons, indeed the House till the full effects of the first Reform Bill were felt, was so small, its members so preponderantly came from the upper class of society as to give the Assembly the air rather of a family party than of a national forum.

From 1707 to the beginning of this century, the English, Welsh and Scotch numbered 558. The Act of Union at the beginning of the century added 100 to the House of Commons of 1801. The additions to the House made by the Reform Bill of 1832 in the case of Wales and Ireland 5 each, of Scotland 8, were exactly compensated by the reduction of English Members. The Measure, therefore, which created popular constituencies and with them a popularly representative Chamber left St Stephen's numerically unaltered. As to quality, it socially modified rather than, as is sometimes said, revolutionized the Assembly. Nor, as to figures, did the Household Franchise Bill of 1868 enlarge the Chamber. The 7 fresh representatives to Scotland, and the 1 to Wales were balanced exactly by the disfranchisement of 8 English constituencies. The House of Commons remained therefore 658. An increase began with the Reform Bill of 1885. The emancipation of the agricultural labourer by the franchise on the same conditions as his urban brother involved the sole increase since the Irish union to the numbers of the House of Commons. Even that is only represented by 12. The whole of this increase was for the benefit of Scotland. Two new Members were indeed received by England under the latest franchise re-arrangement. Two were also lost by Ireland. Thus the Irish disfranchisement balances the English enfranchisement. The sole nett profit in the transaction accrued therefore, as has been said, to Great Britain beyond the Tweed.

While the House of Commons as to arrangements, occupants and visitors has changed more than once during the period comprised in this survey, there has been in the opinion of experts like Mr Gladstone no diminution of ability in its general debates. The amount of varied and accurate knowledge displayed during discussions in Committee by the rank and file of its members has increased appreciably since the Derby-Disraeli Reform Act. But, it is said, as our constitution has become more democratic, our popular legislators have grown unmannerly. Those who know the volumes of parliamentary history summarizing debates in the House during the French Revolutionary epoch of 1793-5 may be disposed to doubt the justice of this censure. The violent personality of the recriminations between individual members of the two Whig sections at this period; the revolting grossness of the metaphors and the epithets by which the intellectual majesty of Burke stooped to express his loathing for the new Radicals on both sides of the Channel; the personal menaces exchanged by competitive debaters of smaller calibre; leave no room for doubt on the point. Two years after the first Reform Act, Church rates and other ecclesiastical topics gave rise in the debates upon them to scenes and noises, cockcrowing amongst them, that scandalised the parliamentary decorum of the period, as disgraceful beyond all precedent. These incidents were attended by a degree of parliamentary disorder which was habitually in excess of the ebullitions however scandalous, provoked during the session of 1893 by the

Second Irish Government Bill of Mr Gladstone. The great change of recent years in parliamentary methods is of course the organized obstruction on frivolous and irrelevant pretexts raised during debate. Even this is not the novelty that some have seemed to suppose. During that distant era when no chandelier hung over the heads of Members, the only illuminants known in the Chamber were candles. A formal motion was made that these should be brought in. The early practitioners of obstruction seized upon this issue to delay the discussion. Motions for adjournment became effective instruments for delay during the Reform discussions of 1832. They were then employed with success generally, and with humour sometimes by the popular Sir Charles Wetherell, and in case of unpalatable amendments by Mr Sheridan. While motions for adjournment have thus always been used as methods of delay, they naturally have had different aspects at various times. Thus when employed for fighting a Bill to which conscientious objection was entertained, these motions differed entirely from those to the same ostensible end made by the feigned opponents of perfectly harmless Measures. Mr Pope Hennessy was practically the founder of this later and indiscriminate opposition to all attempts to legislate.

The late Mr Parnell extended that system to routine business such as the nomination of Committees, also to unobjectionable votes in supply, and finally in 1877 to private Members' Bills as well as Government Bills, with the avowed aim of paralysing the whole machinery of Statute law. The late Sir Stafford Northcote, who more than any other statesman of our time resembled, in his conscientious caution and chivalrous devotion to principle, Mr Perceval, dealt perhaps too gently with this abuse of forms, nor saw fit to employ the new rule that was suggested to him by the consummate experience of the late Sir Thomas May. Mr Gladstone's management of this matter in 1881-2 was more drastic; it would have been successful but for the tactics of the late Lord Randolph Churchill and the present Sir John Gorst. After this came in 1888 the leadership of Mr W. H. Smith, resulting as it did in 15 new Rules. The practical result of the latest changes in House of Commons procedure may be summarized popularly and briefly as follows. The French principle of closure already adopted in all other Popular Assemblies is now part of the law of the English Parliament. This instrument can be moved for at any time. It depends wholly on the Speaker or, if the House be in Committee, on the Chairman, whether the motion for it be put to the House. If put it is generally opposed. Then follow debate and division. For its adoption there must be not only a majority but one composed of not less than 100 Members.

With its larger numbers, the representative character of the House of Commons has been increased also. The steps by which it has acquired control of the executive as well as the legislative machinery of government need not be recapitulated here. Its moral, educational and social influence in the country is probably not proportionate to its actual power. The theory of delegacy so indignantly repudiated by Conservative speakers during the first Reform Bill debates is to-day accepted and actively illustrated by a majority of Members. More and more the tendency is for the constituencies to call into existence a Government to undertake a specific task of legislation whose scope is defined by the individual possessing for the moment the national confidence. To support in that special work that particular statesman, or, if he falls into disfavour, to thwart him, the householders send to St Stephen's men whose discretion is restricted within very narrow limits.

This arrangement immensely increases the authority of the democratic favourite of the moment. It is less favourable to the prestige or usefulness of the Chamber as containing the collective wisdom of the nation. The aptitude for business talk that shall be to the point in Committee has not, when the House has a mind to it, declined. The great speeches, no sooner delivered than they constitute national text-books, are less frequent than the display of excellence in debate. Afraid of boring the Assembly, dreading the imputation of mere rhetoric, the Member who has something to say usually prefers delivering it to his constituents at his periodical reunion with them, or upon some other extra parliamentary occasion. The terse diction and urbane gravity of manner of Sir Charles Dilke made him, during his Foreign Under-Secretaryship, a parliamentary model. Such oratorical efforts as he sometimes made, were reserved for the meetings with his electors. The clever young politician, being on his promotion, speaks when he can that he may give his future chief a taste of his quality. Popular meetings therefore, and the periodical press have detracted from the House of Commons as a school of eloquence, or as a national educator. On the other hand the House of Lords has no constituencies in the background. Its time is less preoccupied. It is to-day far more representative of the English people than was the House of Commons a few years before the Queen's accession. It does indeed chiefly consist now of men whose station and whose antecedents are not very dissimilar from those of the House of Commons before that Chamber had been thrice Reformed. Hence some of those debates, especially on foreign policy, or grave points of constitutional procedure that used to mark epochs in the Elective Chamber are now almost confined to the Hereditary House.

Outbursts of periodical petulance against the Peers will doubtless continue. Such Radicals as may be left in England to-day are at heart far more tolerant of a second Chamber, composed as that at Westminster is, than were the 'root and branch' men not merely of Cromwell's day, but of half a century ago. Something therefore may perhaps be said on behalf of the opinion that any movement which may be successful against the House of Lords is likely to affect the House of Commons as well.[54]

CHAPTER XIX
CROWN, COUNTRY AND COMMONS

Comparative youth not the only point of difference between the House of Commons to-day and formerly. Its reflection of social characteristics of the time shown in the disappearance of the old County Member extinct in the country as well as in Parliament. Modifications in *personnel* of the Liberal party since the great fortunes made in trade and since the first Reform Act; also in that of the Conservatives. Mr Gladstone's opinion and experience on this subject. The obstacles in the way of oratorical efforts or success in the House of Commons, have increased under new conditions. Rivals to House as representative of national feelings. The press, the House of Lords and local debating societies.

The average age of its members is not the only respect in which, during the Queen's reign, the House of Commons has been gradually transformed. If the country squire of the old school of Mr Henley has disappeared from it, that is because he is now as unknown in his own county as in Pall Mall. The social composition of the Whig, or Liberal, party was finally and entirely altered about the period of the first Reform Bill. The change had indeed been going forward from the earlier epoch when the middle class of commerce began to be, as from the days of the Edwards it was tending to become, the greatest power in the country. The replacement of the old Whig, with his territorial associations, by the new Liberal, like Mr Cobden, was only the last stage in the development of self-government in England. In truth, however, the kind of progress now spoken of was not limited to any single political connection. The Nestorian experience of Mr Gladstone testifies it to have been not less noticeable among Tories than among Whigs. There were not, he thinks, in 1835 five members of the Conservative party owing their seats to commercial or industrial influences. The change which has come about in the composition of the party since then is 'simply marvellous.'[55] The specific legislation that has surrounded the English Crown by a democracy, is the extension of the lodger franchise to boroughs in 1867, to counties in 1884, and the cheapening of elections by the Corrupt Practices Bill of Sir Henry James in 1883. Notwithstanding these advances, the blend between authority and freedom has never been more fortunately conspicuous nor more wisely active in this country than since the period of its self-government began. Before 1870 it used to be said that the Pope, shorn of his temporal power, would exercise a prerogative not weaker, but stronger than when he was sole lord of Rome. Whether that prediction has, or has not been fulfilled, the influence that a constitutional Sovereign can exercise in the United Kingdom has increased rather than diminished since the days of absolute monarchy were over. Whatever in the way of political initiative the Sovereign has surrendered has in the department of social ascendancy and civic influence, been restored with interest to the Crown. The late Sir Henry Maine, differing in that respect from earlier political theorists, has in that very suppleness and elasticity which his predecessors praised discovered a source of weakness to the English constitution. So shrewd an observer as Mr Goldwin Smith bitterly complains of the fickleness of popularly elected Parliaments, and their quickness to reflect the external influences of the moment, as of the chief dangers to our political stability. Into that controversy it is needless to enter. It may seem strange to those who have had more than half a century's experience of her loyalty to constitutional principles; but in 1837 no one certainly knew whether the young Queen would not insist upon her technical right to nominate and dismiss her Ministers at will. Less than four years had passed since her uncle William IV. had practically exercised that prerogative. In 1834 Lord Althorp was called by his father, Lord Spencer's, death to the Upper House. Lord Grey had long wished to resign the Premiership. His unsatisfactory relations with the King made him seize this opportunity of doing so. The Sovereign accepted the resignation of the Cabinet with more than alacrity. Substantially therefore, and morally, there would seem something in the statement that William IV. dismissed the Whigs to please himself.[56] As Mr Gladstone in one of his essays has shown, the principle giving cohesion as well as joint and separate vitality to the members of a Cabinet independently of the personal pleasure of the Sovereign had been established before then. First actively applied if not discovered by Sunderland, the son-in-law of the great Duke of Marlborough, the Cabinet system, as Mr Gladstone has shown, can scarcely be said definitively to have triumphed till 1828, when George IV. reluctantly accepted Canning for Prime Minister. William IV., Mr Gladstone's first Royal master, is, it may be noticed in passing, admitted by his early servant to have used his prerogative unwisely; but is defended from the charge of having used it unconstitutionally. So great is the distance in political thought traversed since 1834 by the statesman as well as by others.

No thought of reverting to this family precedent has ever probably occurred to her present Majesty. The comparison of the position voluntarily occupied by the Sovereign to-day to that of the permanent head of a great department of the State unchanged by Ministerial or electoral vicissitudes, roughly but not altogether inaccurately conveys some idea of the practical influence of the Crown upon the politics of the period. Continuous experience of public affairs is not however the sole source of the influence upon them which a constitutional monarch may be enabled or obliged to exercise. The familiar Bedchamber Plot, presently to be mentioned more in detail, and the momentary friction between the Sovereign and her responsible statesmen that followed it, is now known to have originated in a misapprehension. The Minister only desired that a few ladies should give up their places in the Household. The Sovereign resisted the dismissal of her entire suite. If, indeed, a solution of the difficulty had not been found; if, that is, the Queen had pressed her personal wishes to the point of the Premier's retirement, it is by no means certain that she would have lacked constitutional arguments justifying her course. A sort of plebiscite in 1841 had been given to Sir Robert Peel. On some national issues of broader import, the popular feeling at this time notoriously had not been expressed with convincing clearness. On all sides there seemed balance and consequently confusion of public opinion. From the altitude of her throne, and by the light of her ancestral knowledge, the Queen might have argued that she saw the situation more correctly than her Ministers in Parliament or her people outside, and so have vindicated the dissolution of the House had she chosen to adopt that course. This prerogative of sanctioning the recourse of a Minister to the constituencies is one of which the Crown can never finally divest itself. In the last resort, however much he may wish to abdicate his power, the first magistrate of a State must be prepared on that point for a definite individual responsibility. The latest indubitable illustration of this truth was given in 1868. In that year Mr Gladstone's Irish Church resolutions secured the defeat of the Disraeli Government. The Conservative Premier did not, as precedent for doing even then existed, resign immediately. He placed before the Queen the alternative of a dissolution then, or six months later, leaving absolutely to the Crown the responsibility of the choice. If that situation has not since exactly repeated itself, obviously from the very nature of things it is one which may at any moment recur. Thus it will be seen that under parliamentary government, the self effacement of the Sovereign is an impossibility. Years have passed since the sense of popular disappointment at the visible results of the Grey Reform Act found expression in *Coningsby*, and since the Sidonia of that romance ridiculed to his young disciple the imperfect vicariate of a House of Commons. However essential a part of our institutions it may be, its power and popularity are not to-day without competitors in popular favour. These rivals to the House of Commons are in their way as much as itself integral parts of the national life. If, notwithstanding all the gibes against it, the House of Lords, composed as it is to-day, be not a representative body, nothing which exists in England can deserve that epithet. Socially the peers of the later Victorian epoch are as a whole indistinguishable from the Commoners at St Stephen's of an earlier epoch. They reflect at least as faithfully the variety, the interests, the pursuits, and the convictions of the nation. The great difference between election to the Lower and promotion to the Upper House is that the former generally goes by local interest. The latter depends usually on political service, on personal merit, or individual achievement. That distinction was unknown before the present generation. Macaulay, a great writer and the best informed man of his day, received a peerage. His personal claims to the honour were admitted by reason of his place in the party which from 1832 he had continuously served in Parliament. His pretensions to a peerage were emphasized by his services as a State official. He had occupied Cabinet rank; he had been Secretary at War when that office was equivalent to a Secretaryship of State. No coronet was ever given to literary genius alone before that conferred upon Lord Tennyson.

The younger Pitt is reported to have said that any man with £40,000 a year had a right to a seat in the House of Lords. Some of his creations notably that of Lord Carrington gave effect to that opinion. These peerages, however, did but foreshadow faintly the elevations of men actually engaged in commerce as in the case of Lord Armstrong, vicariously through his widow in that of Mr W. H. Smith, and many more. The press, too, is not less representative than the House of Commons. Nor in all probability is Lord Glenesk the last representative of journalism, as he has been the first to receive a seat in the Hereditary legislature. Under any circumstances, the well placed English newspaper is likely to be not less expository of public opinion than any body of gentlemen, by whatever mode elected, sitting at Westminster. Special tendencies of the time make the press an exceptionally lifelike measure of the thoughts and wishes in every department of life of every section of the English people. Newspaper proprietorship has in fact become not less a fashion of the day than theatrical lesseeship was a few years since. A number of men agreed on certain points such as the development or exploitation of particular enterprises, are seized with the conviction that 'an organ' is essential to their success. They combine, therefore, to buy or to press into their service by subsidies some printed sheet which may yet have the ear of the nation but which happens just now to have fallen upon evil times. If no such opportunity as this present itself, newspaper starting has become a recognized industry of commerce. After a time, therefore, a new literary champion of the Empire enters the lists. Its real object may be narrow and even personal. Its managers know that if their end is to be accomplished it must be veiled by a programme of more disinterested generalities, and that popular sentiment should form the first study of its conductors. In this way therefore, apart from the great newspaper oracles of the time which in all but name are national enterprises, the press has increasingly an inducement, that never fails, to hold up the mirror to the convictions, prejudices and sentiments into which public opinion can be analysed. The reptile press of Germany is, upon any considerable scale, not known in England. The connection between most journals whose support is envied, or whose opposition is dreaded, and some or more of the leading public men of the day, has been often very close[57] and is perhaps, still not quite unknown.

The newspaper, however, is but a single agency for the literary influence exercised upon the public life of the day. Of late years periodicals, appearing at less frequent intervals, have among politicians themselves competed in attractiveness with the national assemblies at Westminster. In proportion as parliamentary reports have been in the daily press reduced to a few columns and in the case of all but speakers of the first rank to a few paragraphs or sentences; parliamentarians themselves have substituted the monthly Review for the stenographer or for Hansard as the depository of their views. Technically the presence of reporters in the gallery is even to-day connived at rather than constitutionally sanctioned. Yet the leader of the House of Commons, not very long since, reminded his hearers that those who were not present at his speech might master his points by referring to the parliamentary reports next day. Members with a taste for writing, having some carefully thought out message to deliver on an intricate topic of foreign or domestic policy are increasingly inclined entirely to pretermit the parliamentary stage of their exposition. By reserving their remarks for the monthly periodical, they can be sure of fixing popular attention more conspicuously. Their signatures are appended to their effusions. The editor incurs no responsibility either for the substance or the form of the opinions delivered. The reciprocity of the arrangement is, between him and his contributor, complete. On the one hand the literary impressario secures the advertisement of a familiar if not a famous name, good as he knows it to be for the sale of a certain number of copies, each one of which represents a clear if a small profit. On the other hand, assuming the senator to deserve an audience, he is more likely to secure one when his views are placed before the public for the first time with all the advantages of good type and paper, when they are read comfortably in library or club, not listened to with an effort, and even then but partially heard in the exhausted atmosphere of the House of Commons. Again if the Popular Chamber still be of the same intellectual calibre as of old, it has grown also more manifestly fastidious and more demonstratively intolerant of speakers who do not hit its taste. As Sir James Mackintosh and Lord Macaulay in different words both said, it was always a Chamber whose tastes and verdict were incalculable. Since, under a democratic franchise, it has become an Assembly primarily of business gentlemen, the chances of failure to satisfy it are so alarmingly numerous as to prevent all but the most self assured and impassive from making the effort. It prides itself above all things on its business-like tastes. Therefore, it abhors any approach to rhetoric. It fails not to remember its traditions of eloquence, or the ascendancy over itself which to a master of words and phrases, to a Disraeli, a Gladstone, a Lowe, a Canning, a Peel, it was proud to accord, like a horse that knows, and that takes a pleasure in, its rider. Therefore the House expects from those who address it something more than the bald, business talk of the Board room; an aptitude for clothing sound original reasons in diction which shall be without pretentiousness, but that shall not lack felicity and point always, and epigram sometimes. If these conditions be forthcoming; if the Chamber be in a good humour; if it be neither too long nor too soon since it lunched nor too near the hour when it dines; then the elective legislators will perhaps for a short time give their ear to one who rises at the right moment and in favour of whom they are predisposed. The conditions are obviously severe. It is therefore not to be wondered at that candidates for oratorical honours at St Stephen's tend steadily to diminish.

There is another kind of rivalry to which of late years the House of Commons has been exposed, which may excite a smile, but which is in its way a reality to be reckoned with. This is not that of the provincial platform, of the public meeting room, or of the debating society in its older development. These latter have always, among the lower middle classes, fulfilled a function like that of the University Unions among the classes somewhat better to do. Coger's Hall was the school of discussion in which the late Charles Bradlaugh acquired great power of direct and incisive utterance as well as a perfect control over his temper. London and all the great provincial towns have as many of these places as ancient Rome possessed of gladiatorial schools. A really new growth of the last quarter of the nineteenth century is the local Houses of Commons. These sprung up in and for every quarter or suburb of London, and in many provincial districts as well. They are still known, and sometimes much in vogue. They are not of course recognized by the legislature. Nor, as in the case of the municipal bodies which we have already seen at work, is their machinery controlled by the Local Government Board. A seat in them has been known to be as much an object of rivalry among an increasing class, as a place on the green leather benches of Westminster. The member for Kennington or Lavender Hill in the south of London, for Westbourne Grove or Shepherd's Bush in the west, for Haverstock Hill in the north, may even be as considerable a personage with his immediate friends in the district as the member for Westminster in the Imperial Parliament. The leader in the Hampstead House of Commons, or the Chancellor of the Exchequer in that which meets on Richmond Hill is not certain that he would change his place with his titular equivalents at St Stephen's. These are considerations that may explain why the House of Commons, whose supremacy was unchallenged under a Peel, a Stanley, a Palmerston, a Disraeli, a Gladstone, is regarded no longer with awe, sometimes with the familiarity that breeds contempt.

As yet this diminution of parliamentary prestige, if such there really be, is indicated only by a floating sentiment. It finds expression chiefly in social chatter or in newspaper flippancies. Nor in the present decade of the Victorian epoch are there many positive signs of our representative system being superseded by the controlling will of an individual autocrat for whom the late Mr Froude thought the time was steadily approaching. The same remark might with equal truth probably be made of every part in our national polity. It is certainly true of the House of Lords not less than of the monarchy. The position practically occupied by the Crown to-day, is that which the Prince Consort many years ago marked out for it. Some of these functions he was himself able to assist the Queen in discharging. To him there seemed to devolve upon the monarchy duties analogous to those discharged by the permanent officials in the great departments of State. Amid the vicissitudes of party, the rise and fall of Ministers, the changes of popular opinion, the Crown was in his judgment the one guarantee for continuity in policy, domestic not less than foreign. The occupant of the Throne took, as Ministers of State, those whom parliamentary majorities and public opinion indicated. The Sovereign however had other functions than merely to register and sanction the wish of subjects and the decisions of Commons. Chief among these, as every other page of Sir Theodore Martin's book during the Peelite and Palmerstonian periods clearly shows, was to judge of the quarters whence a stable Administration could be formed; whether, in fact, Lord John Russell, Lord Palmerston, or Lord Derby, in a balanced state of parliamentary feeling, had the best chance of carrying on the Queen's government to the welfare of the realm and the confidence of its representatives. The most familiar aspects of the political and parliamentary situation have ceased to be now what in the Prince Consort's day they habitually were. The doctrine that Ministers are the free choice of the Sovereign was never propounded absolutely by the husband of the Queen. The doctrine was rather assumed by him in the interests of the national convenience than expressed in any terms defining the Royal prerogative. The slow process of absorption of the Peelites into the Liberal ranks; the lifelong rivalry of Lord John Russell and Lord Palmerston produced, during much of the Prince Consort's time, a condition of unstable equilibrium in party organization, which in these later days of popular mandates, general elections which are plebiscites and of overwhelming majorities which amount to commissions of the democracy, it is not easy to realize.

Some there were who thought that the Liberal disruption of 1886 might reproduce in English politics the precarious and fluctuating relations of parties and statesmen that seemed between 1852 and 1865 to have become permanent. Had that forecast been fulfilled, the Sovereign to-day might be confronted with personal responsibilities of Ministerial selection which would have recalled the duty devolved upon her during earlier portions of her reign. Nothing of the kind has happened. The event of ten years ago has resulted not in party instability, but in fresh fixity of tenure to the political conglomerate that the constituencies have as yet shown no wish to dismiss. Of course in time the same conditions as of old must recur. The national organization of which Liberals as well as Conservatives are constituent parts, will at some day or other upon issues perhaps now unsuspected resolve themselves into their elements. Ancient lines of demarcation will again declare themselves. A cycle of government by groups may yet be opened.[58] People and Parliament may still wait for the Royal choice to close an interval of confusion and of doubt. In whatever form this reversion to an older order may present itself, whatever the exact contingencies in store, the occupant of the Throne as has been shown above cannot divest himself of the right, therefore of the duty, of giving a casting vote when his officers of State hesitate, as Mr Disraeli did in 1868, as to the exact moment when the appeal to the constituences most advantageously can be made.

CHAPTER XX
ROYALTY AS A SOCIAL FORCE

> The general power and usefulness of the English Crown strengthened, and not weakened, by the constitutional transfer of political power to Parliament and Ministers. The national aims of Queen Victoria and Queen Elizabeth contrasted. Possibility of the Sovereign more correctly than Parliament or Ministers interpreting indications of national will. What happened under Queen Anne may conceivably occur under some of her successors. The facts concerning the monarchy as they are to-day. Posthumous recognition of the soundness of the Prince Consort's views on the sphere of Royal duties, and the legitimate field of the Crown's activities. His influence still a living force. Court offices, and reforms attributable to him. The present Prince of Wales exactly follows his father's example.

Whatever of power may have been resigned by the Crown in the way of political authority has since that resignation abundantly been recompensed to it in the direction of social authority. The latest predecessor of her own sex upon the English Throne correctly interpreted as against periodical parliamentary majorities the loyalty of the nation to the Anglican Establishment; then a synonym for High Church Toryism. The Legion Memorial,[59] probably drawn up by Daniel Defoe, marks the lowest point of unpopularity ever reached by the House of Commons. No one would venture to say that a repetition of such an experience, however unlikely, is more impossible under Queen Victoria, than at one time it might have seemed under Queen Anne. The chances of a revival, with the national consent, of the personal prerogative of the Sovereign in Church and State affairs, though far from being inconceivable towards this changeful close of the century are too problematical for serious calculation. Like Queen Elizabeth, Queen Victoria, from her accession to the Throne, proposed to herself as an ideal the affection of her people. The Tudor Sovereign, however, amid all her desire for the personal attachment of her subjects, bated no jot of her queenly dignity or hereditary pretensions. The Hanoverian Sovereign who blends the lines of Tudor and Stuart in her own person has always kept before her an object equally distinct, but far more congenial to the graciousness of her sex. An Elizabeth never willingly allowed the tenderness of the woman to eclipse the majesty of the Queen. A Victoria has never, consciously or unconsciously, veiled the motherhood of her people by the pomp of their ruler. The stages by which the conception of English sovereignty that is to-day a national possession has attained its present completeness, must now be examined. From her sex, and the circumstances of her life, it has long been inevitable that some of the social functions (in the sense in which that epithet is now used) of the Sovereign should be discharged vicariously by other members of the reigning House. Whether it be Prince and Heir Apparent, or Royal Duke makes no difference to the present argument. The idea of the monarchy actually operative among us to-day whether in its constitutional, ceremonial, or social attributes is at all points stamped with the impress of one systematizing and controlling mind.

That beneficent intelligence is in human shape no longer with us. Never was there man whose works and projects have lived after him more vigorously and usefully than the Prince Consort. To the generation that has grown up since his death, the notions which he was the first to apply to the Court usages of England, the ends to which, before him, no member of the reigning family had employed the opportunities of the Crown are so familiar; they seem so essential a part of the Kingly office; a Sovereign or a Prince not discharging such duties is so inconceivable by nineteenth century Britons, as to make many persons forget the existence of a time when this portion of the Royal duties was disliked as a novelty, or resented as an impertinence. It is not too much to say that the Victorian England of these later years is that which, more than any other uncrowned individual, the Prince Consort was the instrument of making it. He it was who set the example of that many-sided, almost ubiquitous, assistance in the extra-political occasions of English life which to-day are more conspicuously associated with the representatives of the kingly principle in England than the attendance at levees, or the opening of drawing rooms. Nor must it ever be forgotten that the future husband of the Queen from earliest youth, not less than her future Majesty herself, was trained with an eye to the possibilities of the alliance and the duties that the accident of birth might have in store. Writing in July 1821 to the Duchess of Kent, the Dowager Duchess of Coburg says of the young Prince Albert: 'The little fellow is the pendant to the pretty cousin' (the Princess Victoria).[60] Prince Leopold, who married the Princess Charlotte naturally supplied the first link of cousinly association between his nephew and niece. Other and more highly placed suitors were not of course wanting. But it needed no great experience in the tactics of matrimonial diplomacy accurately to conjecture the relations tolerably certain to be developed between the second son of Duke Ernest of Saxe-Coburg-Saafeld and the niece of William IV., heiress to the English Crown. It is well that the august contingencies of the future should sometimes have been forecast by those around the young Prince. Otherwise it might have proved more difficult than subsequently it did prove, or perhaps have been found impracticable to rear on the foundations of boyish education the fabric of a genuine knowledge of English character, of English life and institutions. Hence it was that the disappointment of Lord Melbourne's over sanguine anticipations of the reception of the Prince by his adopted countrymen was borne with the equanimity which he showed on hearing that the proposed allowance of £50,000 a year, though not, as Colonel Sibthorp suggested, reduced to £21,000, was to be fixed at £30,000. All he regretted was that his ability to help artists, men of learning and of science would be necessarily more restricted than he had hoped.[61]

Naturally the economy of the Court system was the first to feel the reforming influence of the man who afterwards helped profoundly to modify the whole system of English life at large. The first opposition was encountered at the hands not of an Englishman, but of a fellow countrywoman of his own, the Baroness de Lehzen, who, from being the young Queen's governess, had become the head of her household. The abuses and extravagance of the Royal establishment shocked, as they well might have done, the frugal Prince. Nor was it only that the money expended yielded no proportionate return of comfort and convenience. The very rudiments of domestic supervision were found to be wanting. Windsor Castle was only one degree better than Buckingham Palace. Those employed about the Royal dwelling not only had themselves free ingress into the living rooms of the family, a nondescript gathering of camp followers, loafers and errand boys also contrived to pass in and out unchallenged. On one occasion a boy was found, with no felonious intent, to have passed the night under a sofa in a parlour next to the Queen's bedroom. The lad had no wish to have done so. He was simply shut in, unperceived by those whose business it was to lock up.[62] In this work the Prince Consort was confronted by the opposition which the reformer of inveterate abuses never fails in any department of life to encounter. The administration of the Palace household below stairs in a less wantonly wasteful manner was held to threaten the dignity of those about the Throne. A check upon weekly bills in the basement was suspected of veiling a sinister design on the constitution of Church and State. Sir Robert Peel in 1841 had dwelt on the difficulty of domestic reforms in the Palace. In 1843 he acknowledged the economy and efficiency with which the Queen's Household was now conducted. The Minister was vilified in the cheap weekly papers as a joint conspirator with those foreigners who christened their treason by the fair names of retrenchment and order. He was even attacked in clubs and drawing rooms by fine and fashionable people for being ready to compromise the dignity and disturb the equilibrium of the British Crown. The chief point of the Prince Consort's Court improvements was concentration of responsible power upon a single individual in the place of its confused distribution among mutually conflicting understrappers. In this task he was aided by Baron Stockmar who had all the national aptitude of the German for the details small and great in the domestic routine of palaces and princes. The ultimate result of these operations was to invest a Master of the Household identical in all respects with that functionary as he exists to-day, with supreme jurisdiction over the domestic arrangements of the Sovereign, able directly to communicate with the departments for executing the different repairs. Other duties gradually gathered round this personage. To-day, as the Prince Consort had always purposed, it is upon him that there devolves the duty of issuing at the Royal command, invitations to guests to sleep and dine beneath the Queen's roof.

The composition of the Queen's immediate entourage is now practically the same as that decided upon by Her Majesty in conjunction with the Prince Consort. The ladies of the Court, that is, consist of the Mistress of the Robes, the Ladies of the Bedchamber, the Women of the Bedchamber, and the Maids of Honour. The first named of these, the Mistress of the Robes, is in her way, a State official. She must not be below the rank of a Duchess. She changes with the Government of the day. Her attendance on the Queen is limited to State occasions. The Ladies of the Bedchamber, all of them peeresses, are in number eight. One of them is invariably waiting upon the Queen. These are the ladies who in 1839 Sir Robert Peel, when forming his Administration, thought should be changed. The Women of the Bedchamber are also eight. These generally are only in attendance when the Mistress of the Robes is present. One of them is always near the Sovereign. The Maids of Honour are also eight in number. These must be either the daughters or grand-daughters of peers. They have the courtesy title of 'Honourable.' Two of them are always in waiting for a month at a time. The Prince Consort also in selecting the officers of the Household, showed special care and judgment in his choice of the person who discharges the duties of Privy Purse. From the days of Colonel Phipps, or Colonel Anson, to Sir Fleetwood Edwards; these have been men of first rate financial and administrative capacity. Misled by a similarity of terms, some persons seem to fancy there exists a vital association between the gentleman who fills that position in the Queen's Household and the nobleman who, as Lord Privy Seal, has a seat in the Cabinet of the day, and who in 1896-7 was Viscount Cross. Hence the recurrent announcements in the newspapers that this statesman has been summoned to Windsor or Balmoral to assist Her Majesty with her business papers. The present opportunity therefore may usefully be taken to contradict the construction placed upon the character of the visit of that Minister to the Court. This the present writer has the very highest authority for doing. The connection between the Cabinet and Court offices whose names so closely resemble each other is in no sense organic. Lord Cross, now spoken of, is eminent for his knowledge of business of all kinds. He is a man of the widest and most varied experience in every department of civil and political affairs. He had a seat in Lord Beaconsfield's last Cabinet. Than him the Queen possesses to-day few older servants, or more trusty friends. In that capacity, not in virtue of his Ministerial position, it is that Lord Cross finds himself so frequently the guest of his Sovereign.

The Prince Consort's reforms in the economy and administration of the Court itself, though not the least valuable or necessary of his labours, naturally appealed less directly to the popular interest than his other activities, by the results of which the land of his adoption is to-day the gainer. Not a moment had been lost by the Prince in beginning to realize his early idea of associating for the first time since the days of the Stuarts the Sovereign with the promotion of letters, science, and art. The Court of Henry VIII. had been visited by Erasmus, and by other men of letters of the Protestant connection. If the story of Shakespeare's presence in the group that surrounded Elizabeth be apocryphal, Edmund Spenser, Sir Philip Sidney, and Sir Walter Raleigh undoubtedly paid their homage to the Virgin Queen. Charles I. was the patron of Van Dyck and an admirable connoisseur as well as encourager of true art wherever it could be found. Charles II., after his restoration, was less interested in painters and poets than in science.

Before Queen Victoria, the Hanoverian Sovereigns had not identified the new dynasty with any special affection for the accomplishments which gild and refine life. The Prince Consort, at the outset of his career mastered two facts. First, he discerned, that, even in the absence of a national scheme of education, the taste for reading and culture bred not only by improved intelligence, but by the growth of material prosperity and the humanizing influences of foreign travel, must before long result in a marked improvement of the appreciation among the countrymen of Reynolds, of Byron, of Wordsworth, and of Southey, of all that sweetens and brightens daily existence. The Prince perceived, too, that the lines on which English social intercourse was developing must involve a demand for amusements and for recreations upon a larger scale than family reunions beneath the domestic life could provide. The theatre in England had not become then a considerable force. It would have been premature to anticipate the later advice of Mr Matthew Arnold to organize the stage. The demand for good music in public places and on reasonable terms; the growing interest in the works of English artists; above all the newly awakened interest among the whole community in the welfare of their least fortunate members;—these are the features of the time which in his survey of the domestic situation chiefly impressed the Prince.

So early as 1840 his knowledge of musical science and his skill in musical execution were well known to all with whom he had been brought into contact. By this time it was generally perceived that a mistake had been made in not, from the first, establishing the Prince as the Queen's private secretary, and in delaying to entrust him with the control of the whole Household. The Prince's remarkable aptitudes had impressed the leading statesmen of both parties and through them the general public. Thus, in 1840 there existed a growing desire to turn to national account the special knowledge and exceptional talents of the accomplished husband of the Queen. On the 9th of October 1840 Lady Lyttelton, then in attendance at Windsor, has recorded that 'there arose from the room below hers sounds of an instrument which she did not at first recognize, played with such master skill, modulated so learnedly, winding through every kind of bass and chord, finally culminating in the most perfect cadence, then off again, louder first and afterwards softer. I only heard,' she adds, 'the harmony, being too distant to catch the tune, or perceive the execution of the small touches. It was Prince Albert playing on the organ.' April 29 of the year now mentioned was, from the point from which it is now looked at, a memorable date in this blameless and beneficent career. Then it was that the Prince having been appointed one of the directors of the Ancient Concerts, discharged these duties for the first time. All the music had been selected by himself. He had attended the rehearsal with the Queen. Experts in this matter have dated from that day the revival of the public taste for classical music in this country.

Nearly simultaneous with this was his appearance upon a public platform on one of those non-political occasions that his example has specially appropriated to the representatives of English Royalty. In the same year, too, at the very height of the London season, the Prince took the initiative in a function of a graver kind, but not less specially adapted for energies and knowledge to which under a Constitutional monarchy political life is not held to afford a proper outlet. The most important public meeting of the summer of 1840 was that convened for the purpose of encouraging the legislature to complete the machinery for the removal of the last traces of the slave trade. Technically the abolition had already taken place. Well grounded apprehensions, however, existed that the new 'apprenticeship' which was to educate the emancipated negro for the blessings of freedom might sometimes be too much like the old servitude which it was designed to supersede. This occasion produced the first speech delivered on an English platform by the Prince Consort at a time when platform eloquence was less common than it has since become. The address pointed, pithy, without an ambiguous or superfluous word, was the model by which the speaker may well have shaped his subsequent utterances. Its terse felicities of phrase have since often been reproduced by his son, the Prince of Wales.

As a corrective to the innate nervousness of a highly organized temper, he had carefully prepared these remarks, writing them out and rewriting them, so that nothing might be left to the chance inspiration of the moment.

This was the first of a series of princely appearances on non-political occasions. To-day, and in the case of his descendants, these things are taken as a matter of course. During many years no great movement for the improvement by politically unsectarian agencies of human life has been considered complete without the active participation in it of the Crown, or, which comes to the same thing, a nominee of the Crown. That in its popular aspects the artistic movement which fills so large a space in the second half of this century was practically the creation of the Prince Consort's discriminating taste and patriotic industry would, if by nothing else be shown by the course of preparations for the Hyde Park Exhibition of 1851. Sir Robert Peel, at the time, repeatedly stated that without the collaboration and counsel of the Queen's husband, the Commission for the promotion and encouragement of the fine arts in the United Kingdom could scarcely have got through its work. On the other hand, while the public has accustomed itself to regard Lord Melbourne as the nearly exclusive influence for training the Sovereign and her husband in the tasks of Royal routine, one may point out that the Prince himself never failed to emphasize his personal obligations to Sir Robert Peel as his first trainer in the duties of an English public man. Nor from these associations did he acquire only a correct insight into the official ways of his new country. In his tastes and appreciations, the Prince Consort became as patriotic as any of the great men by whom he was surrounded. Some have questioned whether the patronage of a not unmixed English Court has been entirely favourable to the development of native genius in certain branches of the fine arts. The historic facts enumerated by Sir Theodore Martin on this point are worth mentioning.[63]

On December 2, 1841, the Prince met on the official business of the Commission the Secretary, then Mr, afterwards Sir Charles, Eastlake. The latter entered upon the interview with an idea of resigning his post, should the Prince insist on the introduction of foreign artists. His Royal Highness anticipated his visitor by volunteering the remark that to him there appeared no necessity for so much as the employment of a single foreign artist even among those entrusted with the management of considerable works. 'In all that related to practical dexterity (the department in which it was assumed that some instruction for fresco would be necessary), the English were particularly skilful.' Such were the Prince's words as recorded by Sir Charles Eastlake. The same narrator adds that His Royal Highness volunteered many instances of English superiority over all other nations in everything concerned with artistic mechanism. 'Even to the varnish on coaches,' said the Prince, 'it is surprising how much more perfect the

English practice is than that of the Continent.' The talk then turned on the encouragement of fresco painting in England. The words of the Queen's husband are especially noticeable showing as they do his just appreciation of the conditions of artistic prosperity in England. Two great auxiliaries in this country seldom fail to promote the success of any scheme. Of the forces thus alluded to, fashion was one, high example was another. Hence the Prince inferred that if the Queen and himself set the example of having works of this kind done, the taste would extend itself to wealthy individuals. The English country seats which are the most beautiful in the world would acquire additional effect from the introduction of such a style of decoration. With such occupation the school would never languish, and would at least have time fully to develop itself. When on one occasion Mr Eastlake, in reference to the necessary limitation of frescoes compared them to sculpture in which nothing could be concealed, and in which this necessity involved the necessity of beauty also, the Prince replied: 'You have expressed in a few words what I would have said in many.'[64]

This (1842) was the year, too, in which the first steps, both in the direction of officially identifying the representatives of the English Crown with the encouragement of popular culture, and of continuing the work begun by Sir Walter Scott, of popularizing Scotch scenery with English visitors, was taken by the Prince Consort. The opening of the Art Exhibition in Edinburgh; the addresses made by the Prince, with the minute and exact study of artistic and scientific subjects which they showed, not only satisfied experts, but delighted the general public, and practically placed the Queen's husband in the van of the new movement for the encouragement of popular knowledge, then beginning to advance more rapidly than it had previously done. The whole country was agitated with the premonitory risings of Chartism. The Prince's opportunities of good were increased by the proof he afforded of combining manly courage with a technical knowledge then new to the English people. For us to-day the importance of these incidents is not merely biographical. They illustrate, as nothing else could, the growth and the development of the popular conception of the duties outside the Court that Englishmen connect to-day with the Sovereign or the Sovereign's social and ceremonial vicegerents.

Since then the rapidity of the movements of the Heir Apparent as the deputy of the Queen excite admiration mingled with some perplexity concerning the means by which so near an approach has been made to solving the secret of perpetual motion. In all this, for the first time by anyone living within the Royal circle, the initiative was set by the Prince Consort. Now the Prince was visiting with the Queen an English statesman, for example Sir Robert Peel, at his country seat. A few days before, the Royal visitors had been the guests of Louis Philippe in France. On landing at Portsmouth, they at once started for Tamworth. Their visit at the statesman's country house

was scarcely concluded when the Prince Consort was due at Cai his installation in the Chancellorship of the University. As the yea these activities were multiplied. All the great centres of English manufacture, one day Birmingham, the next Liverpool or Glasgow or Leeds, were in turn, and upon the same scale of ceaseless celeri When therefore, the Queen's eldest son first entered upon publi began to dazzle his countrymen by the speed of his movements, or them by the ubiquity of his presence, and indifference to fatigue or mind, it is well to see these manifestations of princely energy historical perspective, and to realize that in this transformation force, which the present reign has witnessed, the Heir Apparent ha much created a precedent as fulfilled a tradition.

The obliging information of Sir Arthur Bigge, of Viscount Cross, and of Sir Francis Knollys, has enabled the writer accurately to state such facts of Court organization as are legitimate matters of interest to Her Majesty's subjects.

CHAPTER XXI
CROWN AND SWORD

The Monro-Fawcett duel turned the Prince Consort's attention, as representing the Crown, to duelling, the abolition of which must begin with the army. Courts of Honour suggested as successful abroad. Why distrusted by English opinion. Views of the Duke and others. Hence the Court first occupied with army reforms to good results. Contrast between military resources 1837-97. Special attention of Court to military education. Old and new schools of officers compared. Duke of Wellington as Commander contrasted with his latest successors. Growth of rifle volunteers; special influences in military education, *e.g.* Edward Hamley. Military democracy. Why necessarily imperfect.

So plausible a case may theoretically be made out for the duel as a social institution that it is not surprising the custom should have died hard in a combatant nation like the English. The ordeal by arms furnishes a simple if barbaric mode of settling personal differences without the scandal and the weariness of law; in an age whose boast is freedom of speech not less than of thought, whose bane is the degeneration of that chartered liberty into the unlicensed malignity and curiosity of small-talk, there always will be ill-conditioned persons whom only fear of the horsewhip, the rapier, or the pistol, can teach to discipline their tongue; all these things have been said in favour of the duel as a mode of social discipline. In practice, however, it was never found that the fear of a challenge ensured social discretion of tongue, or a higher standard of personal courtesy. When these combats were not farcical, as the duel has generally become in France, where it still survives, they proved the instruments of the professional homicide, who, trained to artistic murder, went about society, seeking a feud with those whom he or his patrons desired to be put out of the way. Stung to the quick by the brutalities of O'Connell, Sir Robert Peel, during the early forties demanded, as the story runs, the satisfaction which was not then an anachronism. The great Irishman replied that yielding to the expostulations of his wife, he must

forego the pleasure of the encounter for which he was 'spoiling.' A second invitation was declined on the ground that the entreaties of his offspring had subdued the spirit of the warrior. Hence the point in Theodore Hook's epigram published in the *John Bull* of the period:—

Some men in their horror of slaughter,
Improve on the scriptural command;
They honour their wife and their daughter,
That their days may be long in the land.

The same statesman is known at a little later date to have been persuaded, not without difficulty, to abstain from sending a friend to his chief opponent[65] at the time of the latter's onslaughts on the Conservative concession of Free Trade. Since then, Wimbledon Common or Wormwood Scrubbs has probably never for a moment seriously suggested itself to any honourable gentleman as a possible place to which to adjourn a controversy with a parliamentary opponent.

A duel was the incident which caused the first intervention of the Prince Consort in the social arrangements of English life. On the 1st of July 1843, Colonel Fawcett had been shot by his brother-in-law, Lieutenant Monro. The latter had accepted the challenge most reluctantly; he had been the grossly aggrieved party.[66] Under the then existing code, the survivor's sole alternative to the certainty of being stigmatised as a coward had been to accept the risk of being hung for a felon. Eight years before the Queen's accession, in 1829, however, the great Duke of Wellington had faced Lord Winchilsea's pistol; the memories of the (1809) Canning-Castlereagh and other encounters did not then seem part of ancient history. The Prince Consort, with the military instincts of his race decided that the reform which he was bent on establishing must begin with the army. The authority of the Duke of Wellington was at this moment paramount equally in social, political, and military life. The great general was known himself seriously to have considered the subject. With him therefore, the Prince arranged an interview. Courts of Honour were suggested by the Prince as rational substitutes for the appeal to the sword. The Tribunals des Marechaux were said to have done good work in France; Courts of Honour had been followed with the best results in the Bavarian army. The Duke's objection to the proposal was the English distrust of a secret tribunal; the authorities of the navy took the same view as the Commander-in-Chief. Sir George Murray, then Master of the Ordnance, a serious and accomplished man of the world, bluntly remarked that quarrels would not be made up, or differences composed by the arbitration of others; that the law as it already existed could do all which was practicable to repress the practice. The Prince persevered with his purpose. His suggestion was laid by the Secretary of State for War before his colleagues in the Cabinet. Though the scheme was not adopted in the form suggested by the Prince, his action in the matter led to an amendment in the Articles of War (April 1844). Henceforward it was declared to be suitable to the character of honourable men to apologize and offer redress for wrong or insult committed, and equally suitable for the aggrieved party frankly and cordially to accept the amende. Thus on the initiative of the Queen's husband, there began the organization of public opinion on the lines that have long since made the ordeal by arms as practically obsolete in England as the ordeal by touch.

The Queen's devotion to her army has always been that of a mother for her children; the Queen's gratitude evinced upon all possible occasions to her soldiers for what they have done in the field has ever resembled that of a woman to the protector of the weak against the strong. It was natural therefore that, amid his civilian duties, the new representative of the Throne, himself nurtured in a land that from being the Mark of Brandenburg was growing into a great military monarchy, should actively show his interest in the whole field of military reform. Later, when the post became vacant, the Prince Consort, after consulting with the Ministers of the day, declined more than once the Commandership-in-Chief. His suggestions for army reform, and for national defence during the period of the Crimean War, of the Indian Mutiny, and again during the Franco-Austrian wars were made with a sense of responsibility which the tenure of office could not have deepened as well as with a shrewd perception of the needs and possibilities of the time that no statesman of English birth could surpass. He had already been among the first to recognize the brilliant merits of the Duke of Wellington's plan for the defence of London, during the Chartist disturbances of 1848. To the Prince's discrimination it is largely due that this domestic exploit of the hero of Waterloo, not less memorable in its way than Waterloo itself,[67] came properly to be appreciated by the country. To this day the mighty fortresses which protect the shores of the Solent and Southampton Water, and which make that part of the previously too vulnerable South coast practically safe are to a great extent the memorials of the wisdom and exertion of the Prince Consort. He had already, while our soldiers were before Sebastopol, urged upon the Government of the day the establishment of militia depôts in place of the regulars should they be withdrawn by an emergency, at Malta and elsewhere, along the line of our Mediterranean possessions. When therefore, the national alarm caused by the words and actions of our French ally found its expression in Lord Palmerston's scheme of coast defences, the memorandum on which these measures were based had been drawn up by the Prince Consort at the wish of the Cabinet, and practically formed the basis of the action of Ministers.

Nor of all the army reformers who have lived and worked since the Prince's day, is there one who has failed to testify his indebtedness to the suggestions of the husband of the Queen. In his many talks on this subject with the military advisers of the Government of the day, the Prince often anticipated those improvements in the administration of the land forces of the Crown which since his time have been carried out. As the Prince Consort correctly inferred from the character of the English people as well as from the pace of official movements in England, must be the case, the progressive changes in the English army have been effected piecemeal by slow or minute instalments. The method pursued here has differed not less from that followed in the reorganization of Continental armies than the composition of the army of England differs from that of the great fighting machines of the rest of Europe. In Prussia, after the defeat of Jena (1806); in Austria after France had triumphed for Italy on the field of Solferino (1859) the organic reconstruction of armies was possible. Nothing of the same sort has taken place in England. Nothing, as the Prince Consort perceived, of this kind could be effected here, unless under the conscription. That system the Queen's husband once observed was not likely to be established in England without a revolution.

The changes which the Prince suggested in able memoranda to successive Ministers, which indeed he partly foresaw as coming, may in their general results briefly be glanced at now. The mere enumeration of the military resources of the country on the Queen's accession and on the eve of the sixtieth anniversary of that event needs few words to deepen the contrast. In 1837 the total military strength (regular army) of the country was 101,000. Sixty years later these figures were 147,105.[68] In 1837 India was garrisoned by the Company's army of 26,500. In 1897 the Indian military strength was 74,299 British, 129,963 Native. The increase has been therefore, nearly threefold. In 1837 the Irish troops were 20,000. In 1897 these were between 26,000 and 27,000. As against the 26,000 troops in the Channel Islands and Great Britain in 1837, there were in 1897, 81,516. The entire strength of the horsed-field artillery in the accession year was 72 guns—all at home. On New Year's Day 1897 the artillery total of all kinds at home and abroad was 219 batteries or companies. In 1837 the Horse Artillery batteries were armed with 12-pounder howitzers, and 6-pounder guns; the Field batteries had 9-pounder guns, 24-pounder howitzers. The infantry still used the old flint 'Brown Bess,' which in the cant phrase of the time was warranted at 200 yards to miss a haystack. The Rifle regiments used the Brunswick rifle which at 400 yards, according to Lord Wolseley, could not implicitly be trusted. To-day, the equipping of our troops with the latest weapons of precision which contemporary science designs is of itself a great department of English artificership. Jealousy of the army is as much a bequest from Puritan times to the House of Commons, as jealousy of the Church. Under the two first Georges, bitter and tedious debates on the maintenance of the Hanoverian soldiers were of constant recurrence. As a consequence, the standing troops which in the Napoleonic wars had been 220,000 men were gradually reduced till in three years after the peace (1818), they were only 80,000 strong.

Not without much pressure had Parliament during the earliest infancy of the Colonies provided a handful of soldiers for the protection of settlers in the lands beyond the sea as well as for the maintenance of civil order at home. It was the paucity of the numbers available for his orders which rendered the Duke of Wellington's scheme of London defence against Chartist attack so memorable a piece of strategy. Even the influence and popularity of this great soldier only secured the existence of a small army at home on condition that it did not flaunt itself ostentatiously before the civilian population. To keep up any fighting strength at all the non-combatant portion of the army was reduced to an ineffective minimum. Without exception, regiments were weak in men and horses. The four chief company depôts at home consisted of veterans waiting their discharge, of invalids, and of ineffective, or imperfectly effective, recruits.

Sometimes, as during the Canadian and Jamaica troubles in the earlier years of the reign, additional troops were required for the Colonies. These were composed of volunteers from other regiments and of casual recruits. The *personnel* of our army may be inferred from the Duke of Wellington's oft-quoted remark that the man who enlisted was the worst and most drunken inhabitant of the village. This was the scum of the earth which under officers trained on the playing fields of Eton, the Duke had led to victory in his Peninsular campaigns and in the Low Countries against the consummate veterans of the French army. To win the affection of his men; to make them feel that their commander was also their friend, and of the same flesh and blood as themselves never occurred to the great Duke. His latter-day successor, Lord Wolseley, on the Christmas day of 1896, visited the Wellington Barracks to taste the pudding and test the comforts of the men. That was not the great Duke's way.

The moral and social improvement in the private soldier since the era of humaner treatment began is shown by a progressive decrease in the number of Courts Martial. In 1876 they were 12,187, in 1895, 8,211, a reduction of about one-third. The treatment of soldiers by their superiors was admirably adapted to demoralize them as men without improving them as soldiers. When the recruit took the Queen's shilling, he ceased to be a free citizen. He had said farewell to the world outside the barrack yard. He became a nameless piece of martial machinery; sometimes he was indulged; more often he was flogged. Nothing that could extinguish respect for himself or his officers, was left undone. It had been the Duke of Wellington's business to win victories not to conciliate men. The moral and personal influence of such men as Lord Roberts and others which since the Duke's day has been exercised for the moral and physical advantage of the soldier is not an instrument that the hero of Waterloo often employed; he did not believe in it. Nor was it a soldier, but a schoolmaster, Dr Arnold of Rugby, who formulated the truth, that the best way of improving character is to treat persons on the assumption of their becoming what you wish them to be.

To pass to other details in the military contrast between the sixtieth and the first years of the Queen's reign the short service system which has proved admittedly so effective had occurred as a possibility only to a few reformers of whom the Prince Consort was one, and Sir Charles Napier another. In 1837 enlistment was for life or twenty-one years; the seven years' term had been urged already by Napier. It was not however till 1847 that the reduction to ten years was sanctioned and then only by way of special inducement for recruits when they were exceptionally few. Those who can recall the scenes witnessed outside public houses in the country, in the purlieus of Westminster or Trafalgar Square in London will not consider the term 'crimping' too strong an expression to apply to the process of forcing the Queen's shilling into the hands of half tipsy yokels, and entirely intoxicated or desperate roughs. Nor is it surprising that the Sergeant Kites of the period found all their arts of inventive persuasion, all their largesses of drink necessary to induce the gallant fellows whom they addressed to serve the Queen. Without the stimulating allurement of drums and fifes playing, of banners flying, and unless the future had been seen through a haze of beery or spirituous splendour, the tale of recruits would have fallen lamentably short.

In the eyes of sober citizens of the industrial class, the life of the soldier seemed only one degree less dismal and shameful than the career of the hulks. As a fact the soldier's lot was perhaps half a century ago not much more tolerable than that of the convict shipped for his offences beyond seas. A prison with a chance of being killed in it represented in the popular eye the existence of the private soldier. It involved transportation with hard labour as a matter of course. One battalion first raised in 1700 had been the whole of those 137 years abroad on active service. When his destiny was less severe than this, a life insufferably tedious was led by him in barracks pestilently unhealthy. To-day, upon a different plane of comfort, and on a reduced scale of luxury, the private soldiers may be said to enjoy the same recreations and opportunities of improvement as his officer. He is the master of his own time during several of the best hours in every day. He has no more difficulty in obtaining leave up to midnight for a theatre visit than a Woolwich cadet in getting a Sunday exeat from the Academy. Rooms for study and pastime are provided within his barracks.

Domestic life is no longer incompatible with his military service. But in 1837 married quarters did not exist. Those who had wives and children herded with their unmarried comrades in scandalous confusion. Whatever, with a view of completely brutalizing if possible the men who fought their country's battles, could in addition to these things be devised, was not wanting. Punishments were meted out with indiscriminating severity. The Queen had been on her throne some years before the lash was limited to time of war. Among the officers brought up in the school of Wellington a prejudice in favour of flogging as a simple, efficacious sort of British punishment lingered perhaps till 1880, when on a memorable occasion after an exciting debate that had signalized the opening of a new era of parliamentary obstruction, the House of Commons decreed its entire abolition. As has been already said, the policy to which the Duke of Wellington had from political exigencies been as he thought compelled, was to sacrifice to the maintenance of a small and often invisible body of regulars every other branch of the Service.

Thus sixty years ago the Militia force of the country was declared by the Adjutant-General of the day practically to be non-existent. Before 1815 this force had been a considerable body. After the Peace it dwindled down to less than 70,000; when the Queen mounted her throne, it was seldom or never regularly drilled. There had been no ballot for it since 1831. Twenty-eight years later, December 1895, the strength of an annually trained Militia was 107,742. The Militia, too, in 1837 was administered not as it now is by the War Office, but by the Home Secretary in conjunction with the Lords Lieutenant of Counties; its payment was provided for in the civil not the military estimates; in 1837 its expense was £192,115. The Yeomanry, then called Volunteers, comprised 18,000 men of all ranks, at a cost in round numbers of £105,400. In 1897 the Yeomanry, instructed not less systematically than the Militia, were a force of 11,678 men.

Important additions to the permanent strength of the country against an emergency were made, largely on the Prince Consort's initiative, during the first decade of the reign. In 1842 the military pensioners already enrolled and liable to service were regularly organized, less however as a military power than as an aid to the civil Government, to the number of 7,000 men. This, too, was the period in which (1846) Sir John Burgoyne submitted to Lord John Russell a State paper on that subject of coast defences which had already engaged the Duke of Wellington and had been taken up warmly as mentioned above by the Queen's husband. The Channel Tunnel scheme was then unborn in the brains of future projectors. Our military experts held England sufficiently to be weakened as it was by the isthmus of steam which bridged the Straits of Dover. Sir John Burgoyne's estimate in 1846 was that after providing for Ireland and for home fortifications, only a maximum of 10,000 men could be placed in the field; that the entire United Kingdom did not possess field guns enough for 20,000 men; that there were no reserves of muskets or military stores; that the dockyards were defenceless against any sudden attack. In 1847 the apprehensions caused by these expert disclosures moved Lord Palmerston, when Foreign Secretary in the Russell Cabinet, to suggest a loan for military works along the Hampshire and Dorsetshire coast. Nothing, however, was actually done until the Prince Consort in May 1859 secured the issue of instructions to Lords Lieutenant of Counties by the War Secretary. These resulted in the raising of the Volunteers. Lord Palmerston was himself Prime Minister then. The attitude of Napoleon III. towards England and the Austrian war scare of 1859 supplied the Government with the leverage for the vote needed to strengthen the coast protection of England in accordance with the Prince Consort's proposal of twelve years earlier. On June 23, 1860, the earliest Volunteer Review was held in Hyde Park. A week or so later, on July 2, the Volunteers first met on Wimbledon Common; the competition was opened by Her Majesty discharging her rifle and scoring the inaugural bull's eye.

A quarter of a century later the Volunteers had risen from 119,000 in 1860 to 226,752 in 1886, of whom 220,000 were efficients. At the number then reached subject to fluctuations of some thousands periodically they seem disposed to remain. In Great Britain 800,000 men of military age have passed through the Volunteers. Thus, not counting our natural rampart of sea, and a navy which public opinion, if not official patriotism, insists on maintaining at a high point, the coast fortresses bristling in nearly continuous array from Dover to the Land's End mask behind them little less than 1,000,000 citizen soldiers, who with some help from their brethren of the Royal Artillery could effectively man our coast batteries.

Military education under teachers of the new school and the class of officers thus produced are the immediate outcome of the interest taken in the army by the Court at, and subsequently to, the time of the Prince Consort. The whole scheme of education under which the commanders of the future are trained and a general anxiety for the most beneficent use of the Queen's prerogative, were much in the thoughts of the Queen's husband. The council of military education was largely the work of the Prince, as also was the formation of the Aldershot camp. When a 'governor' was to be chosen for the Prince of Wales, the selection made was the first Commander at Aldershot and one of the chief members of the education council, Sir William Knollys, who, on the Prince reaching his majority became chief of his household. When that veteran was appointed Usher of the Black Rod he was succeeded as Private Secretary to the Heir Apparent by one so thoroughly trained to his administrative methods as his son, Sir Francis Knollys;—a man in whom common sense attains as nearly as is conceivable to the calibre of absolute genius. It was at the period now mentioned and under these influences that officers in the scientific corps began to get their proper share of army staff appointments and commands. So entirely have the old disabilities of that corps disappeared that to-day, in striking contrast to the earlier experience, an officer of Royal Artillery or Royal Engineers who in general respects shows the necessary aptitude enjoys the same chance as anyone else of staff employment in peace. When he has reached the grade of General officer, he will not be at any disadvantage in the process of selection for a command. Here merit alone tells now. Whatever arm of the Service to which he belongs the best candidate practically never fails to be chosen. Generally, in the opinion of the best professional judges, the young officer finds the army a self-supporting profession. The exact experience seems to be that a young man obtaining a commission in the infantry of the Line or in the Artillery can look forward at no distant date to marrying in fair comfort, and that as a bachelor he requires no larger allowance or private means than he would need in any other branch of the public employ, that, for example, of the Colonial Service.

In cavalry regiments, or in the Household Brigade, life is more costly. In these cases, the young officer could scarcely subsist in comfort without private resources equal to those on which young men entering the diplomatic service must at the outset of their career be able to count. Obviously if the army is to be made a career sufficiently attractive for young Englishmen of first-rate abilities as well as of gentle birth, the prizes of the profession must not, for the sake of an unwise national economy, be too severely diminished in value. The complaint is general and just that the emoluments of those who win their way to the top are already unattractively small and few. It cannot be a satisfactory state of things under which no General officer can afford, without private fortune of his own, to take a command. Impolitic retrenchment has touched other positions than these. Thus, quite recently the salary of the Military Secretary to the Commander-in-Chief has been cut down from £2,100 to £1,500; that of Adjutant-General to the Forces from £2,700 to £2,100; that of Governor of the Royal Military Academy from £2,000 to £1,500. The unwisdom of these reductions and the comparative smallness of the highest army stipends, become the more apparent when it is remembered that all military appointments, unlike civil appointments from the Primacy of Canterbury down to a junior Treasury lordship, are for five years only, that the installation in these posts, and the establishment they require are necessarily costly; thus the choice is practically limited to men of means. Nor does a timocratic[69] scheme of military preferment accord well with the democratic ideal of careers unrestrictedly open to all talents.

The reform in the system of officers' education which the Prince Consort launched his eldest son has already lived to see practically accomplished. At the beginning of the reign the average military officer at his best was a keen sportsman or a well-bred London club-man; at his worst, and as not very unfrequently witnessed, the original of him may be recognised to-day in Thackeray's Sketches of Ensigns Rag and Famish; before some Becky

Sharpe of the period had taken them in charge, and had developed them into Captains Rawdon Crawley, to become in due course candidates for the Governorship of Coventry Island. The officer of to-day, naval as well as military, is not less keen a sportsman, is as good a shot, can take and hold a line of his own across country equally well. But he is a soldier first, eager to add to his knowledge from the facts of history, or from contemporary examples of professional achievement. There are to-day no better read men than those who serve their Sovereign ashore or afloat. The training of our sailors of whatever rank leaves perhaps something to be wished for. Scientific seamanship, however, is not merely an ideal, but a familiar experience. Jack Tars or flag officers,—the school wherein respectively they are trained is, as Nelson himself was, and wished to see his sailors, above all things scientific too.

The man-of-war's-man of to-day has educated himself so well from books, with occasional hints from his commanding officer, as to be often a better informed person than the average undergraduate or Admiralty clerk. To speak now only of the soldier. It is not only that like the sailor he has felt the intellectually quickening influences which are part of the atmosphere of his epoch. The military officer of to-day has passed through the curriculum which the Prince Consort was among the earliest to mark out; he has already acquired nearly all that learning which thirty years ago it was predicted would prove the ruin of the Service. Between what he is and what he was, the contrast is not less great than between a future Moltke and Corinthian Tom; yet has he not developed into the spectacled professor with head too big for any busby to fit, to which some looked forward should the British subaltern fail to model himself after Albert Smith's medical student.

Almost till the beginning of the present decade there might be seen any afternoon issuing from the Athenæum Club in Pall Mall, a well-set-up gentleman, scarcely middle-aged, soldierly indeed of figure, but chiefly noticeable for his commandingly intellectual brow. This was Edward Hamley. Should the time now spoken of happen to have been that of the opening of the Franco-Prussian War, Hamley was perhaps demonstrating to a civilian friend the justification of his prediction of a French triumph afforded by the slight advantage gained by French troops at the early affair of Saarbruck; then came the French reverses. Hamley was not cast down. These were tactical moves, only the preludes of decisive triumph; so things went on till the day of Sedan arrived, when even General Hamley was constrained to acknowledge a French failure. If, however, like most of his cloth, this able and upright soldier was sometimes opinionated, he had earned almost a right to be so by having done more than any other man of his generation for the intellectual formation of the new order of English officer who stands in such marked contrast to his predecessor. That young Aldershot, Woolwich, or Sandhurst does not find time hang heavily on his hands when there is no cricket match on, no race-meeting whither to drive his dogcart, no afternoon train to town to catch, is chiefly due to the intellectual habits which Hamley did more by example and writing than anyone else to generate. The most competent critics, by no mean personal partizans of the author, have testified the impossibility of over-estimating the good done by his book on the *Operations of War*. This was the first readable work in the English language on strategy and tactics; in the opinion of experts it is far ahead of any book on those subjects previously written in any language. Hamley took the art of war out of the dull and dreary region of technical diagram, of skeleton charts of battle; he dealt with it as a living theme. Thus Hamley's great treatise, even to those who have been students of Jomini, Clausewitz, and M'Dougall, is a revelation. Its author, not by innate genius alone, but by years of careful practice, had acquired an excellent literary style; the clear and forcible language of this book first taught professional readers how to study all military history, and how to apply the lessons of the past to the campaigns of the future. Such a volume then may, if any, claim to belong to what De Quincey called the literature of power as distinct from that of mere information.

Intellectual quality is not the only respect in which there has been lately witnessed a change among the officers of the army. The Crimean War was followed by many promotions to the grade of officers from the ranks. Since then the average number of commissions given in this way seems to have been about twenty-five a year. Of this number 16 have gone to infantry, 4 to cavalry, and the remainder to other branches of the Service. These promotions, suitable as they are to the day of democracy, cannot of course affect sensibly the tone or the *personnel* of the officers of the Queen's army, who will continue to be, as they have been, men born to the social advantages of gentle station. The social fusion and personal intimacy of men whose antecedents and interests differ, though their official rank be identical, is not likely ever to be more complete than between English and native officers in the Indian Staff Corps regiments; though the difficulty in the way of amalgamation proceeds probably less from the exclusiveness of the older officer than from the indisposition of the new to avail himself of the social opportunities placed technically at his disposal.[70]

CHAPTER XXII
FROM WOODEN WALLS TO FLOATING ENGINES

Great reduction of the navy, as well as of the army, between the Napoleonic wars and the Queen's accession. But silently a reaction soon set in. First beginnings of new policy. Reform in the training of sailors in gunnery; later developments of naval education for officers and men; the existing course compared with the past. Successive stages in the replacement of sails by steam power. A navy transformed by Steam and Iron. Lessons of contemporary experience gradually applied to the English navy, especially those learnt from the American Civil War and the Austro-Italian War.

After the Napoleonic wars the British navy, like the British army, was greatly reduced. In the Navy List of 1837, 132 vessels are named. Sixty years later they had increased to 461. Now the naval policy of successive Administrations seems to have acquired the same continuity as belongs traditionally to foreign policy. It is a first principle to-day with all parties in the State that the iron walls which, as our first line of defence, have replaced the walls of wood, should not be reduced to a point at which they need fear the combined opposition, if not of Europe, still of the two or three most powerful of European fleets. At the moment when the great reductions in our fleet were contemplated, Napoleon at St Helena, in the course of the conversations recorded by O'Meara,[71] said: 'It was bad policy to encourage the military mania instead of sticking to your marine, which is the real force of your country.' In 1832 the naval vote had been 4¼ millions. Two years later, it was reduced to 3 millions. The fleet reductions did not, however, reach their limit until the year before the Queen's accession. Then the naval vote was reduced to 2¾ millions, with the dwindling of our squadrons already noted. Contrast with this the 1896-97 estimate of £22,774,318, providing for the services of a total, every branch included, of 93,750 officers and men, inclusive of the 461 ships already named.

The history of the naval transformations through which during the Victorian age we have passed, may be described as a succession of periodical scares, a steadily progressive instruction by science in its latest application to maritime affairs, and by the lessons contained in the experience of other countries. The English operations by sea during the Crimean War; in a still greater degree perhaps the improvements in naval construction, attack and defence, shown in the hostilities between the Federal and Confederate navies in the civil war on the other side of the Atlantic; later again the lessons taught by the engagements between Italian and Austrian squadrons, notably at Lissa;—these are the incidents that have gradually taught us, as well as our European neighbours, to bring our naval arrangements and appliances up to the latest mark of mechanical perfection.

Even during the time when the security brought by relief after long war was causing England to neglect her navy, some of those movements which in Victorian days have given us our present race of seamen were in progress.

Seven years before the Queen's accession, the 'Excellent,' as a gunnery school for sailors, had been established. Soon after its establishment, it was gradually enlarged and improved till it has become to-day the chief source from which our ships are manned. Before that institution, naval gunnery was taught, or not taught, at the discretion of the captains in command. From being, as at the beginning of the present age it was, always precarious and generally insufficient, the supply of sailors has become fairly adequate and regular. Weeks and months used to be wasted before a crew could be put together. The social haunts of seamen were visited by officers; thus eventually by promises or threats men were induced to join the ship. When the commission of the ship came to an end, the sailors were thrown adrift, usually returning to their civil vocations until a new job was offered. By the time of the Crimean War all this had been changed. Apart from the inducements of prize money sailors flocked in animated by a real enthusiasm. Thus though in France the naval conscription had existed since the time of Colbert the manning of the English fleet proceeded more quickly in Crimean days than that of the French. The continuous service for ten years certain, with the choice of prolonging that term and receiving a pension, has transformed the condition of our navy. Other reforms have given us in time of war a reserve of 20,000 sailors of the mercantile marine, the equivalents of our rifle volunteers on land. These are annually subject to gun and small arm drill on our coasts, and, in the opinion of an expert like Captain Eardley Wilmot, will prove adequate to any demand.[72]

There have been later reforms than this in the professional education of our sailors. Till between forty and fifty years ago men and boys entered the navy without any previous training. In, or about 1855, all sailors entered the service as boys chiefly from fifteen to sixteen and a half years old. They now begin by passing from twelve to eighteen months on board the training ship. Here they are instructed in seamanship and gunnery. They thus bring with them to sea a practical knowledge of their duties. The system which has given us a new race of naval officers dates from nearly the same time as that which began to produce a fresh generation of seamen. Before 1857, no regular system of training midshipmen existed. All their knowledge was actually acquired afloat, exactly as Captain Marryat describes. The large ships only were furnished with regular naval instructors. Since the 'Britannia' was instituted in 1857, all midshipmen receive from fifteen months to two years education in naval subjects and in mathematics. The educational term is not over when the professional career begins. The course of study necessary before the examination for Lieutenant can be passed has been greatly expanded. Formerly acting mates were supposed to satisfy all educational tests for Lieutenant in about three months. Now a year is occupied with these studies; the qualifying standard for the pass examination is pitched far higher than was ever known before.

The transformation undergone by our navy which strikes the eye most forcibly is of course the replacement of the wooden walls by the floating ironclad and the substitution of steam for wind-filled sails as the propelling power of our fleet. A naval officer, Sir William Symonds, instead of a member of the School of Naval Architecture, was appointed Surveyor of the Navy; the first step towards improving ship construction was taken. Almost on the eve of the Queen's accession, certainly during all the earlier thirties, steamers 5 of which in all existed, were only used to tow ships of the line in and out of harbour; or at the utmost for a trip to Gibraltar or Malta. When Captain Charles Napier predicted that steam would soon become to the navy what cavalry is to the army, and have the post of honour, the prediction seemed impossible. The adoption of steam was a very gradual and tentative process. First the 'Active,' a 46-gun frigate was fitted with paddles, but not as yet engines. The result was progress at a maximum of from 2 to 3 knots an hour. Captain Napier carried the experiment a little further; but in no case was steam yet exclusively relied on for working the paddles. When Queen Victoria came to the throne the navy included 5 steam paddle vessels. Each of them had three masts furnished with sails. All were generically known as steam sloops. The largest was 830 tons; the maximum of speed from 8 to 10 knots. Larger steamers called steam frigates, from 1,200 to 1,800 tons were introduced soon after the reign began. They were first actively employed at the bombardment of Acre in 1840, and notwithstanding their old lines of construction, proved the usefulness of armed ships at sea against forts on land. The Acre operations seem to have been important, as showing for the first time the skill of Victorian seamen in gunnery and in the management of the machinery of steam ships. Similarly, long before this only the skill with which English ships were handled had overcome, in their encounters with French, the faults of their design. The weight of metal thrown by the largest guns on board these earlier craft, *e.g.* the 'Nelson,' was 2,750 lbs. Further steam progress was marked when, eight years after the reign began, the 'Erebus' and 'Terror' in which Sir John Franklin's expedition sailed for the Pole, were fitted with the screw.

As yet iron had not been employed on the present scale in ship construction. Both in 1857 and 1858 larger ships than had yet been known, the 'Niagara' first, the 'Orlando,' the 'Mersey,' afterwards, were built, all, however, of wood. Long after steam was partially employed, sails were retained. Even during our Black Sea and Baltic operations in Crimean days, screw and paddle were still combined with canvas. Such success as our fleet secured at this time was not promoted by the excellence of our naval organization which according to Captain Eardley Wilmot, was not much better than our military.The first lesson as to the new mode of motion by sea learnt from the naval operations in Crimean waters was recognized by Kinglake and is confirmed by Captain Eardley Wilmot as being that 'in regions where land and sea much intertwine, steam is stronger for attack than for defence.'

The iron ships now almost as essential to the idea of a navy as steam itself, had been tried for different purposes long before our Admiralty adopted them; the material had been used, first in 1812 for canal barges, secondly, a little later, for the mercantile marine. Iron was not employed for our navy till the last days of William IV. The tragic fate of the first iron ship, the 'Birkenhead,' may well have prejudiced both the Department and the public against the new material.

The iron-plated ship of the modern type appears to have been a French idea, first tried by Colonel Paixhaus in 1825. The floating batteries employed in the Crimean War in which Napoleon III. was specially interested, marked a fresh advance in this direction. Nor does it seem easy to overrate the value of the lessons in scientific seamanship derived from the French and English operations on the Black Sea, 1854-5. The result was the invitation by the Admiralty of designs from all quarters, the ordering of the 'Warrior,' designed by Mr Scott Russell, in 1859, completed in 1861. [74] This vessel was equipped with a battery extending her whole length. Before the fifties were out, the naval and the national mind had been familiarized with the idea of mastless ships, long repulsive to the national sense of the picturesque at sea. The 'Warrior,' however, was furnished with sails in addition to steam and marked an epoch in the development not only of the English navy, but of the navies of the world, as the first absolutely complete iron ship ever built.

The French ships, earlier in point of time were not equally perfect as regards material. They were, in fact, wooden ships cut down and plated with iron. Thus with literal truth referring to the launch of 'Warrior' could our Naval Minister of the day, Sir John Pakington, describe the whole world as interested in the bold experiment. Other ships of the same kind soon followed, and of even larger proportions. It is to the credit of English workmanship that the building of these vessels at Chatham was performed by shipwrights who had hitherto worked only on wood; and that the craftmanship shown by them in the new material was pronounced by experts to be excellent. Timber having been definitely superseded by metal, there followed the long and technical controversy about the relative merits of turret and broadside armaments. The concentration of guns into a single citadel on board ship was first in England powerfully advocated by Sir E. Reed. Since then, the naval warfare between Federals and Confederates on the other side of the Atlantic, followed by the exciting manœuvres off Cherbourg between the 'Alabama' and the 'Keersage,' and in Europe the naval portions of the Austro-Italian war of 1866 have taught lessons the full results of which are not, perhaps even yet, perfectly realized. So long is the experimental stage which has to be traversed before the newest system of maritime defence and attack with its complicated machinery can be said entirely to have reached what is alone to be called properly the scientific stage.[75]

CHAPTER XXIII
TRANSFORMATIONS OF VICTORIAN SCIENCE

The Prince Consort's influence in organizing pursuits and departments of knowledge, a characteristic of the Victorian age. The Prince not only the advocate of the 1851 Exhibition, but most active in the movement that has given us South Kensington as an instrument in the knowledge of art and science. The British Association foreshadowed by a like organization in Germany which may have impressed the youthful Prince Albert, but certainly set the example to the leaders of English science. Like its German forerunners the British Association gradually grew in popular favour. Its progress as shown by facts and figures. Modern course of science summarized. The transforming influences of science traced in all intellectual pursuits.

If in a few words the contrast between the England of the later and the earlier part of the Queen's reign were to be summed up, it might be expressed by the single word, organization. For that process, as for its most impressive results, Victorian England is indebted primarily to the husband of its Queen. To-day Englishmen are reminded locally and visibly of the Great Exhibition of 1851 by the elaborately picturesque memorial of the man who spared no pains to secure its success, situated, as that monument is, on the spot where the great glass house once stood.

That event was the earliest triumph of the new epoch of culture including science in its application to the conveniences or luxuries of daily life. From 1851 too, may be dated the organized encouragement of the inventor in all departments of scientific ingenuity.

Such a world's show might in due course have been devised by the wit of man, even if the Queen's husband had not recalled for reproduction in England the idea of the Frankfort fairs of the sixteenth century.[76] It is quite certain that without the Prince's personal enterprise and sustained supervision, and but for the invaluable co-operation of the late Sir Henry Cole, the movement which has transformed the Court suburb from laundry grounds, or riding schools, into a centre of artistic or scientific education for the whole country had it taken place at all, would not have occurred till many years later than it actually did. The contrast between the South Kensington of the Queen's accession year with its suburban desolations, and of the sixtieth anniversary year, with its palaces of art, its private mansions rivalling those of Park Lane, its Imperial Institute, its provision for educational classes by day, for musical fêtes by lamplight, might have been indefinitely postponed.

The name of Her Majesty written in the clear bold hand of youth when she became Queen may be read to-day in the register of the Royal Society. That entry prefigured the close connection between science and the Court which, for the first time in the history of the monarchy, was to signalize her reign. The period preparatory to the enthronement of science and art beneath the glass roof of Paxton was of scarcely less educational value to the Kingdom than, to most appliances of daily life, the Exhibition itself was to prove. The instructive addresses delivered at this time by the Prince Consort, now to a gathering of artists and writers, now to more popular audiences at Birmingham or elsewhere, may seem to those who read them to-day familiar or even commonplace. They were then entire novelties, not only from their authorship, but from their subject.

In 1897 it appears the most natural and suitable thing in the world that a Royal Prince should vary the more strictly ceremonial functions of State by opening an art gallery in London, a science school in the provinces, an Imperial Institute, a Fisheries Exhibition in South Kensington. Fifty years since such a part seemed of questionable wisdom to some, of dangerous precedent for the monarchy to others; at the best a foreign experiment which the Queen's husband would most wisely have left unmade. In the sixtieth year of the reign, there is no social gathering or private dwelling, there is scarcely a village inn, or country cottage, or a seaside lodging house, that by the paper on its walls, the designs of its furniture, the suspended pictures cut from illustrated prints, fails to remind one with eyes to see such things the extent to which ideas of art or ornament that began with the Prince and Sir Henry Cole have directly from South Kensington penetrated into every corner of the land, and made their humanizing influence felt beneath the roof of peasant as well as of peer.

Even in the thirtieth year of the reign, these forces had scarcely advanced beyond the embryonic stage. Had the Prince Consort himself claimed visibly to exercise the Royal prerogative, on which as a fact he never presumed, he could scarcely have given a greater shock to the prejudices of those high in social position and near the Court who inherited from Hanoverian times a contempt for all distinctions save those of birth and rank.

Up to the moment of his death the Queen's husband was endeavouring to make his wife's Court a centre not only of achievement in war, of statesmanship in peace, but of letters, art, science, and of the most famous among their contemporary ornaments. Death prevented the design from ever being carried out completely. The names of Alfred Tennyson and of Arthur Penrhyn Stanley are enough to remind one of the direction actually travelled by the Prince in producing some resemblance between the Windsor where a Victoria reigned, and the Weimar whose intellectual glories, a Goethe had typified. Here again the intellectual revolution which the Court began has been continued by those who represent the Crown to-day.

Such knowledge of physical science as the Prince Consort's son possesses was largely imparted to him by the teacher Faraday, who was his father's choice. Appropriately enough, therefore, in the winter of 1897 did the Prince of Wales assist in founding the Faraday Laboratory of the Royal Society. The progress now spoken of seems to be symbolized by the acceptance of the word 'science' as the nearly exclusive synonym for that physicism which is strictly only one of the divisions that generically it includes. From the check to the regular teaching of physical knowledge at the disorganization spread through the world by the collapse of the Roman Empire, and by the concentration of human thought upon politics and theology, instead of those subjects first expounded by Thales, after him by Archimedes, Aristotle, Ptolemy, till the day of the modern doctors had dawned, the conquests achieved by man over nature were inconsiderable. Francis Bacon's equalization of human *ingenia,* and his elaborately tabulated apparatus for studying phenomena, created an appetite for mastering the arcana of the visible universe, but did not satisfy it. As the Prince Consort clearly saw, Nature's secret had been yielded in the past, and would be surrendered in the future, not to founders of systems like a Verulam or a Descartes, but to actual discoverers who did not owe even their methods to the Schools.

Half a century after Bacon's labours, Newton, with no help from Baconian methods discovered the law of gravitation, and with it the unity of sequences which pervade material creation. The cause of the slight progress of physical science whether before or immediately after Bacon formulated his method may be partly explained by the want of the material appliances for physical investigation. These in anything like their mechanical perfection of to-day are not much older than our present era. The agencies of glass, of alcohol, of microscopes and of other such appliances were as unknown to the physicists of Alexandria, of Athens, or of the Middle Ages as the electric wire itself. Where the subject matter, the heavenly bodies, the structure of the human frame, could be studied without elaborate machinery, the contemporaries or successors of the Ionian physicists who searched for the origin of all things in some single element, air, fire or water, seem rudely to have anticipated later discoveries. The Aristotelian philosophy and the rudiments of practical medicine, preserved together by Averrhoes, Avicenna, and the whole school of the Arabian thinkers of the twelfth and thirteenth centuries, descended in each other's company to the Italian schoolmen, and were delivered by them to English students. Thus, on the eve of the present century, the indestructibility of matter, however Protean the forms of its manifestations, had been ascertained by European chemists. The year of the Queen's accession was also that of the publication of Whewell's *History of the Inductive Sciences*.

In this age, as in that of Bacon, great lawyers have taken a foremost place among enquirers into the nature of things. Lord Brougham did something to methodize, and more to popularize, the facts of science. A greater lawyer than Brougham, Sir William Grove, Justice of the Common Pleas first, Judge of the High Court of Justice afterwards, was also professor of experimental philosophy at the London Institution during the first decade of the reign. His discoveries with regard to the correlation of forces had not been entirely formulated when Dr Whewell's book appeared. Nor had Charles Darwin completed in his retirement at Down, in Kent, those researches which in 1859, gave the world *The Origin of Species*. This book, if the work of any single man ever did so, created an epoch, not in physical enquiry alone, but in every branch of human knowledge conducted on scientific principles.

The Victorian Court had begun to encourage science before Darwin's great book was published. In 1847 the Prince Consort became Chancellor of the University of Cambridge, and in this capacity he was naturally brought into official and friendly relations with Dr Whewell, then Master of Trinity, as well as with other English leaders of scientific thought. The growing success of the British Association after its inaugural congress had been held, is not unjustly connected with the Prince's name. The idea of an annual parliament of learning was, like that of the Great Exhibition itself, not of English origin. Even in Germany, where the first trial of it had been made, prosperity had been gradual. At Halle, Frankfort, Dresden, and Munich, notwithstanding the personal distinction of its chief promoter Professor Oken, and its encouragement by many of the enlightened Kinglets who then divided the rule of the Fatherland, during the second decade of the century when the enterprise began, its most noticeable meeting does not seem to have numbered more than from 200 to 400. At Leipsic in 1822, the attendance was barely two score; six years later in Berlin, it amounted to 464. Before that assemblage probably had much impressed the young Prince Albert, it had stimulated the most distinguished representatives of scientific thought in England. Sir David Brewster, Sir John Herschel, Sir

Humphry Davy based, upon the German example, an appeal to the English Government. The decline of arts and science in this country was attributed to their total neglect by the State, to the exclusion of men eminent in either of these departments from the titular decorations of the country, and to the heavy exactions from scientific inventors imposed by the fees payable under the patent law.

More than two or three decades of the Victorian age had passed before art, science, and letters began to receive the State recognition now firmly acknowledged as their due. Both Bulwer Lytton and Macaulay had served in Parliament or in office fifteen years before they were ennobled. [77] Tennyson was the first English poet raised to the peerage who knew no politics save those of patriotism; to the same epoch, too, belongs a like honour bestowed upon three men of science at successive intervals:—now a physician, Playfair, now the physicist, Lord Kelvin, and again the latest, and to not a few the most welcome and significant of all, the inventor of the antiseptic treatment which has saved so many lives and limbs, who will henceforth be known as Lord Lister.

It is suggestively prophetic of the new era which in the next reign was to open for letters, science and art in their relations to the English State, that while the country had been preparing for a revolution peaceful but complete in politics, there had assembled at York, September 29, 1831, a company which prognosticated the coming revolution throughout the whole region of popular thought and culture. The York meeting mustered less than 200. It was intended only to launch the programme of the society. 'To point out the lines of direction in which the researches of science should move, to state the problems to be solved, the data to be fixed, to assign to every class of mind a definite task, to amend the laws relating to patents, to agitate for a Government provision to encourage and reward scientific research;'—these are the objects which Mr Harcourt enumerated in the first official document of the body. As proof of the vitality of the revolution which that Yorkshire company, less than 200 strong, introduced, it is enough to mention Dr Rae's Arctic voyages of 1853-4, the Challenger expedition of 1872, and the last Oxford University Commission which at the instance of the first scientific Premier England has ever known, Lord Salisbury, endowed scientific research as one of the estates of the realm, and has done something more than relieve that seat of old learning from the reproach of discouraging the newest sciences. Little perhaps did the doctors of divinity, and classical professors, when, on June 18, 1832, they welcomed the second senate of savants to its session on the Isis, imagine themselves to be fostering a movement which would partially oust from its emoluments and honours in their own Schools the old learning, and give to the new not only professorships for its teachers, but scholarships for the reward of its learners. As against the York meeting in 1831 of not much more than

100, the Oxford meeting of the Reform Act year attracted 700. In another twelvemonth the Cambridge meeting of June 25, 1833, was attended by 900. The Edinburgh meeting of September 8, 1834, mustered 1,298.

Since then the most noticeable figures have been 1855—2,133, 1861—3,138; while 1887 crowns the list with 3,838. The figures necessarily are to some extent governed by the importance or attractiveness of the towns at which the meetings are held. The names on the books of the society are more than half a million. So progressive a thing is English science. The meeting itself is only a part of the work done. Throughout the year committees are investigating various branches of science prominent at the moment, and preparing their reports to be included in the Annual General Report, a document of over 1,000 pages. Social satire at first made merry over the learned ladies and gentlemen who combined mutual laudation of themselves with picnics, excursions and pleasure parties of all sorts in interesting neighbourhoods at the most agreeable season of the year. To-day no one denies the British Association the credit of having promoted the discovery of new facts in science, or at least having been the first agency to draw public attention to them. Within the last few years, it was at one of these Association meetings (Liverpool 1870) that Professor Huxley pronounced against the popular theory of spontaneous generation of the lower forms of life, thus placing on record his adherence to the theory of biogenesis as opposed to abiogenesis; life, in other words, could in every grade of creation only come from life, not from the corruption of death. Thus was a physical tradition that from the earliest times down to the seventeenth century had held its own, finally repudiated by the greatest authority of his day on all biological matters.

Even this pronouncement seems to have been anticipated. A physicist less famous than Huxley, Schwann, some half a century before Huxley's day, is said to have been the first to criticize the abiogenesis doctrine as supported by no sufficient evidence. The tendency towards unity in multiplicity declared by the old Greek thinkers to characterize all true science marked the doctrines of the correlation of force as well as of the conservation of energy, both of them connected with this age. It was also inherent in the theory of evolution as explained by Charles Darwin in 1859, 28 years, that is, after the British Association for the first time met. Even the great Kentish physicist of our day was not entirely the first in the field with the discovery that was to transform the whole region of thought. Early in the last century De Maillet had applied the principle of the survival of the fittest to the world of human life. On the eve of the present century Charles Darwin's ancestor, Erasmus, as well as German philosophers still more famous, elaborated with more ability and knowledge the same idea, which also underlay the discussions between the French Academicians, Cuvier and St Hilaire. However the ground may have been prepared for him, so far as any single man can be said to have discovered any great idea, Charles Darwin must be accounted the author of the theory of evolution as it is now understood.

Whewell's survey of the inductive sciences at the beginning of the reign dimly forecasts some discoveries which have since been verified. It contains no word prophetic of the doctrine by which, in the countless possibilities of its application, every branch of science in little more than a quarter of a century was potentially if not actually to be transformed. The eve of the sixtieth anniversary of the Queen's accession has witnessed the completion by Mr Herbert Spencer of the monumental treatise that applies the doctrines of Darwin to subjects that Darwin had not specially studied, perhaps with results which Darwin himself had not entirely foreseen. Whether a reaction against Darwinism has already, as some think, set in; how far, and with what consequences, that movement may go, are as yet only matters of speculation.

The exploration of the Italian soil has caused many chapters of Roman history to be rewritten more in accordance with the older traditions than with the newer learning. Like processes near the sites of Babylon and Nineveh have done much to vindicate the authors of the Pentateuch as chroniclers of fact; and have even created a reaction in favour of the Mosaic cosmogony, and the sacred narrative of the Deluge. Evolution as a philosophy is not altogether rejected by physicists of orthodoxy so unimpeachable as Mr St. George Mivart. More lately it has been discovered that an Anglican divine may keep an open mind on the subject of Darwinism and yet be made Archbishop of Canterbury. To the unlearned English vulgar the question is whether the visible universe and its inhabitants are more likely to have developed themselves by a series of indescribable processes than to have developed, as the Scriptural tradition has been interpreted as teaching, by a Power external to them and directing every stage of their progress. If it be said that evolution is the method in which that superhuman Power who is behind and above all often chooses to act, there is no reason why the occupant of Lambeth should not be as good an evolutionist as the scientific investigator whose nearest country neighbour at Down, Sir John Lubbock, appropriately presided over the Jubilee meeting of the British Association at York.

The transformations effected in other departments of physical study during our age are not less remarkable. Many of them have been appreciably assisted by the social intercourse of mind with mind which the British Association has so signally promoted. Lyell's *Principles of Geology* was published in pre-Association days and seven years before the Victorian age began. Its influence was in the same direction as that of Darwin; it suggested, that is, the enquiry why the natural processes that are said to explain the globe we inhabit should not explain also the presence of man upon it. Biology and anthropology, the two studies which have most been promoted by the Darwinian doctrine, can consequently be pronounced with truth the creations of the present age. As far back as Elizabethan times, electrical phenomena had been systematically studied. Many of these manifestations, however, especially their relations with heat and light, as well as most of their adaptations to the offices of daily life, belong to the era that opened in 1837.

Photography of course was an unknown art in pre-Victorian days. Even when its predecessor, the Daguerreotype, discovered in 1839, had been considerably improved upon, it still remained a contrivance rather for distorting the human features than for faithfully reproducing them as photography does upon glass or paper, and with the addition of natural colours as photography now bids fair soon to have done.

These achievements of a science which is generically new have not been accompanied with inactivity on the part of those sciences which, like astronomy, are probably in one shape or another nearly coeval with Creation itself. Long before the planet was actually discovered, the telescopes that swept the heavens had brought within their ken the spot at which in 1846 Neptune was proved to be. If the number of the heavenly bodies has not of late received many additions, new asteroids are constantly swimming into sight in the quarters where they had been suspected; comets, less looked for than these apparitions, are often announced to have flashed themselves upon the observer's sight.

The influence of scientific thought and conceptions upon the language of literature as well as of daily life, is only less remarkable than the material conquests of science themselves. The most instructive instance of this is afforded by the scholarly and illustrious woman of genius who will always be known to fame as George Eliot. The popular idea of Mr Herbert Spencer having influenced her studies and her phraseology is not quite true. Mr Spencer was her own, and her companion's, friend. Her diction in her later works was inspired by the intellectual forces of her day. Of the formative power of these she was probably herself unconscious. If Herbert Spencer had a place among them, he was at least only one of several. From George Eliot, in that phase of her genius now under consideration, there has sprung a school. However original the gift of writers like Mrs Humphry Ward, it seems unlikely that their talents would have taken the direction they have received and found their expression in the language they employ unless the author of *Adam Bede* and *Middlemarch* had first supplied a new want or created a fresh intellectual taste by a style that our forefathers might have admired, but might not always have been able to understand.

Of the many transformations wrought by Victorian science, not the least;—unscientific people might think it the greatest—is the assimilation of the idiom of fiction to that of the text books of the schools. The entire ethos of our oral diction not less than our literature has been revolutionized by science. When a parliamentary speaker illustrates his argument by a metaphor, it is not, as his forerunners once did, to the Latin and Greek classics, or even to literature at all, but to the laboratory, to the dissecting room, or to the crucible that he most frequently goes for his *trope*. The similes of the Attic masterpieces are taken habitually from those operations with which their naval empire familiarized the Athenian mind. Nor can these metaphors be understood without some remembrance of the processes which marine affairs involve. A similar acquaintance with the later operations of science is scarcely less useful for a proper appreciation of the most characteristic beauties of Victorian prose, by whatever master displayed. This dispossession of the literary by the scientific is universal. Following unconsciously perhaps the example of a great statesman, those who have in our day most widely differed from him on national affairs, a Randolph Churchill, or a Charles Stewart Parnell have reproduced the taste of a Salisbury in finding their recreations, not in the *belles lettres* that were congenial to the day of a Pitt or a Canning, but in the researches that a Tyndall, a Huxley, a Thomson, have popularized.

Galileo's astronomical views found a useful ally by the incisive raillery of his literary style. The admirable prose of a Huxley and his fellow labourers has been no less effective for popularizing scientific studies with the public they have addressed. The social urbanity with which Nature and training have endowed Sir John Lubbock has prepossessed not a few on his own level in life in favour of those branches of physical enquiry that have enabled him to rehabilitate the moral character of the autumnal wasp.

CHAPTER XXIV
CECILIA'S TRIUMPHS

The revolution in the conditions of English music—effected since its first encouragement by the Victorian Court—illustrated by a contrast between the social status of the musician to-day, and forty years ago. Music always a tradition of the present dynasty. Handel. English machinery for teaching music instituted under the Georgian era, and perfected under the Victorian. Has English organization for musical teaching outstripped English capacity for learning? Certain reforms approved by high musical experts. Other individual agencies than those of the Court favourable to Music during this century. Mendelssohn; his encouragement of John Parry, the forerunner of Corney Grain, and Arthur Cecil. Sir Charles Hallé, Herr Joachim, Grove, Sullivan. Anglo-German ladies. Crystal Palace Concerts.

The transformation, at once artistic and scientific, with which the Prince Consort as the past representative of the Crown, and his descendents as its present representatives, will always be chiefly associated, remains to be glanced at. One need not have reached middle age to be able to realize the revolution in the English capacity for the enjoyment as well as for the performance of music, vocal or instrumental, that has taken place since the Victorian age began. A dowdily dressed young woman, alighting from an omnibus at the street corner, trailing after her a fragment of the straw that littered the floor of her conveyance; her clothes, what was then called shabby genteel. She carried under her arm a roll of papers or a portfolio; she was insolently eyed by the servant who opened the door of the house in Portland Place at which she timidly knocked, and contemptuously motioned to take a seat in the hall until the drawing room was ready for the music lesson to be given to the young lady of the family. A hungry looking gentleman, of foreign aspect, and slightly French or German accent, also descended from an omnibus in the same quarter; he bore in his hand a black case which might be from its appearance a sarcophagus for a deceased cat, but which might be identified by more experienced observers as containing a fiddle. He was received by the servant at the front door not more ceremoniously than the instructress of a few hours earlier. This was the proprietor of a little orchestra which attended private dances. A few hours after he might be accompanying with his fiddle the wind instruments of his troupe, for Thackeray's Mrs Timmins gave that very night her little dance. If the musician played well, and pleased the head footman as well as the mistress of the house, he might as a special favour be invited downstairs to help the servants finish the cold chicken and the champagne heeltaps when the guests had gone.

To-day the lady who condescends to teach the art of pianoforte execution to the young people in a popular London quarter drives up to the house in her own victoria and would no more be kept waiting a minute for her appointment than if she were a duchess in her own right. The accomplished foreigner who plays the violin alights from a brougham drawn by a pair of thoroughbreds. If he is to be induced to honour a friend in Grosvenor Square with his company at dinner, the invitation must be given at least three weeks beforehand. The 'master' must choose his own fellow guests, and supervise the menu before it is finally decided on; the dinner itself must be so arranged that to a moment it will occupy the time which the great man prescribes. The conversation must be so contrived as to coruscate with epigram, and to fascinate with anecdotes all warranted to be new, lest the diner of the evening should have the slightest touch of boredom. If these conditions are not satisfied, this arbiter of taste may refuse to sit through the meal. He is the chartered libertine of the dining rooms and drawing rooms of the great.

England has always possessed a considerable school of national composers. These might have achieved the highest triumphs of genius without acquiring a fraction of that social ascendancy for their art which it has gradually won. Under the auspices of the Prince Consort first, the patronage of the Court was secured for the art of St Cecilia. That day already mentioned on which Lady Lyttelton first heard the Queen's husband playing on the organ at Windsor was an eventful one for the social esteem of music in the adopted country of the Royal executant. After this came the Prince's directorship of the Ancient Concerts, and the arrangement of its programmes on special occasions by himself. The club principle during the married life of the Queen had in its popular illustration not gone beyond infancy. Otherwise, one of the Royal Family would, as he has since done, regularly have handled the conductor's baton; while for the special amusement of another a series of smoking concerts might as to-day have been arranged in Piccadilly palaces.

Music of course has always been a tradition of English Royalty. The Royal Academy of Music now domiciled in Tenterden Street, Hanover Square, was founded in 1822 with the King as patron. It was opened March 24, 1823, with a small and precarious attendance of pupils seldom exceeding two or three score, even at the date of its receiving the Royal charter, June 23, 1830. The number of students at Christmas 1896 was 500, all of whom were regular in their visits. The Royal College of Music at Kensington Gore was first founded as the National Training School in 1875. Its avowed motive was to honour the Consort's memory. It was due partly to the efforts of the Prince of Wales with a Committee of which the then Duke of Edinburgh was chairman. He was also a most indefatigable promoter of the whole scheme from the very first. Its first Principal was Dr, now Sir Arthur, Sullivan. Some years later, again at the Heir Apparent's initiative, as a result of a meeting held at St James's Palace, February 28, 1882, this institution was re-formed. It was opened in the building formerly occupied by the National Training School by the Prince and Princess of Wales, May 7, 1883. Of this Sir George Grove was the first director, holding the post till Christmas 1894 when he was succeeded by Dr. C. H. H. Parry. The Charter of the Royal College was obtained in 1883. It has to-day an endowment of £130,000 which provides some 60 different scholarships. This, too, in its existing shape was opened by the Prince Consort's descendants, the Prince and Princess of Wales; it had at the Christmas of 1896, 300 regular pupils. A very important part of the institution consists of the Donaldson museum of musical instruments; these were given to the College by Mr G. Donaldson in 1894.

The Guildhall School of Music was founded in 1880 by that same Corporation which has done more perhaps than any other single body since the Queen's accession to promote the humanities of life. Its first Principal was Mr Weist Hill; he was succeeded by Sir Joseph Barnby, who again in 1896 was followed by Mr W. H. Cummings. This Guildhall School is undoubtedly the most popular institution of the kind which we possess. Its pupils at the Christmas of 1896 were 3,496. The other great metropolitan school of music is Trinity College, London. This was incorporated in 1875 under the Companies Act. Six years later, in 1881, it was reorganized upon a wider basis. The number of pupils at Christmas 1896 shows a steady increase.

These and other institutions less important are only some of the national monuments to the progress of the study of music as an art during the last two or three decades.

The organization and the educational machinery of music have now, in the opinion of those competent judges to whom the writer of these lines is indebted, reached a point beyond which further development is neither necessary nor desirable. Production and execution leave perhaps little to be wished for. Appreciation, however, of musical excellence is not universally proportionate to musical activity. Audiences more intelligently critical and better trained are apparently the chief *desiderata*, if composers and performers are to rise above mediocrity. Instruction in the art now spoken of has, of course, shared in the advantages incidental to the transformation of London from an insular into a cosmopolitan capital. As a result, the best teachers from all countries are available for the London learner.

Nor in this respect does England to-day, as thirty years ago it did, compare disadvantageously with Leipsic, Paris, Berlin, Stuttgardt. There seems however reason to fear that, like Gwendolen Harleth in *Daniel Deronda* before Klesmer, we fail in that important and indefinable quality, style. The best critics complain that, when a student has been through the regular course here, and has perhaps become a first rate technical musician, he seldom seems to get any further; he never, in other words, develops any individuality. To some extent this result follows the collective teaching of all academies. The area of level mediocrity is, however, it may be feared, larger here than in France or Germany. There is more of delicacy and daintiness in the French student; there is more of individual expansion and thoughtfulness in the German. Both are trained in academies. The quicker intuition and more intelligent appreciation of French and German audiences are in the opinion of unprejudiced critics attributed to this cause. Hence the expert, if consulted by an English student, probably would advise him to go abroad for a year or two when his technical course has been finished in England. Unfortunately the advice too often resembles that of a medical man who might prescribe a generous diet and a glass of port wine to an invalid labourer, earning less than £1 a week.

In respect of education, cheapness and free scholarships seem to have been carried at least as far as is conducive to the real interest of learners in this country. A reform, favoured by many good judges, is to make payment for teaching universal with a few exceptions; then to give to students of promise an allowance sufficient to enable them to go abroad and complete their education. As it is, some risk is run of gratuitously training mediocrities, launching them on professional careers which can only land them in disappointment and poverty.

The late Prince Consort, though the most highly placed, is only one of several individuals whose personal influence has conspicuously encouraged the growth and the gratification of a musical taste more or less cultivated. The discussion which agitated English taste in the eighteenth century as to the merits of German and other music is summed up in a familiar epigram as the difference between tweedledum and tweedledee:—

> Some say, compared to Bononcini,
> That Mynheer Handel's but a ninny;

Others aver that he to Handel
Is scarcely fit to hold a candle.

The commanding genius of the great German composer is enough to account for the traditional complaint that native genius in England has been eclipsed by foreign products. The Elector of Hanover had recognized Handel's genius before he became George I. of England, but began his reign by showing little favour to the composer, who had absented himself without leave from his duties at the Electoral Court. Already in Queen Anne's reign Handel's *Te Deum* had celebrated in St Paul's Cathedral the conclusion of the Peace of Utrecht. It was not till after his *Water Music* had procured his restoration to favour that the new English monarch took him back into his service. Gradually, however, till in 1741 it was confirmed by the *Messiah* produced in Dublin and by his operas in London, the triumph of the German over the Italian school thus advanced. Neither then nor later did it involve neglect of the great English composer of the seventeenth century, our own Henry Purcell,[78] organist at Westminster Abbey at eighteen years of age, and author of a greater number of songs, anthems, operas, glees and cantatas, at once famous and popular, than probably any other musician whom England has produced. Felix Mendelssohn of Hamburg, not less precocious than our own Purcell, also at eighteen produced an opera. His personal influence in England was scarcely less great than that of Handel, and of course tended towards the further popularization of Teutonic art: he lived on terms of intimate friendship during his different sojourns in this country with English musicians. The popular and accomplished pianoforte improvisatore, John Parry, who was familiar to the English public of this age from his connection with the German-Reed company, 1860-9, the forerunner of the Corney Grain and Arthur Cecil of a later day, might almost be called Mendelssohn's pupil. By Mendelssohn, Parry was first encouraged to adopt music as a profession; the present writer well remembers how he heard from John Parry himself the account of Mendelssohn's listening during half a winter night to the piano improvisations devised by the versatile genius of the then young man.

Charles Hallé, born in Westphalia in 1819, and so just ten years younger than Mendelssohn was driven from Paris to London by the Revolution of 1848, to which England was indebted for such an influx of foreign genius of all kinds to her shores. Beethoven, like Handel, first became known in Europe through a German Elector, him of Cologne. He died in 1827. Though the charm and fame of Beethoven had been steadily growing upon English critics and musicians first and upon the general public afterwards, to Charles Hallé[79] belongs the distinction of having done much towards popularizing this great author of classical music with the English public. The Musical Union which preceded the Popular Concerts was then directed by John Ella, whose programmes included Beethoven's sonatas, played by Hallé with great applause.

The English public, if by voluntary culture it had not been disciplined into a genuine admiration for Teutonic music, as interpreted by various foreign executants, would have been wooed to its love by the educating influences of the Hungarian violinist Herr Joachim, deservedly reverenced by all circles of English society, ever receiving his homage with the dignified modesty of great genius. This director of the Royal Academy of Music at Berlin had, before that appointment, received the degree of Doctor of Music at Cambridge. The bow with which he elicited entrancing strains from his instrument was a social sceptre as well. When George Eliot was writing *Daniel Deronda,* Herr Joachim's social and artistic ascendancy had just reached its culminating point. A scientific musician herself, George Eliot visited those circles where first-rate music was to be heard. No writer more artistically found the suggestions of her characters in real life. The Herr Joachim whom English society knew is reflected so strikingly in the Herr Klesmer of whom the *Daniel Deronda* public reads as to warrant the conjecture that the master before whom Gwendolen Harleth trembled had been suggested by the violinist at whose feet the aristocracy of birth, beauty, wit, intellect and wealth with unfeigned admiration knelt down.

Other individuals deserve a place in the catalogue of those who have helped on the musical movement of our times. Sir George Grove made a substantial addition to the musical wealth of the world by contributing a chapter to its musical romance; that which relates his discovery of the lost scores of Schubert in a Vienna cupboard. His dictionary of music will survive when the honourable record of his Directorship of the Royal College of Music may be forgotten. Sir Arthur Sullivan has not only illustrated with melodies, that have at once caught the ear of the town, the fantastic conceptions of Mr W. S. Gilbert's intellect; he has used his personal popularity on all levels of social London to diffuse improved notions of musical taste. Agencies of the same kind, collective as well as individual have not, during the Victorian age, been wanting.

The *personnel* of upper middle class society in England has been perceptibly affected by the entrance into it through the gate of marriage, of ladies of German origin, of great taste and accomplishments generally, and like all their nation, devoted to music. Hence among other things the increased patronage of the Italian Opera, of all high-class concerts in public as well as of musical artists in private by that well to do section of the Queen's subjects which combines the tastes of culture and of birth with the resources of trade. Its composition of the veritable materials of Paxton's Glass House for the Great Exhibition is not the only respect in which the Crystal Palace at Sydenham is connected with that enterprise of the Prince Consort as a reformer of English taste. To mention only its connection with the subject now being specially considered, the Crystal Palace has maintained its full orchestra since 1854. These concerts have been admittedly during near half a century prime instruments of metropolitan and suburban civilization. They have practically revolutionized the home life of tens of thousands of the prosperous commercial class which fixes its household gods out of earshot of Bow Bells. The impulse thus given to the study of the art on a basis wider and deeper than anything formerly existing can scarcely be exaggerated. It is of itself enough to explain why the number of English students of music in the nineties is so vastly larger than it was during any of the preceding decades.[80]

CHAPTER XXV
TRANSFORMED AND TRANSFORMING ART

English art stimulated and strengthened to a degree second only to science by the movements with which, through the Prince Consort, the Victorian Court identified itself. Contrast between the social consideration of artists now and fifty years ago. From Gandish to Gaston Phœbus. Progress in the association of art with the government of England, and general gain to all concerned in consequence. Gradual endowment of art by the State and establishment of the existing machinery for teaching art and displaying its triumphs to a cultivated public. The work of South Kensington. Success of the Academy tested by figures and facts. Reciprocal benefits to art workers and art patrons. Foreign recognition of English art. The past, present and future of English sculpture.

The popularization and improvement of art in all its manifestations followed the 1851 Exhibition and the initiative of the Prince Consort in a degree second only to the development of science and music themselves. That the Court of Victoria and Albert should have been to the painters of a later day what the Court of Charles I. was to Van Dyck could not have been expected. The Consort's interest and judgment in pictures were inferior to his genuine concern for science. The complacency with which he regarded the canvases of Winterhalter could not promise much enthusiasm in the patronage of English painters. His rescue from disorder and decay of the Raphael cartoons, long before the Prince's day belonging to our Court, but by him first properly cared for and arranged, was not a work of creation, but was one of artistic development. His were the active mind and useful hand that rendered available for national instruction or delight the hereditary treasures of Crown and country which before his day were not indeed unknown, but were not perhaps properly appreciated in the country which possessed them. The rise of a moneyed and fairly cultivated class in English society was the chief element in the improvement of the social and commercial position of the English painter. These agencies happily coincided with the example set by the Prince to his successors of assisting at the great artistic gatherings of the year.

Before May 3, 1851, the Crown had not been represented at the Royal Academy dinner. It has seldom been unrepresented since. Sir Charles Eastlake, in whose election to the Presidency the Queen and Prince had been much interested, had not brought oratorical euphuism to the same perfection as his successor, Lord Leighton. He was, however, a man of cultivated mind, of acceptable presence, and of well-bred speech. His proposal of the Prince's health was made in words that have to-day an historical value. The reply of the Prince blended a philosophic criticism less English than German, with an appreciation of our national masters which was entirely patriotic. It was, he said, the fate of all aristocracies to be assailed habitually from without, sometimes from within. The Academy being an aristocracy of the brush, must accept the position and turn to practical account any hints for improvement which it might contain.[81]

These were still the days when art and artists had not migrated from the gloomy studios of unfashionable Bloomsbury to the gleaming palaces of modish Kensington. Sir Charles Eastlake's predecessor had been Sir Martin Archer Shee, who, very faintly disguised, appears in Thackeray's Mr Smee in *The Newcomes*. Gandish, the unappreciated genius of the palette at whose school, on Mr Smee's advice Clive Newcome is placed, is not a caricature at all of the most serviceable art teacher of that period whose real name was Sass and who counted among his pupils John Everett Millais. What has taken place since then is that in the smiles of popular favour, Thackeray's Gandish has blossomed into the Mr Gaston Phœbus of Lord Beaconsfield's *Lothair*. Colonel Newcome thought it a condescension to ask the painter of 'Boadishia' to dinner. That artist's later and transformed self would have resented an invitation at short notice as an impertinence; he would have bluntly excused himself on the plea of being pre-engaged to the Prime Minister,[82] the Heir Apparent, or to Windsor three months ago. The social prejudice, confined to a small section of the upper middle class, against the studio which lingered so long and so unintelligently in England is easily explained. It is identical in its origin with an equally unreasoning and antiquated feeling against doctors, singers and players. This superstition had disappeared in the days of Sir Henry Holland who, half a century ago was a welcome and honoured guest at the most exclusive houses; under men like Sir James Paget and Sir Richard Quain it has long since ceased even to be a memory. In each of these cases money is regarded as passing directly between the patronizing public and the employed professional. The purse is opened at the door of the theatre, the concert hall, or in the consulting room of the physician. That the payment is in the other cases as real though not as sensibly direct is ignored. The terms on which Sir Charles Eastlake was a visitor at the Victorian Court are those that have marked the subsequent relations of his successors with the Crown. The intellectual influences of a whole school of intelligent and highly educated critics following as nearly as they could the example of Mr Ruskin, has shed a dignity on the painter's calling that could not have resulted from material prosperity or the favour of high place alone.

Sir Edwin Landseer, elected R.A. 1830, it may be said, years before the transformation now spoken of, was welcome in any house whose threshold he pleased to cross. His was rather the exception which proved the rule, and for these reasons; he flourished most just when Court patronage was making the Scotch Highlands fashionable; he was the painter of hounds, horses, animals themselves so eminently aristocratic that no Englishman with any pretensions to social breeding could affect disregard for them, or for their reproducer in art without losing caste. Hence it is that while fifty years since, the Clive Newcomes who took to painting were spoken of by their families in a low voice much as if they had taken to drink, the painter of repute to-day who chose to receive pupils[83] would have no more difficulty in filling his studio twice over, than a fashionable crammer for the army or Civil Service in filling his lecture room. As a fact it is not in the private studios of great artists that the Royal Academician of the future, unlike the intending exhibitor in the Parisian salon, is to-day generally trained. Sass had a rival, or a professional descendant, in the father of a clever versifier H. S. Leigh. Since that day, English artists have generally learnt their craft in the Royal Academy, or the Slade or other schools of England, or in foreign ateliers. These have transformed the surface of Victorian England. The same organization of art teaching, which is to-day at the disposal of all is said to have discouraged the development of individuality. Where genius exists, it is not very likely to be strangled by the conventions of a public school, nor to be prevented from exchanging State teachers for those whom native inspiration prompts it to prefer.

The South Kensington[84] machinery is not the only artistic growth of the Victorian age. The National Gallery had been in existence more than ten years before the reign began (since 1824). It was not a popular institution until a year later, the architect Wilkins having made the design, the present building in Trafalgar Square was opened, April 9, 1838. The nucleus of the collection was the Angerstein pictures, thirty-eight in number, bought by the Government for £57,000. Twenty-seven years had still to pass before the Trafalgar Square structure was enlarged to its existing size by a parliamentary vote of £50,000. The immediate era of the Queen's accession was marked by the purchase of a masterpiece of Murillo, a landscape by Salvator Rosa, and an important picture by Rubens. Still the Gallery lingered below the Imperial dignity of the nation to which it belonged. The Vernon bequest enriched it only when the Queen had been on the Throne ten years.

It was not till after the Crimean War that Parliament could attend to artistic claims, and that under the Directorship of Sir Charles Eastlake, deservedly trusted by Crown and country, the rooms designed by Barry were added to the block which Wilkins had shaped.

The institution, now endowed with the paintings that had belonged to Sir Robert Peel, began steadily to approach towards the dimensions and the dignity of an Art Gallery comparable with that of any other capital in the world. Nor probably have its perfections or its premises yet reached their final limit.

While this was going on in London, the entire provinces were vigorously taking their part in the new movement. The death of the Duchess of Gloucester in 1857 was not allowed by the Queen's representative to interfere with his opening in that year the Manchester Art Treasures Exhibition, the completeness of which was largely due to the Royal encouragement to private owners to send their statues and paintings to the show. Thirty years later the Jubilee anniversary of 1887 was observed in the same city by a like display of the creations of British genius. Then the objects exhibited were the property no longer of the leisured, or a patrician class. They belonged also to the new patrons whom, during less than half a century, success in manufacture and commerce, accompanied by the liberal agencies of travel and education have stimulated to competition with the social order whose exclusive appanage art encouragement once was. The material proof of art progress is the increase of art values. Many instances of these were given in an earlier chapter. During his lifetime David Cox was glad to sell his landscapes for £20. Cox had formed his genius amid the rural scenes of Hereford. He never liked London. After living there fourteen years he settled at Birmingham. Here, during his lifetime he had the satisfaction of seeing his masterpiece in oil colour bought for £40. Ten years later, when the painter was dead, it secured £50 in the open market. In the early seventies a Birmingham manufacturer, the former partner of Mr Chamberlain gave for it £2,300. In the same way De Wint's landscapes during his lifetime seldom commanded more than £50. To-day they sometimes fetch £1,000, and are reckoned cheap at 700 or 800 guineas.

The social consideration, and with it the commercial possibilities, of any professional calling have in England always been regulated by its degree of connection with the State. The department of practical art established at South Kensington with the encouragement of the Prince Consort under the Directorship of Mr Henry Cole in 1852 had no sooner expanded into the science and art department under the President of the Council instead of under the Board of Trade than the social repute of practitioners in all branches of decorative art appreciably improved.

About this time, too, Marlborough House, up to that date an asylum for exhibited pictures and a receptacle for the Duke of Wellington's funeral car, suggested itself as a future residence for the Prince of Wales when he came to have an establishment of his own. In 1856-7, therefore, the House of Commons, without demur, allotted £10,000 for the removal of the chaos of artistic treasures from their temporary resting place in Pall Mall to their permanent home in South Kensington. Hither, therefore, were sent the national purchases made at the sale of the Bernal collection, a full account of which has been given in an earlier chapter.

Directly art was in this way officially and substantially incorporated by the State, the golden stream of private munificence with no check and in great volume flowed towards Brompton. Most readers of these lines will remember the consignment to this wealthy spot of the Dickens manuscripts and relics as well as the library and paintings bequeathed to it by the friend and biographer of Dickens, the late John Forster, in 1876. These had some years earlier been preceded by the pictures, bric-à-brac, and foreign furniture collected by various private connoisseurs, now stowed away in the glass-covered cabinets which line the galleries and which, studied daily by English artizans, have probably done more than the '51 Exhibition ever effected, towards improving the designs of English manufacture.

South Kensington, it should be remembered, is richer even than it appears. Its activities are ubiquitous. It is a bank of art treasures on which institutions affiliated to it throughout the Kingdom can draw at discretion. To-day this department of State, decorative as to its purpose, but distinctly remunerative as to its results, is supported by an annual endowment of nearly half a million. That outlay not only gives profitable holidays to countless pleasure seekers from every quarter of the Kingdom; it enables a yearly average of 30,000 pupils of both sexes to pass through its art and science classes.

This apparatus for developing and training the future artists of England has been accompanied with an increasingly lavish expenditure by the State when a chance has occurred of permanently adding to its artistic wealth. Thus, during the early eighties the Treasury paid for a single painting from the Blenheim collection, the Ansidei Madonna of Raphael, exactly the same sum that, thirty years earlier, had been voted for the entire collection of Sir Robert Peel.[85]

The transformation effected during the Victorian age in the position of English art is illustrated by the statistics of visitors to the Royal Academy exhibitions not less significantly than by the increase of prices itself. Only within the last few years has what is called the 'private' view of the Royal Academy become a fête day of fashionable society;—a promenade for the display of the latest devices in Parisian or Bond Street toilettes. Long after the great Exhibition or even the Prince Consort's death, it was that the view of the critics, from being confined strictly to the judges of the press, began to be transformed into an immense meeting of authors, scholars, divines, novelists of both sexes, art fanciers of every degree; all of them able to produce some credentials of critical aptitude or profession, and of some slight connection with periodical letters. The figures themselves shall tell their tale. To the earliest exhibition at the Academy rooms, then in Trafalgar Square, of the Queen's reign, the admissions were less than 79,000. Ten years later they just fell short of 91,000. Between 1846 and 1866 the increase was 94,000. The additions steadily continued till in 1879 the high water mark of 391,197 was reached. Since that date they have fluctuated: depending, as one might naturally expect, upon the state of trade in the country, upon the weather in town, or upon the general character of the London season. Thus, in 1896, which was not a very brilliant season, the admissions were 10 less than in the preceding year, or in the Queen's jubilee year of 1887.

The mutual relations of art and wealth are probably for the most part beneficial to each. The painter, during the latter half of the whole Victorian age, has been the chief educator of the plutocrat, as Dante Gabriel Rossetti shrewdly anticipated must prove the case. If the intellectual teaching of the brush were not easily apprehended, there would, for the representatives of the new wealth, have been no special training in the humanities at all. As it is, the aristocracy of wealth, following the creditable example of the aristocracy of birth, in England as well as Italy, has secured for itself mental culture not less than social distinction by its patronage of the creators of the nation's art. To that rôle it brings the shrewdness already displayed in making its fortune. Such a patron may be a generous paymaster; he insists on having value for his money; he is quick to detect scamped work, or shortcomings in technical detail; he no longer, as he was once fabled to do, buys his canvases at so much per square foot any more than he fills his library shelves by the yard. That no meritorious artist in Victorian England is now likely to live and die so miserably as Haydon is due to the fact that the newest wealth finds its natural outlet in the encouragement of the oldest art. No aggregate of spiritual or intellectual interests has ever been firmly established in England without being subject to some great organic movement as a test of vitality before its roots struck deep in the soil of British minds. Literature experienced many such phases. So did science. So also, in the Oxford Anglican movement and in others since then, did religion. Before, therefore, the new art was firmly enthroned in our midst, it was at once shaken and quickened by that nineteenth century revolution known as pre-Raphaelite; about this so much has been written by recent experts as to absolve one from the duty of dwelling on it in detail here. Art in the hands of Rossetti, Burne-Jones, Holman Hunt, and other men of genius entered upon this ordeal as a sectional and limited pursuit. It came forth a new national interest or rather one of European concern as well. Without that severe process of discipline, Leighton and Millais, to mention only two typical names, would not have taken their place as masters of the brush for a continental as well as for an insular public. Nor would the fame of the English school first known through the Paris Exhibition of 1855, extended by the Paris Exhibition of 1868, have secured for English artists representation in all the great galleries of the world, and have added to British painters or to their national themes the crown of foreign recognition and of cosmopolitan esteem. Later chroniclers of the Victorian age may be able to record the same progress in the sculptor's, as in the painter's art. Our climate is not favourable to the out of door triumphs of the plastic art. But those who have examined the statue of Outram in Pall Mall; who have gazed upon the effigy of the great Duke of Wellington by Alfred Stevens in St Paul's; or have noted the growing power as well as popularity of Hamo Thornycroft, still a young man, cannot doubt that, apart from the successful labours of a naturalized but most patriotic foreigner and his school, Sir Edgar Boehm, the English chisel is in a fair way of emulating the progress of the English brush.

Commercial prosperity in art, as in other things, moves in cycles. The years between 1870 and 1885 were very prosperous to English painters. The lean years followed then, and are still being experienced while these lines are written. As to the high prices given at Christie's and set forth elsewhere in this volume, they have been generally for the works of old and departed masters. With very few exceptions, the decade between 1886 and 1896 has witnessed none of those prices for contemporary artists which marked the preceding period. This, too, notwithstanding the standard of artistic work to-day is infinitely higher than it was; and that the paintings which were hung on the line and were the talk of the town thirty years ago, would have a very slight chance of being accepted at all to-day.[86]

CHAPTER XXVI
POPULAR CULTURE IN THE CRUCIBLE

Translation into fact of ideals not less than transformations seen in the People's Palace, Whitechapel, and in the free libraries, originated by the Ewart Act, affecting as they do all contemporary life. The working of these in town and country. Proved connection between popular education and morality; what books free libraries like best. Analogous work for upper classes done by Mudie's, and by the London Library. Their progress traced. Help rendered by these to public servants and literary producers. Carlyle, Thackeray, etc. Eclectic and educating influences of these shown in detail. The new public and the new magazines. General review of influences at work. Great services of minor poets and prophets of the period.

Not only transformations, but translations of ideals into fact, mark our age. A popular novelist gave a fancy sketch of a palace in which art, pleasure, and instruction should meet together to gladden the lives of the London poor. Almost as soon as could have been done by the genius of Aladdin's Lamp, the People's Palace shoots up in the Mile End Road.

In 1841 Thomas Carlyle sighed for the day when a 'people's library' should be as much a part of every town as Her Majesty's jail, or in his own grim words—Her Majesty's gallows. The reign was still young when the philosopher's vision began to take shape and substance. In every centre of population from the Tyne to the Thames, from the Thames to the Tamar, a place where, without payment, upon no other conditions save those of reasonably clean hands, and silence, the working man is as well off for newspapers and books as a Bishop at the Athenæum Club, has changed the Victorian landscape. These buildings, comely to look at, comfortable to enter, have competed with the later board schools in transforming the appearance of London suburb and provincial town. Where Knightsbridge merges into Chelsea first, and Fulham afterwards, there, during the early days of the reign, desolate fields and miry ways used to stretch their unlovely length. After dusk there were few lamps to light; the roads were not more safe than Hounslow Heath had been some generations earlier. To-day this district is covered by a mass of buildings in red brick or stone, of aspect rather more academic than the new quarter of Victorian Oxford. Among these are the free libraries, built, partly out of the public rates, partly out of private funds. If it chance to be Saturday night, hundreds of working men, decently clad, with parcels under their arms will be seen passing to and fro near these buildings. They are not going to the public house. The packages they carry do not imply a negotiation with the pawnbroker. The men are, in fact, returning to the library the books which, taken out some days earlier, have given them their reading during the week after the day's work has been done. Certain processes supplementary to these studies have still to be performed. Even in our age of improvement, the reference library kept by an artizan at his fireside is not extensive. Nothing quickens the intellectual appetite like its earliest gratification. As our student has travelled through the volumes which have occupied him, he has become aware of allusions for the full understanding of which fresh information is required. He has, therefore, while going along, made notes of points to look up. This, therefore, is one of his errands to-night.

No professional visitor to the British Museum sets more systematically to work than our day labourer in the Fulham or Pimlico district. Before his visit this evening to the place of silence and of books he has, perhaps, had recourse to a member of the University Settlement in his neighbourhood, or possibly even to his own employer if the employer happens to be better read than the employed. The local librarian presently to be consulted needs to combine patience and method with something like omniscience. The note book is produced by our working man in which the points for enquiry have been jotted down. In a few minutes the official has placed the researcher on the right track. Before his studies are ended that night he will have hunted up facts and figures enough to furnish forth a leading article for a journalist, or a speech in Committee for a Member of Parliament.

Not only in the industrial suburbs of the capital, but throughout the Kingdom, this is the sort of thing which takes place at least on one evening in every week. It is one among the many agencies which, nowadays, make the humblest reader so terrible a critic, and which cause a working man's meeting to be not less intolerant of mere rhetoric than the House of Commons itself.

Like everything else which during our age has been brought towards perfection, the free library movement existed among us in germ from the earliest days, before indeed the books themselves were known. When

Lancashire monasteries had ceased to be gratuitous places of literary study, their manuscripts and parchments were housed in the Chetham Library, with its old oriel windows at Manchester; in the Guildhall Library at London, certainly coeval with Whittington; in the libraries of Bristol or Liverpool which compete with London in antiquity, and with which the Protector Somerset is said to have made somewhat too free.

The patronymic of the man who was the father of the free library as it is known in England to-day is preserved in the second name of Mr Gladstone. Mr Ewart belonged to an old Kirkcudbright family. He had been at Eton with Dr Pusey and Speaker Denison. In the spring of 1843 he obtained a Committee of the House of Commons to enquire into the conditions of popular reading throughout the United Kingdom. Disraeli, Monckton Milnes, Cardwell, Kershaw, were among the more famous names that the Committee included. Less than ten years after this, the Ewart Act, based on the Committee report was the law of the land.

In the early autumn of 1852, the new legislation was celebrated in a very practical manner by the opening of the free library at Manchester; the town which had been the birthplace of the movement.

Sir John Potter, the father of the present Mr T. B. Potter, took the chair. On the platform among the speakers were John Bright, Bulwer Lytton, Sir James Stephen, the future Lord Houghton, Dickens and Thackeray; Charles Dickens made a speech in his happiest, and therefore incomparable, vein, on the Manchester School, an expression then in many mouths. The success of the experiment first illustrated on the Irwell was gradual. The provinces led the way which at last the capital followed. So late as 1886, only two parishes out of the sixty-seven within the metropolitan area had adopted the Acts. By August 1891 this number had risen to thirty. Other London districts have since followed.[87] With time the result has been more than satisfactory. In the manner already seen it has affected the life and appearance of every town in the country, and has certainly provided a machinery without which as a supplement the educational apparatus of free schools would do little.

To-day, therefore, in any large district, London or provincial, it is the exception for the Free Libraries Act not to be operative. That the power to read and the taste for reading does not always make good citizens, is of course true enough. On the other hand the close connection between ignorance and crime is instructively shown by a few historic statistics cited by Mr T. Greenwood, in his valuable volume on *Public Libraries*. These figures are to the following effect.

In 1856 the number of young persons committed for indictable offences was 14,000. In 1866, when the State had, by the action of the Privy Council, since 1833 assumed educational responsibility, and cheap literature of the better sort had, thanks to Charles Knight, and his many public-spirited imitators, become general, the number was decreased to 10,000. When School Boards were fully at work, there was a yet further reduction to 7,000; and this though the population had risen from 19 to 27 millions. Passing to a later date, out of 164,000 persons in prison between the years 1880-90, 60,000 were entirely uneducated. Nor is it less suggestive that since the teaching of the people was seriously taken in hand by the State in 1870, no new prison has been built; while several buildings which were prisons have been changed into public libraries, or, as in the case of Milbank, have been converted into a fine art gallery.

An objection is sometimes raised against the multiplication of free libraries on the ground that they promote exclusively the perusal of the most worthless fiction among the class least likely to be proof against the social dangers of this class of writing. No novel, perhaps, is so entirely mischievous as not to be preferable to the occupations from which for a few hours, it may withdraw the illiterate reader. In truth however a very careful examination of the facts by enquiries made at representative free libraries throughout the country justify the statement that novels form a stepping stone to books of a more seriously improving kind.

The same statistics show the demand for fiction already to be on the decrease. Thus, in the case of the Newcastle-on-Tyne library; during a recent twelvemonth, of the books issued to readers 65·69 were fiction. The next year the proportion was 64·28. A year later it was 61·81. In 1896 the figures were 55·22. The latest enquiries show this decline in the demand for fiction to be steadily going forward. Further, the category of fiction is stretched by free libraries to include not only the coloured paper boards containing the latest sensational romance of the day, but all the masterpieces of Fielding, nearly all the writings of Defoe, the *Arcadia* of Sir Philip Sidney, the *Tristram Shandy* of Lawrence Sterne, the *Don Quixote* of Cervantes, and the Dialogues of Lucian.

The remarkably elastic connotation with which the word fiction is thus invested, may make one doubt whether a case might not be established even for novel reading. As a fact the works most in demand at any typical London library, *e.g.*, that of Chelsea, are not novels at all. Here the favourites seem to be Herbert Spencer's *First Principles,* thrice asked for on the day this library was visited, his *Ecclesiastical Institutions,* twice asked for. Aristotle's *Ethics,* the works of Spinoza, Martineau's *Types of Ethical Theory,* Adam Smith's *Wealth of Nations,* J. S. Mill's *Logic,* Professor Sayce's *Vindications of Revealed Religion by the Light of Ancient Monuments,* all Sir Charles Dilke's works of travel, Carlyle, Froude; *Cassell's Popular Educator,* Todhunter's *Euclid* are in greater demand than any fictions. However many copies of these there might be, none, it is thought, would be often out of hand.

It is not only what are called the industrial classes whose literary resources have been expanded and transformed during the Victorian age. Libraries for a different class of readers have of late years increased throughout the Kingdom, in the provinces not less than in the capital. Mudie's is, in the most literal sense of the epithet, a national agency. Its headquarters are in London. There is no town or village book club in the country, which is not fed from its metropolitan shelves. Mudie's Library was founded by the late C. E. Mudie, in 1842, two years after the St James's Square London Library. If light literature were alone in demand, this library would not flourish as during more than half a century it has done. Without it, many of the candidates for the Indian, the Home Civil Services and other such examinations would be unable to get up their books. A theologian like Canon Liddon turns new light on old truths. A pious and picturesque impressionist like Dean Arthur Stanley presents the scenes and incidents of sacred story as he has himself seen or imagined them. A Darwin propounds a fresh theory for the origin of life; a Froude rehabilitates a Tudor; a Freeman refutes a Froude; a Livingstone explores a Dark Continent; a Stanley recovers a reluctant Livingstone or an indignant Emin. A Green illustrates the growth of an English people; a Lecky supplements the work of a Buckle or makes the eighteenth century real as the nineteenth.

Mudie's is the channel through which these streams of culture are conveyed to the majority of English readers; for, highly educated as the Victorian age may be, it is with books that its economies begin To buy volumes that can be borrowed or hired, is accounted wanton extravagance. A work which requires more study, which holds public attention longer than a novel, must obviously be most profitable to the circulating librarian. Nor would self-interest let him be a distributor of fiction alone or even primarily.

The increase of novel readers as of novel writers is indeed the great literary feature of the day. Not less characteristic of the time are the new periodicals which have created a fresh public for themselves. The sixpenny magazines count their circulation by millions, and are borrowed from the library as well as bought by their readers. But it is the standard works, as shown by the instances already specified that give to Mudie's its deserved epithet of 'Select.'

Rather more grave in its contents, and didactic in its origin and purpose, the London Library, in St James's Square has during more than half a century been a most productive agent in the culture not less of the whole upper middle classes than in the equipment for their tasks of writing men and women.[88] On the Mid-summer Day of 1840, with Lord Eliot in the chair there was held at the Freemasons' Tavern a meeting, the object of which was to provide literary workers and others at their homes with those books for which they then had to go to the reading room of the British Museum. The result was the formation of a Committee of the leading literary persons of the period, the drawing up of rules and of a list of desiderated books, the acquisition of premises in Pall Mall. Towards the end of December in the same year, the new institution was opened in its first home in Pall Mall with, on a smaller scale, the same kind of accommodations that it possesses to-day in St James's Square. As the earliest prospectus reminded the public, no less a person than Edward Gibbon had first lamented the lack of any lending library befitting the dignity of an Imperial capital in London.

When, in the May of 1841, this library was first in working order, its stock was some 3,000 volumes. A year later these figures had risen to 13,000. Since then, at an outlay of some £50,000, its contents have been increased to nearly 200,000. Situated in the heart of clubland, the Library has done for the education of clubmen, including penmen of every degree, all that Mudie's can have done for the instruction of families. Not that the London Library is without claim to be considered a domestic institution. Its reading room is frequented by as many lady journalists of the new school verifying references for their articles, as by male writers of an older type. There are few households where its books are not to be found. Carlyle and Thackeray are only two of the many well-known men who have been helped by it in suffusing historic descriptions with local or personal colour. It was to ascertain the exact hues of George Washington's waistcoat[89] that Thackeray consulted the late librarian Robert Harrison as to the classical authorities.

Nor are there many writers of recent years in the English tongue, who have not been indebted to London Librarians from the days of Cochrane, the first of the line, to those of Hagberg Wright, his latest successor,[90] for seasonable hints as to what authorities most usefully to consult.

As has been already seen, in the theory and practice of the culture now popularized in England, there is a growing tendency on the part of science and art to trench upon the ground formerly occupied by literature. The fashionable vocabulary of culture is itself an instance of this. Metaphors from the palette, the scalpel, the crucible, the retort, are applied to indicate the commonest and oldest literary phenomena. Or we hear of loaded epithets, of dynamic diction, of sonatas in sentences, of fugues in periods, and of new stratifications in style. Amid all our improvements we are a little mixed, and have still to decide where the province of the writer ends and that of his brother in some other art begins. This is a transient, as it is a transitional phase. It may perhaps confuse posterity which will scarcely recognize as the same language the lectures of Sir Joshua Reynolds, the orations of Lord Leighton, the art criticisms of Steele or Addison in *The Spectator*, of Walter

H. Pater, of J. A. Symonds, in *The Cornhill Magazine*, or one of the monthly Reviews.

The survey of the agencies now at work upon different social levels, shows that even thus the education which comes of reading, competes at some disadvantage with the instruction that is the result of lectures in class rooms, of demonstrations in scientific 'theatres,' of days and nights spent in museums of sculpture or in galleries of paintings.

During the second or third decades of the present reign, the literary system of the country, as shown in the introductory chapter to this work, was dominated by the presence of a few illustrious men, who naturally became models for imitation to a host of workers. During their lives, Dickens and Thackeray both founded schools. The former was, through the weekly magazines he edited, the founder of newspaper descriptive writing, especially of the picturesque Parliamentary narrative recently brought to so high a point of perfection by clever writers now alive. The entire company of satirical essayists in the weekly press, was first inspired by Thackeray. Each master was surrounded by personal admirers and literary imitators in a degree unapproached by any of his contemporaries or successors. The author of *The Newcomes* was outlived[91] by the accomplished writer of that series which began with *Pelham* in 1828 and neared its end with *The Parisians* almost fifty years later.

While the anniversaries of the Queen's accession were few in number, Lytton by the side of Dickens, as a popular master of the pen, filled something like the place which Thackeray had occupied before him. During most of his time, another man of letters belonging like Lytton to the titled classes divided with Lytton the social patronage of literary beginners. No man of his day did so much as Lytton to help younger men with the booksellers, as in his old-fashioned phrase he was apt to call the publishers. He had indeed a rival or a colleague in these good offices in Lord Stanhope, then Lord Mahon, the historian, as also in Mr Monckton Milnes, afterwards Lord Houghton, the timely friend of Coventry Patmore, and the rescuer from great troubles of a forgotten but deserving poet David Gray.

When as yet journalism as a profession was not fully organized, and young authors still looked first to the pillars of Paternoster Row, an introduction to Lord Lytton or to Lord Stanhope was the surest stepping stone to print. In this way Antonio Gallenga, then an obscure refugee, with associations of the dagger and bowl about him, having won the good word of Lytton, found a publisher for his *History of Piedmont*. This in its turn opened to him the office of the *Times*. Here he made his name not only as among the most brilliant, best informed and versatile of newspaper writers but, together with William Howard Russell, as a founder of that school of graphic newspaper narrative since represented by Archibald Forbes,

Edward Dicey, B. H. Becker, G. A. Henty, George Augustus Sala, and John O'Shea.

The development of the press has changed most of the conditions of literary life. For very many Englishmen of all classes, the periodical, daily, weekly, or monthly, is practically an exclusive synonym for literature itself. This fact of course has reacted upon the whole class of professional writers. The most commercially successful of men and women of letters are, as, since the days of Sir Walter Scott, they have been, authors of some novel which hits the taste of the moment, and fixes the interest of the town. When George Eliot wedded in her writings the artistic to the scientific spirit, she invented a combination unknown till then; she opened a gold mine for herself and the more dexterous of her disciples. Dickens and Thackeray both realized high prices for the labour of their pen. Wilkie Collins and Charles Reade were not far behind. But the men of this class were either original creators of literary types that will take their place with the characters of Shakespeare, and Cervantes, or else were masters in the manufacture of exciting and dramatic plots.

Lord Lytton knew a little of everything, science included. He was indeed not only a marvel of varied productiveness but a consummate student, summing up in his own person all the intellectual interests and tendencies of his time. During his most industrious period, before he had attained Cabinet rank in politics, and before Carlyle's deeper studies of Fichte and Goethe had familiarized the English public with modes of German thought, Bulwer did more than anyone of his day to educate the average reader on lines, and in subjects, which now seem commonplace, but of which, when the dandy who dashed off *Falkland,* as Byron dashed off *Beppo,* had matured into the student who travailed with *Rienzi,* Englishmen knew nothing.

The mental inquisitiveness and activity of a newly enlightened generation, resolved, like Bacon, to take all learning for its province, finds the reflection of some aspect of itself in every page of Bulwer. The polished conceits, the recondite illustrations drawn from every sphere of human thought or achievement, the similes sometimes as far fetched, and obscurely ingenious as those of Sir Piercie Shafton or of Euphues himself, suggest at times the inspiration of an universally-informed, and precociously-gifted youth who displays his cleverness before it is yet quite disciplined, and parades his patchwork learning before it is fully digested.

In all these things Bulwer was essentially the product and the mirror of the new and eclectically educated Victorian age. He had been a young man of great fashion, a good specimen of that social school of which the younger Disraeli at his *Vivian Grey* period was a bad specimen. A dandy of the older type through life Lytton remained. Tennyson's lines in *Punch* on the padded man who wore the stays, stuck to him throughout life as did

Thackeray's caricatures of Sir Edward Bulwig. People therefore insisted on finding affectations in his manner, and insincerities in his nature.[92] He saw his time in its entirety abroad as well as at home more clearly than most of his contemporaries. The reforming zeal and humanitarian spirit of his age were not expressed more powerfully, if to many persons more intelligibly, by Dickens himself than by Lytton.

All the modern masters of English fiction are in their different ways as much the products of that series of movements comprehended in, or grouped round, the French Revolution of the eighteenth century as Byron himself was in England the immediate progeny of that organic upheaval of thought and faith. The year of the accession produced Carlyle's *History of the French Revolution*. Four years later, the most powerful picture of these episodes presented by any writer of fiction was given to the world by Bulwer in *Zanoni*. To the same era of revolutionary influences belonged *A Tale of Two Cities*, in which Dickens not only illustrated after his own manner the age of Robespierre, but produced a work not inferior in literary art to the *Esmond* of his great rival. Lytton's genius impelled him to mysticism, as George Eliot's associations inclined her to positivism. Both after their own manner dealt with human problems from what they respectively thought the scientific point of view. Add to this that Lytton remained a student annexing new domains of interest, thought and knowledge to the last; that he showed himself the prophet of the new and better France in *The Parisians*, as he had been the bard of the new England beyond the seas before the curtain fell on the fortunes and the friends of Pisistratus Caxton.

Enough is said to vindicate his place as among the most representative writers of the age, as well as to explain the recent renascence of his writings in France and the growing popularity of his works as attested by the fresh editions issuing from the house of Routledge in England. Macaulay, though never a newspaper man, is in point of manner, the father of the leading article. The terse impressionist style which has much superseded the Macaulayan in the press may be referred to George Borrow, author of *The Bible in Spain*, than whom no one has influenced periodical writers more beneficially; to Kinglake in his *Eothen*; to his literary disciple, Lawrence Oliphant in *Piccadilly*; to the late Grenville Murray, whose 'Roving Englishman' in *All the Year Round* contains the happiest of travel sketches, and whose Young Brown in the *Cornhill Magazine* is a miracle of clever writing. Each of these has contributed to make such happy writers of concise prose as Jehu, Junior, in *Vanity Fair*, and Violet Fane, now Lady Currie, in her clever and original novel, *Sophy*. Carlyle, Ruskin, Tennyson, Robert Browning, Matthew Arnold complete a representative list of educators of popular taste during our age. They are, however, heroic instances. Others, with not a tenth of their fame have reached at least as far in their influence, and have brought their refining mission home to the masses with an intimacy not approached by their mightier rivals.

Emerson's writings, his visit to, and lectures in, London in 1847 leavened English thought with the same spiritualizing quality which had long since penetrated the American mind. For one Briton who was inspired by Emerson, hundreds were charmed and humanized by Longfellow first, and by Whittier afterwards. If Longfellow's simple ballads had never been written, the higher offices of poetry, notwithstanding a Tennyson or a Browning, would have remained a mystery hidden from the toiling millions of the Anglo-Saxon world.

The same gentle and gracious offices have been performed by less known and not always respected writers, Martin Tupper of the *Proverbial Philosophy*, and the late Hain Friswell of *The Gentle Life*.

CHAPTER XXVII
NEWSPAPER PRESS TRANSFORMATION SCENES

The newspaper press of all kinds, largely, the penny press, exclusively, a Victorian product. Its recent growth reviewed. A valuable rival to Parliament because its publicity assures parliamentary efficiency. Growth of the cheaper journalism summarized. The *Daily News,* the *Daily Telegraph,* the halfpenny press, morning and evening as a special product of the age. The press and party.

'Barnes is the most powerful man in the country.' Such, in reference to the then editor of the *Times,* was the remark made a year or two after the Victorian age had begun by Lord Lyndhurst, himself an ex-journalist,[93] to Charles Greville, the Diarist. Like opinions by equal authorities as to the successors of Barnes have been delivered frequently since, but are less known because the memoir-writer has not yet stamped them with immortality. No attribute of skill or power belonging to Barnes was wanting to Delane. To his weight with the public a characteristic tribute was once paid by a shrewd judge of editors as of men generally, Lord Beaconsfield. 'I think,' were that statesman's exact words, on a social occasion to Lord Granville, 'I had better postpone giving you my views of Delane till he is dead.'

On her accession the Queen was congratulated by some 479 newspapers representing the collective press of the United Kingdom and its outlying islands. Her sixtieth commemoration gives a theme to 2396 journals published within the same area.[94] The English newspaper press which in effect began under one Queen, reached its final term of greatness under another Queen. 1837 is a landmark in newspaper history, because it was the first year in which the public press published the parliamentary division lists, and thus made another stride towards equality of influence with the legislature. Its effect was to increase the usefulness of Members of Parliament, as well as of the press itself. The Long Parliament made English freedom, but gagged the press.

In 1712 Harley had taxed newspapers at a penny a sheet, and one shilling for each advertisement. Under North and Pitt successively, these taxes were raised to prohibitive figures. In 1836 Spring Rice had fixed the stamp duty at a penny, so that the first step towards newspaper prosperity was made on the eve of the Victorian age. The Victorian press means the penny press. That was only possible after the fourteenth year of the reign, and the repeal of the paper duty in 1851.

Popular politics are changed as little by newspaper articles as are political votes by parliamentary speeches. The press rather organizes political opinion. Existing convictions are deepened. But the average reader chooses his newspaper not because he wants to be converted, but because his self love is flattered by seeing his formed ideas reflected in its columns. The modern newspaper is therefore a Victorian creation. In its best form it belongs to England alone. In no other country is there a second *Times*, as since 1788 the older *Universal Register* has been called; no such epitome of foreign history from day to day; no such reflection, in letters to the editor, of English opinion.

So far as the cheap newspaper is due to any one man, it may be connected with the name of the first proprietor of the *Athenæum*, like its latest, a Charles Wentworth Dilke. In the twelfth year of the Victorian age the *Daily News*, to which the short editorship of Charles Dickens gave literary distinction rather than commercial success, its proprietors, Bright, Cobden, Walmsley, called in Mr Dilke, as the great newspaper organizer of his day. He at once reduced the price, though not yet to its final penny. In 1865 the proprietary was enlarged by the late Mr S. Morley, Mr Labouchere and others, with the intention of turning it into a penny paper. That was done. Its success was made by its foreign correspondence during the Franco-Prussian war of 1870-1. Meanwhile, the *Daily Telegraph*, started by Colonel Sleigh in 1856, had been acquired, enlarged, and improved by the strenuous ancestors of its present owners. It at once electrified the town by its original writing of all kinds, notably its Paris correspondence. The letters to the *Times* from the Crimea of William Howard Russell, first caused the Sebastopol enquiry;—then in 1855 produced the Roebuck motion[95] and with it the fall of the Government of Lord Aberdeen. In this way the whole conception of the province of the press was enlarged. Soon there sprung up a new and organized profession of the pen. If to-day the political writing of the great London dailies be below the mark of that of the two *Couriers* and some later publicists in France, its special and descriptive correspondence by a Forbes, a Henty, a W. W. Knollys, a Pearce, a Becker, a Conan Doyle, a G. W. Steevens, in point of graphic vigour, of accurate and comprehensive swiftness of execution, is superior to anything which other periodicals of Europe can show.

The Jubilee Year of 1887 witnessed the completion of a revolution in the public press, that had in fact begun a twelvemonth earlier. Hitherto the great London broadsheets had either been affected really if not professedly to one of the great political parties; or had, as in the case of the *Times*, not less than of the chief weekly journals, made some show of impartially criticizing both parties alike. In 1886 the Liberal party was rent in twain by the Irish policy of its greatest member. The result with the press was to divest political writers of all show of independence. Those journals which accepted the great leader's view were converted into uncompromising champions of the scheme that their opponents said would dismember the monarchy. Those, on the other hand, which resisted the great statesman's plan found themselves by the force of events they could not control detached from their earlier traditions of independence and converted into the enemies of political Liberalism not only on one issue, but on all.

From that day newspaper criticism of men and measures has practically ceased. With a few able exceptions, signally that of the *Daily Chronicle*, the paramount task of the press in the sixth decade of the epoch is to support a combination of groups rallied not under a party flag, but an Imperial banner. About the same time another newspaper change may be said to have taken place. Hitherto, the anonymous system had been fairly preserved. The names of newspaper writers were not known beyond their office, or at least beyond Fleet Street. Now, however, English journalism was undergoing two distinct and mutually antagonistic processes. On the one hand it had by the agency of the great newspapers with their enlarged staffs and various departments been organized into a liberal profession, attracting specialists of all kinds to its columns. On the other hand its pleasures and its profits had gathered a host of camp followers who as amateurs vied with the older professionals. Next, persons of fashion or of quality took to the proprietorship or editorship of new journals, as, till then, they had taken to the owning and management of theatres for the benefit of personal friends. In *Lothair*, someone advises the hero to amuse himself with theatre proprietorship 'as being the high mode for all swells.' The paper next enjoyed the same vogue as the playhouse.

The former secrecy now became impracticable. As had long been the case with the monthly periodical, the weekly print first and the daily print afterwards showed a tendency towards a transformation from an organ of collective opinion into a platform for individual display. The new editor's chief business was not as formerly to point the gun for the marksmen of the pen to fire, but to recruit writers with well known names. If their signatures were suppressed, the authorship, as it was intended it should do, speedily transpired. Fleet Street became a whispering gallery of press gossip. Its murmurs were heard throughout the land.

What the sixpenny magazine is to the monthly press that the halfpenny newspaper is to the daily. The first daily journal at this price, the *Echo*, after some startling vicissitudes came into the capable hands of John Passmore Edwards, a Celt of Cornwall with all the characteristics of his race. Morning as well as evening rivals at the same price sprung up like mushrooms after rain. *Evening News* or *Star* at night, the *Morning*, the *Leader* are only a few of the fresh notes added to the music of the London street vendors. No urchin so ragged that he does not proclaim the printed wares of a millionaire *in esse* or *in posse*. Believers in literature as part of popular education will think it a good sign that book reviews, and articles of a kindred sort are features in characteristically Victorian newspapers. Signally in the arrangements for supply of foreign news, a revolution extending throughout the whole press of the country has been effected by the enterprise of these journals. The telegrams on which for its tidings from abroad the public used exclusively to depend, have been often superseded by the dispatches of special representatives of their journal stationed abroad.

Every journal has now become its own Reuter. Men like Alfred C. Harmsworth, being millionaires as well as resourceful journalists, thought no more of having their own agents in every capital at the end of a telegraphic wire than of arranging a little Arctic expedition on their own account. They have thus forced the hand of newspaper proprietors all round. The leisurely descriptive writing has gone out. The condensed three-line paragraph has come in. The *Daily Mail* has shown a busy generation which reads its papers as it takes its lunch standing at a buffet, that the essence of the day's news of the world can be read in a few odd minutes as easily as the *Iliad* and the *Odyssey* were once packed into a nutshell.[96]

For this new journalism new men have been needed. In most cases very young men; generally fresh from Balliol or Trinity where they have perhaps won Fellowships as well as First Classes, but in appearance often not much older than a public school sixth form boy. Youth is an error which unfortunately time too soon corrects.

In ability, in conscientious use of increased power; in education, in social position, in all the best guarantees of responsibility, the British press has improved immeasurably within the present age. Even now it shows signs of perceiving that a certain amount of political impartiality towards the great leaders of State and Church renders its praise, its censure, and its criticism the more effective because the less mechanical. The condition of things which has made so many great newspapers patriotic partizans instead of independent guides must in its nature be temporary. When it has gone by, and a more normal state of affairs is re-established, there will be perhaps no compensating disadvantages to the increasing influence with which the Victorian age has endowed and is yet endowing what is really a fourth estate.[97]

CHAPTER XXVIII
TRANSFORMATIONS IN INVALID LIFE

Legislation for the helpless in health or in sickness the exclusive feature of the Victorian age. Early interest of the English Court through the Prince Consort in the housing of the poor. This coincided with, and helped forward, the organized public movements for popular sanitation. General summary of these, as shown by results. The new nurse contrasted with the old. Hospitals to-day twice blessed.

Specific progress of sanitary reform. Demonstrable connection between these improvements and figures of the death rate. Preventive and curative medicine also entitled to credit. General course of medical progress. Special researches of English physicians. Their ascertained usefulness and their latest aspects. Improvement in English doctors, with particular instances.

Before the Victorian age, there had been no legislation for the purpose of helping the helpless, housing the homeless, providing for the health of those whose birth-right was the squalor, the starvation, the disease, that come from systematic neglect. Here, as in other things, the representative of the Crown, transformed from a political power into an agency of social good, led the way. The Prince Consort, moved by the condition and by the address of the ballast heavers in the East End of London took the initiative; the legislature gradually followed. Thus was the principle established and acted on that one of the prime duties of the State is to those for whom from any other quarter there is no help.

The last instance of that wholesome truth was the Dilke Commission for the better housing of the poor aptly presided over by the Prince Consort's eldest son in 1885. Exactly forty-five years earlier than this, Colonel Slaney's[98] motion in the House of Commons produced an enquiry into the health of towns. Local Improvement Acts had been multiplied to the number of 500. There was still no proper drainage. The Duke of Buccleuch's Commission of 1848 led to the Public Health Act of the same year. As the cholera invasions of 1853 and of 1865-6 showed, the Local Boards established by the Act of 1848 were too permissive in their operations to be fully effective. Edwin Chadwick, and Southwood Smith had from the first co-operated with the Queen's husband. Their activity did not cease when the earliest steps to reform had been taken: 1858 witnessed fresh improvements. [99]

It was not till 1875 that the confused mass of sanitary laws was consolidated. Then the Local Government Board which, with the powers of the superseded Poor Law Board, had been established in 1871 was in full and in most beneficent work. Still the Commission that last investigated the matter, due as it was largely to Lord Shaftesbury, showed many evils still to remain. Overcrowding was worse in the West London rookeries than it had been in the East. In 1885 the Dilke Commission Act gave fresh power to local authorities to destroy unhealthy dwellings.

The machinery which thus exists as the sixth decade of our epoch draws to its close, is therefore tolerably complete. Guarantees for its promptly being put into motion are still wanted. Not only the credit, but the very conception of this wholesome function of the State belongs entirely to our era, and arises out of the enlarged idea of Royal service which fills the modern mind.

Strictly consistent with family tradition is the effort of the Prince of Wales to help those who are only one degree more helpless than the dwellers in city and suburban alleys and courts in time of need. To free the London hospitals of debt will crown the edifice of sick relief that in Crimean days the Queen and her husband began.

From the departure of Miss Florence Nightingale[100] and her trained staff for the Crimea in 1854 must be dated the birth of nursing as a polite profession. But for that mission of mercy one would hear nothing of the contemporary parade of nurses in the height of the London season in the grounds of Marlborough House. The fashionable vogue of the vocation may sometimes attract modish recruits who have not counted the cost.

Amiable sympathy is not the sole qualification which the lady nurse needs. Self-consciousness is as much a disqualification as a shuddering dislike of sick room scenes. It is also the attribute that the patient is the most quick to observe. Not a few of the sick whom the ministering angel of the new school desires to relieve may still sigh for the presence by their bedside of the displaced Mrs Gamp instead of the young lady in the coquettish muslin cap and dainty grey frock who casts complacent glances at herself as she passes the mirror, and with an air not quite suited for a sick room offers her patient his medicine or his barley water as if she were suggesting black coffee, green Chartreuse, and a cigarette after a whitebait dinner. These defects will no doubt be mended when the lady nurse is more habituated to her calling. Decayed billiard markers, and scripture readers who have gone wrong, will not eventually figure so largely among the self-sacrificing males who also find their career in tending the invalid. The scandals of which the nurse (old style) was sometimes the heroine still live in the pages of Dickens. They arose from the rumoured hastening of the sick man's death by the scriptural practice of laying a wet cloth over his mouth. Any scandals with which the nurse (new style) might be connected would perhaps come from the desirable marriage that she arranges for herself in the sick room or from the legacies made to her by grateful patients, but disputed by thankless relations. These things, therefore, should be no doubt regarded not as slurs upon her disinterestedness, but as tributes to her efficiency.

Inside the hospital the same transformation has been effected as in the aspect of the ministering angels themselves. The grave young gentlemen in training for the medical profession have nothing about them left of the lamp breaking, policemen baiting, medical student of Albert Smith. If sometimes one reads of the too engrossing attractions for these youths of the sylphs who flit to and fro in the wards, the answer is obvious—'Evil be to him who evil thinks.'

Hospital management is the subject not for a few pages in a single book, but for a library in itself. One or two not controversial facts may be given. Throughout the Victorian age a marked feature in medical charities has been the supplementing of the historic hospitals with many new dispensaries and establishments for special diseases. If the latest hospital endowments are smaller than those originating in an earlier century, the explanation is less a decline in eleemosynary purpose or power than the development of the value of the property assigned to the older foundations. [101] Thus the revenue of St Bartholomew's in the middle of the sixteenth century seems to have been only £371 a year. Towards the close of the nineteenth century it is £32,000 a year. During our own era hospital benefactions approaching a quarter of a million are far from unknown. These do not include such special and comparatively recent hospitals as that for consumption, with the 40 new dispensaries connected with it.

To epitomize the facts; the total of London hospitals or infirmaries with wards for the sick amounts to 49. The movement still goes forward. So vast is the scale on which these buildings, less houses than towns in themselves, were first planned that in many of them there is yet room for fresh beds. This is only a specimen of what has been, and is being, done throughout the kingdom. There thus seems a fresh argument in favour of continuing to London itself an institution like St Thomas's, Southwark, the removal of which to the country was not long since suggested.

Like all gracious works, these places are twice blessed. They relieve those who are in need. They humanize those whom prosperity and comfort might make callous. Before our age began, no one thought of sending game or fruit to the sufferers or convalescents within these places of refuge. Now it is the exception for the millionaire not to make the spoils of his fashionable battue pay tithe to those for whom such food is often the best of physic. The costly flowers that decorate the drawing rooms or dining rooms during the season are not discarded as rubbish when the festivity is over. They are scrupulously tended so as not to lose their freshness. Presently their hues and fragrance will relieve the bleak expanse of white-washed wall in those places where our sick are nursed away from their own homes.[102]

The contrasts of our age include a marked connection between the organization of the healing art and the advance of medical science on the one hand and the reduction of the death rate on the other. In 1855 the mortality of the United Kingdom was 23 per 1,000. In 1875 it was 21 per 1,000. In 1895 it had fallen to 18 per 1,000. The figures,[103] and the conclusions to which they point, are tributes, not only to medical skill in healing disease, but to sanitary reform in preventing it.

Before the Victorian age began the whole population of these Islands awaited the periodical onsets of pestilence with the resigned fatalism of the Turk, or with the passive submission of latter day London to the incubus of snow. The notorious consequences of unhealthy living prompted no preventive measures. Divine wrath was believed to express itself in deadly epidemics. When that anger was assuaged health would return. Till then human remedies could do little. Meanwhile, the truth that Providence helps those who help themselves was being scientifically shown. Hence in 1838, a State enquiry into the whole matter was instituted. In 1848 the legislation began which, by promoting cleanliness, at once disarmed disease. John Simon proved the propagation of pestilence to proceed by impure particles. In 1858-65, on his initiative, the Government strengthened the defences of public health. The entrance of foreign plagues was stopped at our ports. Three sons of a clever West of England doctor named Budd[104] had been trained from their childhood in practical medicine by their father. These doctors showed the connection between impure water and typhoid fever, as before them Snow had shown between cholera and water. When the improvements suggested by these researches were adopted health generally benefited. Consumption statistics became less alarming every year. Fevers of all kinds were successfully combated. Since vaccination had become general, smallpox cases had fallen by at least one-half.

Meanwhile, the discovery of anæsthetics, of chloroform by Professor J. Y. Simpson of Edinburgh in 1848, of ether in 1846 by Morton and Robinson of the United States, at once robbed surgical operations of their terrors, and rendered them practicable in cases where till then they could not safely be tried. In 1860 came the antiseptic treatment of Sir Joseph, since Lord, Lister. Before then, the nervous system had been explored successfully by Carpenter.[105] Instruments for examining by reflected lights the hidden parts of the human frame had been invented by several English surgeons. Operations for certain internal tumours, that had hitherto defied removal, were first performed by Cæsar Hawkins, born 1798, brother of the famous Oriel Provost, a pupil of Brodie at St George's; and more recently by Spencer Wells.

More than a half of the medical discoveries of the period are English. The latest perhaps, certainly not the smallest if the least known, was the treatment by the late Sir William Gull of the swellings technically known as myxœdema by an entirely new process, that of supplementing deficiences of the thyroid gland with matter taken from animals. The throat specialists of Germany found much to learn from the late Morell Mackenzie. Not till 1860, was the scheme of medical education perfected in its present shape by the College of Physicians, which to-day, under its President and two Censors, arranges all examinations; while the Medical Association represents the whole profession, bringing its grievances and needs before the legislature. The average of ability throughout the practitioners of the country is as noticeable as the achievements of its scientific pioneers. The treatise on *Heredity* in disease by Dr Douglas Lithgow, on gout and allied complaints by Dr Robson Roose, and on the medical uses of electricity by Dr W. S. Hedley, are instances of permanent contributions by busy practitioners to the scientific knowledge of their daily labours.

The late Dr Quinn, the late Oscar Clayton, are men who have improved the status of their calling by their social services and gifts, and have helped to extend the authority of the physician over every department of life. We have long since shaken off the rule of priests. Some may think we have already placed ourselves under a despotism of doctors, who by their word can make or mar the reputation of places and climates if not of characters and of men; and on whom the obligations of professional etiquette seem at least equal to their sense of responsibility to the public.[106]

CHAPTER XXIX
TRANSFORMATIONS OF RELIGIOUS THOUGHT

The vicissitudes of religious thought in the Victorian age illustrated by the quaint saying of an Oxford verger. Changes in the organization of the Church of England during the present reign. The revival of Convocation; the Ecclesiastical Commission. Facts and figures illustrating the results of these and the progress made at home and abroad. Activity and efficiency of other religious bodies, Protestant and Papist. Special influence of individuals in the Churches. In the Anglican, Dean Arthur Stanley, Professor Jowett, Professor Mansel. In the Nonconformist bodies, R. W. Dale, and C. H. Spurgeon. A friendly critic on the abuse of religious liberalism. How this re-acts, even on the new High Church critics, *e.g. Lux Mundi* and *The Sermon on the Mount*.

A verger at St Mary's Church, Oxford, during the sixties used devoutly to thank his Maker that after having heard University sermons for thirty years, he still remained a Christian. Conflicts within, attacks without, at least as severe as any to which either was exposed during the Georgian epoch, have been the lot of the Christianity whose depository is the Church of England during the Victorian age. Neither Christian faith, nor the Church that is its national expression, has come forth maimed or weakened from that ordeal. Modern scepticism scarcely aims at substituting for a Divine Being any tangible object of faith. It retires from the discussion with the remark that high and invisible things are beyond human knowledge. Hence nothing in agnosticism, however hostile its tendency to, need be inconsistent with, Revelation. The mere statement of difficulties in the way of belief and of purely abstract alternatives to belief makes no proselytes.[107]

Freethinkers of the last century appealed, and were limited, to the rich. The secularists who are their successors since 1840 pose as the friends of the poor. Neither school can consider itself a power. The Victorian age is in fact above all others an age of religious revival. This has been largely due to the influence of the Court. From the *entourage* of the later Georges and of William IV. the best of their subjects held aloof. Had the year of Revolution come then instead of in 1848, the English throne, whose possessor lacked all personal hold of the people, might have shared the fate of continental crowns.

The Queen saw nothing of any Court until she presided over a transformed Court of her own. Her subjects no sooner knew their fresh ruler than they were powerfully impressed by the contrast of her blameless life and society to anything of which they had read, heard, or seen. Under such a sovereign, a change in the whole spirit of the nation's religious life naturally followed. Thinking minds had indeed long been in a state of spiritual ferment. The Tractarian movement had begun with Keble's Assize Sermon five years before the Queen's accession. Its full results were not to be seen till 1846.

Meanwhile, in the third year of the reign the idea of reviving Convocation, which since 1717 had been suspended, of which Burke had said that it was without functions save to pay compliments to the king and then dissolve, took form; since 1850, that body has met. Unreformed this clerical parliament still remains. As in 1864 it declared *Essays and Reviews* heretical, but could not punish the men whom it branded, so, to-day, a canon of Convocation, though approved by the Crown, has no binding power. But the days when the *Times*, long since convinced of its Erastian errors, could sneer at Convocation as 'a clerical debating society with a long name' are altogether gone by.

Many who are by no means ardent Churchmen, or are outside the Church Communion, are interested to know the actual opinion of Convocation on social and industrial questions of the hour, as this opinion is expressed by educated men who reflect the views of their cloth at least as faithfully as the House of Commons reflects the views of the people. Thus, during the recent sittings of a single year, Convocation in its two provinces with their divisions into lower and upper Houses, has discussed and suggested solutions of subjects so varied as sisterhoods and deaconesses, betting and gambling, popular education, soldiers' marriages, marriage law amendment Bills, spiritual provision for workhouses, clergy discipline Bill, the relations between the Church and State in the Colonies. Even in its unreformed condition, this body can scarcely fail to be of some use in officially telling Parliament men the opinion of the Church, which, on any view of it, is at least a considerable corporation, on matters affecting clerical interests or popular morals. In the remote event of the Church being disestablished, Convocation is a useful drilling ground on which Churchmen of all degrees can be trained to collective action.

What are the facts relating to the Church to-day? At the opening of this age, the beneficed clergy were often unfit for their posts; they were very largely indifferent to their duties. The attacks on the Establishment led by the Lord Henley of that day and others, shortly after the 1832 Reform Act, were more organized and plausible than anything which has been witnessed since. There are, after all, not many things more national in England than the Church. Even the differences of the clergy, and the professed desire of some among them to be free from State supervision, have not lessened the national regard for the Established Faith. The attack from within, therefore, seems likely to be weathered not less successfully than the attack from without.

The parochial system of the Church—its clergy resident in every village where the squire is often an absentee, has struck its fibres too deep into the soil of English life, to be rooted out by any sectarian agitation. The best proof that Church endowments do not check, but rather encourage, private beneficence is the amount of money donations to the Established Church during the present age. Gifts to the Church, whether in the shape of lands, tithes, other rent charges, stock or cash, represent roughly a sum of £5,500,000, yielding a perpetual yearly income of £181,940.

The second of the two Acts establishing the Ecclesiastical Commission is of Victorian date. The operations of this body have increased the incomes of Church livings by £1,016,775 a year, or by a capital sum of £30,599,100; and this during the twelve years ending 1896-97. Queen Anne's bounty does not, indeed, seem to have been uniformly administered with such wisdom. Its funds have sometimes been granted to incumbents to enlarge houses, schools, and other buildings beyond the point at which there was an assured income for the maintenance of these fabrics. The Tithes Commutation Act is not blamed for the periodical return of hard times for the clergy. The distress itself is partial, sometimes exaggerated. Still, there seems to have been a general reduction of incomes in rural districts by 25 per cent. No offertories, which in towns greatly help the clergy, can make the country deficiency good. The suggestion of repealing the Act which put down pluralities so as to concentrate several poor preferments in one incumbent is not likely to be acted on. But some relaxation of the Act might be a feasible concession to a growing opinion. Rich livings are sometimes the worst served. Some re-adjustment of stipends after a new enquiry seems, therefore, likely to be proposed.

So much for the purely English aspect of clerical activity in our age. The alliance in the foreign enterprise of the Church with the State coincides exclusively with the Victorian reign. In 1841 the Colonial Bishopric fund was begun. By 1851 the Colonial episcopate was fairly organized. Four years after the Queen's accession there were 10 Anglican dioceses out of

England. Sixty years after that accession there are 92.[108] These sees are grouped into provincial Synods. This foreign Church, one in doctrine with the Established Church at home, is modified in its agency and development to suit the soil to which it is transplanted. The late Sir J. R. Seeley, with respect to its calming influences amid jarring faiths, has in a familiar passage dwelt on the Christianity of the English Church as a reconciling element between the rival creeds of the Eastern world. Add to this the organization of episcopal Protestantism of the Anglican type, not only in the West Indies and in our Canadian Dominion, but in the United States themselves.[109]

A fair idea may thus be formed of the State Church in its character of a veritable catholic, not less than a national, power. Improved organization does not always argue increased efficiency. The machinery of the Roman Empire was never more elaborate than when it was in a state of atrophy. Coinciding, however, with the unmistakable signs of spiritual life at home and abroad, the domestic resources and the foreign work of the national religion are tributes alike to the efficacy of the Church as a world-wide instrument of righteousness, and to the increased motive power of religion during the Victorian age. With the spiritual work that has been done, certain names very briefly must be associated. The Oxford Tractarianism between 1832-46 is only one of many manifestations of religious life which mark that epoch, and which nearly perplexed into infidelity the Oxford verger aforesaid. In extreme Evangelicalism outside our Church, the followers of Wesley, regardless of their founder's injunction not to form a separate sect, were perfecting their system when the reign began. In 1833, an English clergyman at Plymouth, J. L. Darby, left the National Church and founded the sect of 'Brethren' who take their name from the Western seaport where he had officiated. Fifteen years later, in 1848, Plymouth Brethrenism was itself divided by one of Darby's followers, named Newton; he created a clique of his own now called by their rival religionists, the loose, or open, Brethren. The missionary and literary activities of this little sect are really remarkable. In 1843 Presbyterianism across the Tweed had a schism of its own. The secession of Chalmers on the issue of State patronage resulted in the founding of the Free Kirk. The religious activity of the epoch has been universal. Among the older dissenting bodies, Congregationalists, in point of numbers, influence, in national repute of their leaders, perhaps come first. These in 1837, numbered 170,000 full members. Now they number nearly 400,000. Of the Baptists there were, in 1837, 125,000. Sixty years later they are 340,000. This increase is due to the single agency of C. H. Spurgeon, whose personal influence is not yet fully realized but may be judged from the circulation by millions of his posthumous Sermons, as well as by the pulpit imitations of him in all Communions, not excepting the high Anglican pulpits. Hence of course Nonconformist numbers depending largely on individual attractions, are subject to greater fluctuations than in the Establishment. Roman Catholics have increased in the large towns of England and in the Colonies. In 1837 their priests were less than 1,000. Fifty years later they were in round numbers 2,500. Their Churches have risen from 600 to 1,350. The activity of British Evangelicalism is farther shown by the doubling of the income of the British and Foreign Bible Society during the reign, by the cost of a New Testament being ten-pence in 1837, a penny in 1897. Similarly the income of the Propagation of the Gospel Society is very nearly twice, and of the Church Missionary Society almost thrice, as much to-day as it was in the Accession year.

Among Nonconformist bodies, numbers vary according to the eminence of individual leaders, rising by bounds with a Spurgeon, diminishing temporarily with some of his successors. Similarly, among Anglican Communicants numbers fluctuate according to the influence of the leaders of the great schools, a Liddon, or a Ryle, a Maurice, a Webb Peploe, or a Lefroy. R. W. Dale, of Birmingham, whose work on the Atonement is a recognised text book, even among many Anglicans, did as much as A. P. Stanley of Westminster, to soften down sectarian differences, and to command the respect of other Communions. Nor has Dale had any lack of worthy successors now living. Unless religion had been ineradicable in the national, because in the human, mind, results very different from this general increase in the number of all religious Communions, judged by whatever test, would have been witnessed.

Scarcely had the Church recovered from the shock of Newman's secession, and the agitating effects during two decades of High Church and Low Church controversies[110] when Dr Mansel, then an Oxford tutor and professor,[111] in his ardent, but not wholly discreet zeal, expressed views on the relations of the Infinite to the finite which, as F. D. Maurice perceived, declaring the Deity to be unknowable by man, might be perverted into an apology for agnosticism. That religion did not really suffer is due in some degree to Benjamin Jowett. This good and honest scholar's life was spent in educating young men into useful Christians, into serious citizens, and into sincere believers. He claimed liberty; he loved truth. He ridiculed with quiet satire the religious nescience and despair which Mansel's terrific propaganda had been distorted into making the vogue. When Dr Temple was made Primate:—the first and greatest tribute was paid to the variety of Oxford ecclesiasticism that would be rightly described not as the broad, or high, but as the hard Church. There could be no more striking instance of the transformation in religious ideas witnessed during our age than the fact that the volume to which Dr Temple and Mr Jowett both contributed, *Essays and Reviews*, was branded by Convocation as heretical during the sixties, and is discovered to be harmless during the nineties.

So qualified a judge on these matters as Mr Stopford Brooke deplores the declension of religious liberalism into something indistinguishable from unbelief. But as Professor Mansel's orthodox zeal for the dignity of his faith helped his enemies rather than his friends, so the services rendered by his devout successors are not always unmixedly conducive to the old faith. The 'higher criticism' has been a dubious ally of Biblical Christianity. *Lux Mundi* distinguished between the historic and mythic elements in the *Pentateuch*. The gifted editor of that work has more recently[112] applied the same method to the sayings of the Founder of Christianity, and has seemed to some to sanction the evaporation into proverbs of some Divine utterances.[113]

CHAPTER XXX
THE QUEEN'S SUBJECTS AT PLAY—ACTIVE OR SEDENTARY

The new Court as head of the old society. Social transformations which would most strike one revisiting the London West End in 1897. Going to Court. Multiplication of clubs in St James's and Pall Mall, but disappearance of gambling clubs. Socially transforming effects of the Parliamentary Committee in 1844. Then and now. 'Play and Pay' betting modified by its recommendations. Necessary connection between horse breeding and horse racing. Cricket—then and now. The new football or the old prize ring. Indoor amusements. Transformation, by development, of Victorian chess. The men and events which have made it what it is. Ladies' drawing room work. Middle class English ladies the great readers nowadays. Fashionable needlework of all kinds from 1837-97.

The transformed society of the Victorian age may be regarded as a new combination of old elements. The interests, and the pursuits represented in it have always existed. The grouping and the mutual relations are the only novelty. Even during the Prince Consort's time, the Court had begun to be the federal head of the many coloured corporation which, under the name of society, has superseded the 'genteel' or 'polite' world of earlier days. That all liberal professions or worthy pursuits should find their natural head among the representatives of the Crown was the central idea of the Queen's husband. So far as the opportunities of a short life allowed, he translated this notion into practice. It was reserved for his eldest son to witness, and himself largely to promote, the full realization of Prince Albert's purpose. The result is that to-day not only diplomacy or soldiership, statemanship or wealth, sends its envoys to a transformed Court. There is no sort of human achievement or distinction that, directly it has won the approval of the people, lacks the recognition, personal or vicarious, of the people's rulers.

Each of the callings noticed in the present survey, clerical or lay, sends its deputies to Marlborough House or Sandringham in the same way that diplomacy and arms are represented at a Royal drawing room or levée. For a reflection of the chief currents of thought, of the favourite pursuits of the most absorbing interests and influences of Victorian England, the historian will have to consult the list of visitors to the Heir Apparent's house, or read the account of his doings. The Prince Consort was attacked by the Tories in 1846 because he listened to Peel's speeches on Free Trade from the Peers' Gallery in the Commons. In 1897 the Prince of Wales attends daily the State trial of South African celebrities at Westminster, and is praised for a fresh proof of his interest in Colonial affairs. No artist or author; no sailor, soldier, cricketer or actor, makes his mark upon his age without some tribute from a popular Court to prowess that is already a household word with the multitude.

Thus in its relations to those aspects of national life in which the people itself is most interested, the Court of to-day has been transformed into a federal head of the entire motley system. If the competition of individuals for personal recognition in the highest quarter sometimes embitters social life, that is not the Royal patron's fault.

Among the changes which would make the fashionable quarter of the town most difficult of recognition to-day by one who knew it only in the early years of the reign, is the multiplication of joint stock palaces called clubs, which are really co-operative homes for poor gentlemen.[114] The absence of the gaming houses of which Crockford's was only one among many; and the widely representative quality of the ladies and gentlemen whom our stranger might notice driving to Court on a presentation day during the season is as visible as the disappearance of the West End hells.[115]

In the seventh year after the Queen's accession, the House of Commons' Committee on Gambling began its sittings. It was presided over by Lord Palmerston. Among the witnesses it examined were men well known in every section of London or of national life. Trainers, jockeys, magistrates, policemen, all contributed to the remarkable picture of contemporary life and manners, contained between the covers of this document.

The state of the law as regards gambling was then, as now, obscure. Magistrates shrank from giving constables a chance of confirming their suspicions as to houses of shy-looking exterior; but generally in the streets off St James's nearly every third house was a place of play. Between Pall Mall and the east side of Leicester Square, some 36 gambling houses were proved to exist. At Crockford's itself the tables were honestly managed. It was the perversion of Crockford's example which did the harm. Thus, some half dozen years before the Great Exhibition, Crockford's ceased to exist; its humbler but more mischievous imitators were also weeded out. An improved epoch began. Before the twentieth anniversary of the Accession, the building at the top of St James's Street described by Disraeli in the first chapter of *Sibyl* had become under the style of 'The Wellington' the best restaurant of the kind then, or for many years, known to London. Thereafter, indeed, it reverted to a club, the 'Argus' first, and then the 'Devonshire;' but a gambling club no more. The periodical flutter caused by rumoured scandals, is itself evidence of the improved standard of social morals. One other result of this Enquiry[116] is probably felt among sporting persons to-day.

Lord Palmerston's Committee pronounced against play and pay betting, that is, the system under which the bet is valid whether the horse runs or not. In betting at the post for ready money the bet is off to-day if the horse does not start. Not only is the Turf more popular than it ever was before. It binds sections of the polite world more closely together than they are held by any political or ecclesiastical cement. It is thus a social interest of the first importance which a prudent statesman makes a point of conciliating not less than he would the clergy, the lawyers, or even the licensed victuallers. The constantly increasing encouragement given to the Turf by men who have no personal end to serve, and whose refinement must be revolted by the aspect of many of its accessories, justifies the conclusion that the racecourse is indispensable to the breed of horses.

From the Plantagenet and Tudor period the best horses in England were raced; they were made better that they might be raced more successfully. Hence the wise introduction, for beauty as the crown of strength, of Arab blood, especially under Charles II. and onwards. The early excellence of stallions followed. The sires of racers begot also English hunters, so that the best horses in the hunting field to-day derive their pedigrees on one side from the founders of the best racing blood. The general utility animal, seen in carriages and cabs, is bred in the same way but has just fallen below the hunter level. Thus, without thoroughbred sires, the excellence of our horses generally must decline. The expense of breeding the best quadrupeds of the stud book is so heavy that without the stimulus of racing, the stock could scarcely be maintained.

The long distance plates on the Turf dating back to the time of Anne have been replaced by the Queen's premium stallions, periodically on view at Islington, and at the disposal, for a small fee, of horse owners throughout the country. These fine animals are almost all the winners of races. The necessary expense of racing suggests the usefulness, as in an earlier chapter was seen, of the sporting plutocrat to the Turf, and hence to the national quadruped generally. Unless the sport gave to its followers some sort of social diploma, the wealthy breeders whom the mart has furnished to the racecourse, from the earliest of the Rothschilds down to the latest of the Hirsches or the Maples, would scarcely have given time and money to their own pleasure as well as to the country's good.

To pass to the horse in another aspect, the conjectural estimate of packs of hounds at the beginning of the hunting season in 1837 was 28. At a corresponding date in 1897 the ascertained figures were 61. This does but faintly indicate the change undergone by the national sport. Not even John Leech's pictorial satire in *Punch* could deter the Cit from the hunting field, or discourage him from educating himself into a more than passable rider across country. Capel Court has or had a cry of beagles of its own. At longer distances from London than the Surrey pastures 15 per cent. of the wearers of pink and buckskin wear on ordinary days the glossy uniform of the brokers and jobbers of the House. A little earlier in the year, these sportsmen were tramping after partridges by the early September twilight that they might be at their business in the City before the West End sits down to breakfast. This is a specimen of what goes on throughout the kingdom. On the outskirts of all great cities, co-operative shootings are as common as co-operative stores.

Other pastimes are too much in daily evidence to need many words or to allow the apprehension that the male acceptance of the feminine lawn tennis implies any degeneration in the Victorian race of youth. The addition of Scotch golf to English games, and the vast improvement as to pace, style, and time shown by crews at Henley or on the Metropolitan waters in 1897 over 1837 may dispel any fears of a deterioration of youthful stamina or of muscular zeal. Whether as regards its own surface or the meadows which it waters, the Thames in the South, like the Tyne or Mersey in the North, is still a river that feeds the sea of English manhood.

As regards cricket, it is impossible to compare ancient or modern players, batsmen or bowlers; so entirely have the conditions of the game been transformed. The high scoring of the later Victorian days which would have amazed earlier players seems due, first, to the vastly improved pitches, making as they do, almost any bowling fairly easy; secondly, to the great increase of good players, consequent of course upon the evergrowing popularity of the game. The first of these facts, the improved pitches, explains why the difficult shooter that before 1875 was so fatal to batsmen at Lord's has now become a very rare ball. Although the power of the bat seems to-day greater than that of the ball, the ground had no sooner become easy and overhand bowling allowed, than the utmost was done to equalize the attack and defence. Hence the bowling is much straighter than of old; long leg and long stop no longer have a place among the fieldmen, and the absence of long leg hitting and fielding makes the game less interesting for spectators; still the grounds improve, the scoring consequently increases.

The feature which has transformed the bowling seems to be that now the best bowlers are fast with a break even on a hard wicket: whereas formerly they only broke on a sticky wicket. The still astounding power of the best bowlers is shown by the havoc they make when they get a sticky wicket to bowl on. In fine weather there is no serious obstacle to the stupendous scoring; the batting is of a more monotonous type than it used to be, and the play therefore less interesting to onlookers.

Here, as elsewhere, individual influence has been a transforming power. Between 1871 and 1883 when W. G. Grace was at his best, no fast bowler could do anything with him. Slow bowling, therefore, was adopted to keep down his run getting. As this batsman has taken his place among the veterans the old swift style has come into vogue once more. In the opinion of the greatest experts of modern cricket, as W. G. Grace is the most formidable bat, so Richardson of Surrey first, after him, Spofforth, the Australian, in his middle career, have been the most difficult bowlers.

The popularity of football, whose vogue is a recent Victorian growth is shown by the collection of 50,000 spectators at the Crystal Palace, to witness a final tie for the Association Cup. Admissions of 20,000 and 30,000 are daily events in all great towns; the money thus paid by the public has created the professional football player. Hence many questions on which authorities differ. The subject has divided the different football unions: the northern Rugby clubs having seceded to found a union of their own. The feuds among football legislators are thus as varied and violent as the forms of muscular ferocity which the game itself allows. That these can be minimized by a strenuous and keen referee is probable; that when this functionary is slack, professional football resembles the revival of the prize ring in disguise is admitted.[117] Football may seem to the mere observer almost to have become a misnomer, when carrying the ball is part of the game; when hands, shoulders, chest, fists, are nearly as active as legs and feet.

Among indoor games chess is that which has been transformed the most during our age. Here something may be attributed to the example of the Prince Consort, who was not, however, an invincible player, but more to his youngest son, the lamented Prince Leopold, who did a good deal to popularize the game. In point of universal popularity chess will never quite rival whist or billiards. It lacks the element of chance in the first, and the display of physical skill in the second which must ever chiefly fascinate men. The chess player, too, when well matched, uses more brain power than the whist player. Each has to keep the judgment perpetually alert. But the conventions in chess are left behind when the opening has been matured into the mid game, while the conventions of whist relieve the whist player continuously during the progress of the rubber.

Throughout the whole of this age chess has grown in favour among us. In most of our large towns for every chess club existing in 1847, there are ten or fifteen in 1897. On the Queen's accession English chess players still felt the stimulus given to the game in London from 1780-95 by André François Danican, commonly known as 'Philidor.' Hence may be dated the earliest English chess clubs, and the scientific study of the game. Three years before the Victorian age began, a series of matches was played by the English Alexander MacDonell and the French Labourdonnais. In 1844, the English Howard Staunton defeated the French St Amant in a match which decided the championship of the world. This, followed in 1847 by the publication of Staunton's *Chessplayer's Handbook*, brought hundreds more to the board.

Another agency in the same direction was the presence in Europe of a young American, Paul Morphy. His play was, upon the whole, the finest the world has ever seen. He crossed the Atlantic in 1857; at the close of 1858 he had beaten every European noteworthy enough to try conclusions with him. The effect of these triumphs, won by a youth of twenty-one in the most difficult of all games, was electrical. No considerable town in the country was without its chess clubs. Nor is the influence more recently exercised by J. H. Blackburne less remarkable in its way. His skill in playing games without the board, exhibited in all parts of the United Kingdom, has raised up many imitators, but scarcely an equal.

With these great players there have come also fresh scientific discoveries in the conduct of the game itself; the first of these as to time was the Scotch Gambit, partially anticipated indeed by Italian writers in the last century, but owing its new name and later vogue to its adoption by the Scotch players in the correspondence match between Edinburgh and London, 1824 to 1826 and subsequently improved upon in 1837. About that latter year, too, W. D. Evans, of the Royal Navy, invented the Gambit which now bears his name. Stimulated by these British achievements, the Austrian players hit upon the Vienna or Queen's Knights game which was first made famous during the tournament of 1873. In this country, most of these advances have been sensibly helped by the movement that the *Illustrated London News* began in 1842, which the whole press has since followed, of publishing chess problems.

An exhibition of feminine needlework justly forms a feature in the Commemoration shows of the period. In 1837 the decorative functions of the needle were oftener shown by English women of the middle classes than by acknowledged fashion leaders. In 1867 it is the middle class ladies who do most of the reading and the ultra-fashionable ones who do most of the fancy work. What transformations has this latter passed through? In 1857, as it had been in 1837, the mode was to work patterns for cushions and screens with Berlin wool on canvas. The squareness of the cross stitch was fatal to artistic effect; the covering thus decorated went out of fashion soon after Rowland's Macassar hair oil ceased lavishly to be used, and heads no longer gleamed with unguent. The frame work was succeeded by that known to the Afghans as 'boning,' and to Britons as crochet, while chairs and sofas still needed some protection from locks not yet wholly unanointed. Even the crochet coverlets, tied with little pink ribbons, began to disappear when people left their hair to nature. But the artistic instinct was slowly helping forward this sort of work.

More popular than crochet had ever been, leather frames for pictures, cut out of leaves copied from Nature, or the pinning down of fern leaves on a soft cloth or silk began to be; for these Indian ink, used with a fine brush made an effective background. Ruskin's gospel of following Nature had not been preached in vain. Accomplished women like the late Lady Marion Alford began to revive, with improvements of her own, the art of embroidering flowers, plants, birds and butterflies in wool or silk; while the stately arum lilies were used for screens, and gorgeous poppies for curtains. Next came a renascence of lace work. Many amateurs produced beautiful samples of pillow and point; but the work was trying to the eyes, and competed unfairly with the poor professionals of Honiton or Nottingham.

The early days of Ritualism popularized the copying of the borders of the old painted missals and prettily occupied many drawing rooms. Oil painting on pottery, wood, and glass came in during the early South Kensingtonian period. All young ladies now were water colour artists, or busied themselves with colouring panels and dados on their friend's walls. Brass work was a later and not very long lived development. It was costly; it was noisy; the long suffering male gradually rose up against it. Iron work, the torturing into fantastic shapes of ductile strips of metal, was a little more enduring; but it required too much accuracy and too many instruments ever to be very popular. The beautiful glass painting in churches of Lady Canning and Lady Waterford was admired rather than reproduced.

Irish cabins supplied a modish industry to English drawing rooms in drawn linen work. The principle of this seems to be hem stitching, or unbinding work into the spaces left by the drawn threads. Poker work done within the outline traced by this simple instrument on a wooden board, is practised successfully by ladies of genius who could touch nothing without adorning it, but is scarcely to be commended to bunglers or in school rooms. [118]

CHAPTER XXXI
THE REIGN OF LAW AND ITS TRANSFORMATIONS:— HOME AND COLONIAL

Significance of the New Law Court buildings in London. Early efforts after law reform in Parliament. No appreciable result till 1841. Slow progress and subsequent changes, culminating in the 1869 Commission, and the 1873 Judicature Act. The popular consequences of this, and general view of our legal system as it affects to-day the Colonies as well as the mother country.

Transformation in our Colonial system shown by the latest facts and figures. Special usefulness as well as Imperial value of the Colonies to England. Social fusion of the mother country and the Colonies prefigured by the presence and influence on both sides of the Atlantic of the American element in the best society in London. Individual influences which have promoted this movement, and are doing the same thing for our Colonial cousins, as for our American.

No architectural change during the age has more affected the perspective of Fleet Street and the Strand than the disappearance of Temple Bar and its replacement by the griffin which marks its former site, and the erection of the Royal Courts of Justice that now flank the central thoroughfare. This is the outward and visible sign of a transformation not less great, as regards the administration of the law within the new palace of justice itself.

The Reform Act of 1832 was followed by various movements in Parliament in the direction of law reform. The proposals and their very slight results were solely technical; the public reaped no appreciable benefit so long as the separation of the Common Law Courts from the Court of Chancery existed, and on different sides of Westminster Hall two legal systems, often mutually antagonistic, were at work. Ten years after the

Accession, the monopoly of Serjeants of Law in the old Court of Common Pleas was swept away. Still justice was delayed. During the early days of railway enterprise, commerce was obstructed, by the postponement, for inadequate or vexatious reasons, of the trial of cases arising out of bills of exchange on which large sums of money depended, and which, till they were decided, blocked commercial enterprise. This may be looked back to now as the scholastic era in nineteenth century law administration. The categories into which causes and kinds of legal action and pleas, were divided, in their pedantic complexity, recalled the tortuous refinements of the logical school men upon the comparatively simple predicaments of Aristotle.

In 1851 a flagrant and inveterate anomaly was removed by the success of those law reformers who had long in vain protested against the absurdity of disallowing the evidence of persons immediately interested in the suit. After this, the movement did not pause till the Commission of 1869 was appointed, with the result that in 1873 there passed the Judicature Act which has amalgamated conflicting usages into a homogeneous system, and produced the long desired fusion between Equity and Law. The ancient divisions are perpetuated to-day not in different Courts but in different divisions of the same Court. The result briefly stated is that notwithstanding the real difference which still exists between Equity and Law, and the practical division of the Bar into two branches, Law and Equity can to-day be administered by the same Courts and one judge can give suitors the same relief as any other judge.

There is now no possibility of a question being decided by one tribunal according to Common Law principles, and by another according to the principles of Equity. To prevent any chance of confusion it has further been enacted that wherever the rules of Equity and Law seem to conflict, those of Common Law are to prevail. The principle of a division of labour still exists. Every judge, that is, does not transact every sort of business. The judges in the Chancery division are still specially charged with the execution of trusts and other such matters, even as happened in the case of their predecessors fifty years ago. To do justice with as little regard as may be to forms and precedents is the visible object of the administrators of the law in every department. That professional prejudices should have disappeared was not to be expected, and, perhaps, not to be desired. But the exclusive etiquette of judges and lawyers is not greater than prevails in other professions, among doctors, diplomatists, or divines. The plaintiff in person is no more welcome in the reformed, than in the unreformed, Courts; nor, in the interests of public time and of common sense, is it probably to be wished that he should be. The two principal and practical defects in the administration of English law that still need attention would seem to be—one, the barbarous system which still obtains through the imperfect arrangements of the Circuit Courts of keeping untried prisoners unreasonably long in prison. Of late cases have been noticed in which persons, proved on trial to be innocent, have been detained in prison for weeks or months. The second defect is the undue licence allowed to the legal profession of protracting the hearing of cases secondary in their importance by the accumulation of unnecessary evidence and cross-examination. This has often been objected to, but has seldom been firmly controlled by the judges.

The great public benefit conferred by the reforms whose monument is the New Law Courts hard by the church of St Clement Danes, may be condensed into the remark that whereas from 1837 to 1875 it was an accident whether the right party won his case, the presumption in favour of his success in 1897 is so strong as almost to amount to a certainty.

Of another sort of fusion, that between the two divisions of the legal profession, solicitors and barristers, much has been heard. But in Canada and some other Colonies some inconvenience and disadvantage are found to result from the absence of any distinction between barristers and solicitors. Gradually, perhaps, a solution in practice is being arrived at. Without mentioning individual names it is the fact that among the men who now stand highest, whether at the Bar or on the Bench, many while students at the Inns of Court have perfected themselves in the practical details of law by voluntarily attending the offices of great firms of solicitors, whether in Westminster or elsewhere.

The palace of justice whose opening marked the close of the fourth decade of the reign, commemorates, in a fashion of its own, the unity of the Empire as well as the late achieved unity of the administration of justice.

Among the Queen's subjects are nations not only of every creed and of every colour, but trained in obedience to every code of law which human skill has devised. Since the modern era of our Colonial Empire began in 1836, the practice has been to continue to those dependencies the laws under which they were when they came into being, or when they were first acquired by diplomatic cession or military conquest, always provided that these pre-existent systems do not contradict the fundamental principles of British jurisprudence. Thus, in British Guiana, in the Cape Colony, and in Ceylon, the letter and spirit of Roman-Dutch law have been continued under English rule. In lower Canada, French forms have become so confused as to be impracticable: the laws of this province are to-day identical with those in vogue in England at the time of its acquisition in 1763, periodically of course improved by modern lights. In the Mauritius, the French Code Civile and the French Code de Commerce still exist. It is for the sovereign embodying in her own person the unity of the Empire to decide through the Privy Council, that is, to-day, through the Judicial Committee in all disputed cases what the particular law of the locality may be.

On page 227 of the writer's earlier book *England*, etc., the Colonial as well as ecclesiastical jurisdiction of the Privy Council Judicial Committee was explained in detail. Since those words were written an important step has been taken under an Act passed some years ago by Lord Herschell. By this, the Chief Justice of the Cape Colony, Sir Henry de Villiers, Chief Justice Sir Henry Strong of Canada, Sir Samuel Way, Chief Justice of South Australia, have been added to the Judicial Committee of the Privy Council, in order to strengthen that body with special reference to the Roman-Dutch, French-Canadian and Australasian law, in legislation and practice. Here too, it is well to refer to the recent formation of the Society of Comparative Legislation. This body is actively engaged and has already done good work in classifying materials throughout the Empire, as well as in accumulating a compendium of information which will greatly promote the simplicity and uniformity of the laws of the world.

Some distinct idea must, however, be formed of the concrete reality connoted by the familiar expression 'Colonial Empire,' beginning, as in truth for our generation it did, with the founding of the Australasian capital called Adelaide, after his Queen, in the last year of William IV., but practically co-extensive in its growth with the reign of his successor. The area of the United Kingdom is 121,000 square miles. That of its possessions in foreign parts is 8,725,000 square miles. In other words the mother country is only in extent a seventieth part of the Empire of which that mother country is the nucleus.

To put the facts somewhat differently this British Empire, covering some 9,000,000 square miles, occupies a fifth part of the habitable globe. No other world power such as this has been known to past or can be found in present history. The British Empire of the Victorian age is five times as large as was the Empire of Darius five centuries before the Christian Era began. It is four times the size of the Roman Empire at its zenith. Among modern Powers, the Empire of Great Britain is larger by an eighth than that of Russia; it contains 230 millions more people. It is sixteen times as great as the foreign dominions of France; forty times as great as the Empire of Germany. Seven days and nights of continuous travelling are required to cross the American Continent. The lands which owe allegiance to the monarch of these Islands are three times as extensive as those composing the Republican Empire of the United States.

The relative progress, according to the population test, of the mother country, and the nationalities, voluntarily incorporated into her government, beyond seas will best be judged by the facts and figures of a comparatively recent contrast, such as is alone practicable in the case of an essentially modern experience. Between 1871, then, and 1881, the increase in the inhabitants of the United Kingdom was at the rate of 10 per cent. In the case of our American Colonies it was 19 per cent.; in the case of our Australasian it was 42 per cent. The same progress which has marked our recent history in other respects than numbers at home, has not been wanting with our kin beyond sea. Thus, in respect of education; in the single province of Quebec, then fairly typical of our other possessions, in 1837 barely one-fourth of the population could read; less than one-tenth could make even a pretence at writing. In 1897 there are in the same province 4,000 schools, with a total of 200,000 scholars, each of whom is periodically certified by examiners to be making gradual progress in the prescribed standards, according to age, and qualified individually to swell the claim upon the Government grant for efficiency.

As for higher teaching, all our principal Colonies have their Universities. In the mother country, corresponding progress since the legislation of 1870 was at work was shown by the ability of the framer of that measure, the late W. E. Forster, himself well known in the Colonies, before his death in 1885, to point to the fact that the school attendance from being seven per cent. before his Act was passed had within fifteen years' operation of that measure risen to seventeen per cent. In the Australasian Colonies the results are not less striking than in the mother country or in the Canadian. In 1837 New South Wales was without a constitution as well as without any elementary education machinery of its own. Within rather less than half a century the institution of responsible government had been followed by an Education Act on the same lines as the English Act of 1870, but providing inter-mediate schools as well, with the result that the last census in Victoria shows that, of every 10,000 children of school age, 9,500 could read, and more than 8,500 could write.

These are specimen cases which establish the point that the extension of English power is accompanied by the spread of whatever advantages modern civilization can bring. As was seen in the preceding chapter, since the Colonial Bishoprics movement of 1851, religion has followed everywhere in the wake of our Empire. So, too, has education. These are the things which distinguish the Colonial methods of Great Britain from those of any other country whether in earlier or in contemporary times.

Dependencies, *i.e.* places necessary for the maintenance of Empire, but not suitable for permanent British habitation; Crown Colonies, controlled by a Governor, and legislated for by orders in Council, with, as soon as the soil is ripe for it, some representative Council on the spot, reduplications of the mother country under foreign suns, with Constitutions of their own and representative Government after the pattern of the United Kingdom; these are the different heads under which the Colonial Empire that has grown up in our age may be divided. As this Empire is in itself new, so the machinery for its central administration in the form in which it now exists is a product of the present reign. Evelyn the diarist, writing under date February 28th, 1671, mentions his appointment as a member of the Committee of the Privy Council, that had been established in 1660 for controlling the foreign plantations. This Council in 1672 was joined to the Council of Trade, the entire body being called the Council of Trade and Plantations. That was reconstituted in 1695, and again in 1748, when India came under its charge, continuing to remain under it until the appointment of the Board of Control in 1784.

At the beginning of our century, War and Colonies formed the province of a single Secretary of State and continued to do so till 1854. The first Colonial Secretary holding that office alone was Sir George Grey, followed in 1859 by the Duke of Newcastle. This was the Peelite duke whose father had founded the Newcastle scholarship at Eton, and who himself accompanied the Prince of Wales to Canada in 1859. The Colonies were not the department he had desired when Lord Palmerston formed his last Government, but he did his work not unsympathetically and bequeathed his post in good order to Cardwell. The ablest of the earlier Colonial Secretaries was without doubt Lord Grey, son of the Reformer, who held the office in Lord John Russell's Administration. During the forties, especially in 1849, Colonial sensitiveness was wounded by the perpetual motions brought forward in the House of Commons by Joseph Hume and others of his party for reducing the salary of Colonial Governors,[119] accompanied as these motions were by language not complimentary to the new polities. Not without party criticism had the office of Parliamentary Under Secretary been created in 1810. The same opposition was called forth by the appointment of Permanent Under Secretaries, and Legal Advisers to the Home Government in 1867, in 1870, 1874, and by the vote for the new Colonial offices in Downing Street first occupied in 1876. In 1897 politicians of all parties take the same patriotic pride in the Colonial Empire, while an ex-Radical leader is that Empire's Minister. The increased popularity of Colonial in preference to United States emigration is shown by the fact that in 1837 35,264 persons went to the Colonies, and some sixty years later the number was 52,029.

The pride that the Queen's subjects take in the Empire beyond seas, created by Anglo-Saxon enterprise, and the honour they derive from it are accompanied by the growing interest with which the Colonies are regarded by political thinkers who see in their development an anticipation of the constitutional movements soon to be witnessed on British soil. The Australian legislatures have not only kept pace with, they have stolen a march on, the socialistic Radicals of the old country. New Zealand generally has led the way. This and three other Colonies, New South Wales, Victoria and Tasmania, have adopted Woman's Suffrage with the legislative freaks which seem to be its sequel. To the action of this franchise is attributed the proposal recently made in one of these Parliaments to give every domestic servant a statutory holiday once a week. Tasmania, too, will not apparently be satisfied till she has secured the Swiss Referendum for ending disputes between the two legislative Chambers by submitting the single point in issue to the constituencies. Tasmania, also, has made several efforts, as yet unsuccessfully, to acclimatise the Hare system of proportional representation which is now forgotten in England, save when some theorist uses a periodical re-adjustment of our franchise, to revive its interest. South Australia, Victoria, and New South Wales, have also attempted, but not as yet carried, the establishment of national banks; perilous experiments enough for any new, or for that matter old, country.

Individual effort gave England its Colonies. The same agency—as embodied in a Gibbon Wakefield, who began life by being Secretary to Lord Durham in Canada 1838, who, 1839, obtained the annexation and colonization of New Zealand, and who in 1849 published *The Art of Colonization*; in a Sir William Molesworth, the pioneer of Colonial self-government; who, obtaining from Palmerston the great object of his ambition, the Colonial Secretaryship 1853, died shortly afterwards; more recently in the fourth Lord Carnarvon, Colonial Secretary (1866-7; 1874-8)—applied the social cement which has joined the new countries with the old in personal rather than in merely political relation. Colonial patriotism was also reasonably gratified on its intellectual side by Mr Lowe's sojourn in New South Wales 1843-50, and by Sir Robert G. W. Herbert's share in the Administration of Queensland before he became Colonial Under Secretary in London.

A shrewd Colonial statesman not long since observed that if another flying Australian, but a born and bred Colonial horse, were to win the Derby, no whisper of separation from the British Crown would ever be heard among the most advanced of Colonial democrats. Popular enthusiasm at the Antipodean winner of the Blue Ribbon would spread from Epsom Downs throughout the kingdom; it would be flashed along every wire or transmitted by every cable to the four winds of heaven; the Colonists would cease to complain that they, or their products, were not appreciated by the mother country. This half serious remark contains more than a grain of truth; it points to the fact that the grievance alleged by our kinsman beyond sea against the headquarters of their race is sentimental, rather than practical. Pending the Derby winner from beyond seas, the less sternly democratic of England's Colonial cousins have appreciated the peerages bestowed on a few of them, and can point to other substantial proofs that they have become a power in English society. Thus they have founded clubs in London; they possess a party of their own in the House of Commons, and entertain the social leaders of the old country at their balls and parties during the season in famous restaurants, or at their own homes.

Till the Victorian age was well developed, the latter day American elements in London fashion were unheard of. To-day these leaven the whole of our social life. It is those born under the Stripes and Stars who relieve, at a princely rental, English nobles of house property which its owners are not occupying, and supply Countesses and Duchesses to the English peerage. The great feature of our time has been the concentration of our people in the Metropolis. A like gravitation to towns has indeed taken place throughout the whole country. Between the eighties and the nineties, the increase of the urban population has been 3,016,579; the decrease of the rural has been 139,545.[120]

With respect to this movement, as in other matters, London has shown itself the true mirror of England. For a proof of this, it would be enough to mention the Langham Hotel, and those caravanserais which have followed it, down to the latest and most palatial of all, the Hotel Cecil. That the capital thus socially re-created has been successfully reorganized as the most cosmopolitan and modish centre of fashion for two hemispheres is due largely to the agency of American dollars and American arbiters of elegance. In the thirties and the sixties the gifted men who were sent to represent the United States in the old country, a Washington Irving, and a Lothrop Motley, made their Embassies social centres for the most pleasant company of the time, attracted famous men from their own country, one of whom, the Rev. Cleveland Coxe,[121] formed a lasting link between the two chief branches of the Anglo-Saxon Church, most of these Transatlantic visitors left behind them brilliant reputations as conversationalists.

More recently a Russell Lowell and a Bayard have adorned this tradition. In their day, the American season following hard upon the London season proper has become a regular, and to all concerned most profitable, observance in the social calendar. The dictatresses of polite life from the other side of the Atlantic generally have been educated in Paris, not a few of them by the daughter of Emile Souvestre at that institution for turning intelligent girls into charming women, Les Ruches, Fontainebleau; they always bring with them to their London homes the tastes of citizens of the world. These tastes are gratified as successfully on the Thames as on the Seine; it is *la belle Americaine* who has most visibly impressed her image on the capital where, since the Second Empire fell, she has chiefly delighted to dwell; she decided that English life needed enlivening: she has enlivened it and continues to do so effectually. Some restlessness is constitutional to her, as also to the Anglo-Indians and Colonials who are perennially so much with us; thus largely to please her the London season is now subdivided into innumerable parts. It would be truer to say some form of that season lasts all the year round. The constant locomotion from one centre, or from one country seat to another, began, as has been already seen, with the Prince Consort. It has not been discouraged by later representatives of the Crown.

From the day that in 1860 the Prince of Wales visited the tomb of George Washington, he has never lost the American heart. The new London régime exactly suits the future peeresses of the old country when they are fresh from New York.

The constant alternations of Hyde Park promenades, not only with suburban racecourses, but with long days under summer suns given to Thames-side picnics, or with rapid flittings on any opportunity to and fro between Mayfair on the one hand, the Boulevard des Italiens, Monte Carlo, or Homburg on the other: these innovations have been brought about by the American Londoner more than by any other single person. The Colonial millionaire or millionairess has not yet been so fully developed as their Transatlantic equivalents. But the process is going steadily forward, no doubt with similar results to follow.

The contrast between the amount of international friction that was caused before the Oregon Boundary dispute, and the Trent difference, between the two countries were composed in 1846 and in 1863, respectively, and the comparative ease with which the Venezuela Question in our own day was settled, suggests the solid international advantages of the arrangement under which New York and London have become socially one and the same capital, having their pleasures, their lions and lionesses, their favourite composers, authors, dramatists and players, in common.

The late Mr Samuel Ward, who is as well remembered in London as in New York, and who liked to be called the prince of *bon vivants* at Delmonico's, the king of the lobby at Washington, was a cultivated little old gentleman, of whom it is difficult to conceive as ever having been much less, or more, than some seventy-odd years of age. He was known throughout the whole Anglo-Saxon world as 'Uncle Sam.' He had become popular in English society soon after the examples of the then Lord Hartington and Lord Rosebery included America in the grand tour of every educated Briton. He really did something to entitle him to his universal sobriquet. He was the founder of a social and literary Anglo-American school which has struck its roots deep in the chosen homes of English fashion. As Californian gold preceded Australian, so the Transatlantic force that has transformed the social England of our day has come before the fully organized exercise of a Colonial power of the same sort. But every year brings one visibly nearer its final development, with all the international advantages which will no doubt accompany that event.[122]

INDEX

D

F

H

I

J

K

L

N

O

P

U

V

W

Y

FOOTNOTES

[1] Edited by Dr Ernst Regel—Berlin, 1894.

[2] The grandfather of the fifth Marquess. As Lord Henry Petty, he had so long since as 1806 been Chancellor of the Exchequer. In 1848 he was President of the Council, and led the peers in the Russell Government. Died 1863.

[3] But much of the Forest being saved by the Common rights had not at any time been enclosed.

[4] *The Age of Gold,* vol. i. p. 37.

[5] While these lines are being prepared for the press there appears in a London newspaper a statement of the prices current at the Western Australia gold fields in the summer of 1896. They may be compared with the figures given in the text and are as follows:—Tea 3s., flour 10d., sugar 1s., bacon 3s., beef and mutton 4d. to 8d., cheese 2s. 6d., coffee 3s., tobacco 8s., and preserved potatoes 1s. 9d. per lb.; milk (condensed) 1s. 9d. per tin; flour 20s. per 50 lbs.; and eggs 10s. a dozen; but the cost of living generally, as compared with earnings, is low. On the Ashburton River gold fields mutton is 4d., beef 6d., flour 10d., tea 3s., sugar 9d. to 1s., preserved potatoes 1s. 6d., salt 1s., rice 1s., and oatmeal 1s. 3d. per lb. On the Yilgarn gold fields meat is 9d. to 1s. a lb., flour 10s. to 30s. per 50 lb. bag, tea 3s. 6d. a lb., and other provisions are equally scarce and dear. At Coolgardie, to the east of Yilgarn, flour costs £3 per 200 lbs., bread 1s. per 1½ lb. loaf, butter 2s. 3d. per lb., potatoes 6d. per lb., sugar 8d. per lb., tinned milk 1s. 3d. per lb., bacon 1s. 9d. per lb., salt 6d. per lb., and board and lodgings £3 to £7 a week. On the Murchison gold fields in the North, the prices per lb. are: Flour 8d., sugar 8d., tea 3s. 6d., tobacco 6d., fish 1s. 6d., mutton 8d., beef 8d., butter 3s., and tinned meats 1s. 3d.

[6] Still more than this was given to get men on the home voyage from Melbourne.

[7] See *Our Railways*. By John Pendleton. Cassell & Co.

[8] Brought down to 1897 instead of 1881, these *mutatis mutandis* figures are derived from Mr Mallock's most useful book.

[9] In the West of England, with which the writer is specially acquainted, this is generally the case.

[10] These figures are taken from 'Art Sales,' by George Redford, privately printed, 1882.

[11] Now Sir William Agnew.

[12] All the details of art prices given in this chapter are derived from Mr G. Redford's authentic record of art sales, first privately printed in 1888. For other information the writer is indebted to the late Sir J. E. Millais, P.R.A.

[13] See Picciotto's Anglo-Jewish History for all these early facts about the Jews.

[14] The idea of the Exhibition being 'universal' was not that of the Prince, but of the Committee of the Society of Arts. It was first suggested in fact by Mr Thomas Winkworth.

[15] Most of the time he was at Ghent. His stay there is known in French history as *La cour de Gand*.

[16] These anecdotes are given from Mr Reeves' volume already mentioned. They are suggestive of incident if not uniformly accurate in fact. The correction of the Waterloo incident given above commended itself to some among Baron Lionel's friends who would be likely to know.

[17] While Lord Palmerston has become a historical name, Lord Beaconsfield's precedents are daily, alike by friends and foes, cited as living forces.

[18] See *Quarterly Review*, July, 1896.

[19] This anecdote was often told by Lord Shaftesbury.

[20] Not, however, the most appreciated by his master.

[21] Now of course Battersea Park.

[22] Who, to the regret of all who knew his abilities, died February 1897, having exercised influence rather than achieved distinction.

[23] While he yet lives, his enduring monuments are his blocks of working men's dwellings in the King's Cross district and elsewhere.

[24] The guarantees against undue delegation are stringent and successful.

[25] Opinions vary as to the workability of this clause in the shape in which it left the Lords.

[26] *E.g.* In a typical Surrey village, where there are no Nonconformists, the Chairman is the Vicar, but of 38 Gloucestershire parishes, where dissenters abound, only in two or three.

[27] Urban District Councils have taken the place of Local Boards; they are in fact town councils of those districts which are not incorporated into municipalities.

[28] Molesworth's *History of England*, vol. i. p. 19.

[29] As a fact, the County chairman is most likely a J.P. already.

[30] For valuable facts and figures, bringing this chapter down to the latest date the writer is indebted to Mr Henry Chaplin and his staff at the Local Government Board, as for much other useful help to Sir Henry Fowler, Sir Charles Dilke, the Rev. Charles Cox, D.D., and to Mr G. W. E. Russell.

[31] In addition to Sir Charles Dilke, Sir Henry Fowler and others already mentioned, the writer is indebted for invaluable help in the preparation of facts and the revision of proofs in this portion of the book to Mr W. J. Soulsby the accomplished private secretary to a succession of Lord Mayors of London.

[32] An account of the University Settlements in East London. Edited by John M. Knapp, Oxford House, Bethnal Green. Rivington, Percival & Co. 1895.

[33] *England: Its People, Polity and Pursuits.* 2 vols. Cassell & Co. 1 vol. Chapman & Hall.

[34] This usage varies under different Administrations and at different epochs. Mr Forster [1870] was an actual Education Minister. His Liberal successors have been so since; his Conservative successors only in a qualified sense.

[35] See Report of the Secondary Education Commission, vol. i. *passim*, but especially, pp. 44, and seq.

[36] These have produced not a few famous men even in this generation: Thus Bishop Stortford shares with Oriel, Oxford the honour of educating Mr Cecil Rhodes.

[37] As the writer has a personal reason for knowing, this is the year in which the amalgamation first took a definite shape, though it was not perhaps fully carried out till a little later.

[38] This point was dwelt upon strongly in the letters of London correspondents to the French press at the time of the 1887 Jubilee.

[39] Recent legislation providing for the information of the working classes on this point, by the display of lists in factories, has not given entire satisfaction to the persons interested.

[40] The statistics showing the new rungs in the educational ladder in this chapter have been supplied to the writer by Mr G. H. Croad of the London School Board, by other gentlemen in like positions and by private

friends in the Education Department. Thanks are also due to Sir John Gorst, and to Mr Mundella for the kind trouble they have taken in checking the facts of the narrative portion, and for making valuable suggestions.

[41] This, during the youth of the late Rev W. G. Cookesley was said by that authority to be, not hyperbole, but historical fact.

[42] This title has been denied to the King here named, but Waynflete, also an Eton benefactor as well as official, was himself transferred by Henry from Winchester to Eton, becoming Headmaster and Provost successively.

[43] For the facts and figures in this chapter showing the relations of the old public schools to the new educational tests, as for the facts of Eton expenditure, the writer is indebted to the Rev. Edmond Warre, D.D., the Headmaster, who has placed at his disposal all the necessary data.

[44] See *Eothen,* edn. 1896—Blackwood, p. 7.

[45] Now in vogue at nearly all the pleasure towns in southern England.

[46] The name of Frank as well as of Charles Mathews was often on the bills of this theatre during the sixties.

[47] Census of England and Wales, 1891. Vol. iv. General Report, pp. 64 and fg.

[48] For a valuable dissertation, to which the present writer is much indebted on this subject, see A. J. Ogilvy—*Westminster Review,* 1891. Vol. 136, pp. 289 to 297.

[49] W. Cunningham on the Malthusian theory—*Macmillan's Magazine,* Dec. 1883.

[50] In addition to the published official statistics from which the above facts and figures are taken, the writer is indebted to the Registrar-General for much useful information, and to Mr G. Shaw-Lefevre for further friendly help.

[51] See Molesworth's *History of England.* Vol. i. p. 90 and fg.

[52] Commons Journal, xci. 319.

[53] In the Upper House, there is perhaps no one to whom the classics are more familiar as literature than Lord Morley.

[54] For nearly all the details as to the structural arrangements of the two Houses of Parliament, and to the particulars of what may be called their social life, the writer desires to express his grateful acknowledgments to Mr Archibald Milman, C.B., a Clerk of the House of Commons. On other parliamentary points, he is not less indebted to Sir Charles Dilke, and to many more Members of Parliament, only a few of whom now survive.

[55] See the following extract from the *Daily News,* Dec. 16, 1896:—

Mr Gladstone on Parliamentary Changes.—Mr Gladstone having read an article in the *Westminster Review* entitled 'The Old M.P. and the New,' by George A. B. Dewar, writes that, speaking from recollection, he thinks there were not five members of the Conservative party in 1835 who sat in the House of Commons by reason of their connection with trade or industry. He describes the change which has come about in the composition of the party since then as 'simply marvellous.'

[56] 'It is the Queen's doing,' is the statement of the newspapers of that year; but seems to apply not to the dismissal of Lord Grey, but of Lord Melbourne who had followed him.

[57] The reference to Lord Palmerston and the *Morning Post* is historical.

[58] It might be argued of course with much plausibility that this order of things has begun long since, and that, the verbal distinction notwithstanding, government by party has always, from another point of view been government by groups.

[59] This (1701) followed the Kentish petition to the Commons protesting against distrust of the King, and desiring that the addresses of the loyal petitioners might be turned into Bills of Supply.

[60] Sir Theodore Martin's 'Life,' chapter i. These references are in all cases to the People's Edition.

[61] 'Life,' p. 11.

[62] Before Prince Albert's reforms, the jurisdiction of the Palace interior was divided between the Lord Chamberlain and the Lord Steward. The Lord Chamberlain was responsible for providing the lamps, the Lord Steward for lighting them; before a pane of glass or cupboard could be repaired, months sometimes passed; all external repairs were in the hands of the Woods and Forests, on which it therefore depended how much daylight should be admitted through the windows. More than two-thirds of the indoor servants seemed without control, coming in, going out, when, and with whom they chose.—'Life,' pp. 26-27.

[63] 'Life,' p. 21.

[64] 'Life,' p. 21.

[65] Not, as was long said, Mr Disraeli, but Mr Disraeli's then titular leader, Lord George Bentinck.

[66] At this interval, traditions as to the merits of the quarrel may differ. The account here given is from the most authentic source existing.—Martin's 'Life,' p, 29.

[67] This opinion used to be expressed very strongly by Lord Raglan who commanded in the Crimea. It was shared by the French military experts of the day.

[68] The figures in the earlier estimate are taken from the *Imperial Federation Journal*, June 1886: Those of the later date are supplied by the Army Estimates, and by the courtesy of Lord Lansdowne and his colleagues at the War Office.

[69] This (*i.e.* distribution of honours according to property) seems from *Ethics*, Book viii. ch. 10, the exact meaning of the convenient compound.

[70] For the chief facts in these remarks on the army, where they are not directly drawn from the Blue Books, or as above specified from the Imperial Federation Journal, the writer is indebted, and would express his thanks, to Lord Lansdowne, Secretary of State for War; to Field Marshal Lord Wolseley, and to his old and distinguished friend General Sir Henry Brackenbury.

[71] Quoted by Captain Eardley Wilmot in *The Development of Navies*, p. 1.

[72] *The Development of Navies*, p. 12.

[74] The 'Warrior,' at this time standing by herself, was a vessel of 9,210 tons. Thirty-five years later the advance made in our ideas of dimension and power may be judged from the fact that on Jan. 31, 1895, the 'Majestic' was launched. Her tonnage was 14,900, an increase of 5,690 on her predecessor. Unlike the 'Warrior' of an earlier date, the 'Majestic' was only one of several, the building of which began at the end of 1894, the last parliamentary record of which reaches to the spring of 1896. Briefly to summarize the results that emphasize the contrasts between the two epochs, the average size of vessels built at the present time approaches thrice that of twenty years ago. Then too, steel was not used for ship building; now it is gradually supplanting iron. Of late there have been more ships built than formerly on a less colossal scale. The result is partially due to the dimensions of the Suez Canal whose depth is not equal to an ironclad of the first magnitude. Time, apparently, is still needed to show if our seamen can develop a skill as great in handling these iron leviathans as in controlling those wooden craft, their management of which was the admiration of the world.

[75] Apart from the parliamentary papers bearing on the navy, Captain Eardley Wilmot's *The Development of Navies* is the literary authority that has been found most useful in preparing this chapter. The writer is however, chiefly indebted to the details with which he has been kindly and

copiously supplied by the present First Lord of the Admiralty, Mr Goschen and his staff, especially Lord Encombe.

[76] In the nineteenth century, on a much smaller scale, exhibitions had been held in Paris 1801, 1806, 1836, 1849, as well as in Belgium, Germany and Spain. The true precursor of the '51 Exhibition has been discovered by Mr Molesworth (History ii. p. 363) in the Covent Garden Free Trade Bazaar 1846.

[77] Macaulay's House of Commons speeches in the 1832 Reform Bill debates are famous. When he was best known as a writer, he had been Secretary at War (1839) and Paymaster General (1846). Lytton at the zenith of his literary fame had been Colonial Secretary under Lord Derby in 1858, before he was made a peer in 1866.

[78] The vitality of Purcell's fame at the 200th anniversary of his death was attested by the celebrations of 1895. Since then a very remarkable tribute to his greatness has been given accidentally in an unexpected quarter. The great German classical authority, the Bach Gesellschaft (vol. xlii. p. 250) prints as a doubtful work of Bach, Purcell's Toccata in A which is given in the Harpsichord and Organ volume of the Purcell Society (p. 42). That a work of Purcell's should have been mistaken for one of the very greatest organ writer's who has ever lived, and that by Bach's own jealous countrymen, is a panegyric more significant than words on our own great national composer.

[79] *Life and Letters of Sir Charles Hallé* (Smith, Elder & Co.) illustrates with interesting detail the service rendered to Beethoven by this great exponent of his genius.

[80] For the facts and figures contained in this survey of our musical state, the writer desires to express his special obligations to Sir George Grove, and to Sir Arthur Sullivan, both private friends of many years standing.

[81] Martin's 'Life,' People's Edition, part ii. p. 63.

[82] The habit of inviting other than parliamentary guests, men famous in art or science, to the State dinners on the eve of the session began with Mr Gladstone, and after him Mr Disraeli.

[83] A class chiefly, if not exclusively, represented by, to his honour be it said, Professor Herkomer.

[84] While these pages are passing through the press, the French critic, M. Yriarte, writing in the *Times*, gives the following interesting testimony

to the world-wide value of this British centre of humanity and culture:— To-day for all of us foreigners South Kensington is a Mecca. England there possesses the entire art of Europe and the East, their spiritual manifestations under all forms, and Europe has been swept into the stream in imitation of England. Berlin, Budapest, Vienna, Nuremberg, Basle, Madrid, St Petersburg, Moscow, the large towns of America itself have now their South Kensingtons; but in the original one of England still unfinished, where the splendour of the start (excessive, as it seems to me) contrasts with the inertia of the last fifteen years, the inconceivable treasures are becoming so much heaped up as to be a veritable obstacle to study. How is it possible to study this extraordinary series of textiles of all times and countries, ranged one upon another, overlapping and hiding one another, without proper perspective and proper light?

[85] £70,000, to which the Duke of Marlborough reduced the £100,000 which he originally asked.

[86] For the information embodied in this chapter, the writer is under many obligations to the late Sir John E. Millais, to the late Sir Philip Cunliffe Owen, long Director at South Kensington, and Mr F. A. Eaton, the present Secretary to the Royal Academy.

[87] Greenwood, p. 291.

[88] Thackeray, when writing *The Virginians*, Carlyle, in the preparation of all his later works, are authentic and only the more illustrious instances which could be given.

[89] Such was the precise garment mentioned by Mr Harrison when he told the story to the present writer.

[90] To whom, while at work on portions of this book at a distance from London, the present writer owes much courteous help.

[91] By exactly ten years, Thackeray dying 1863, Lytton 1873. The increased interest in Dickens is shown by Messrs Chapman & Hall's latest editions, the revived interest in Lytton by Messrs Routledge's new ventures.

[92] Personally, Lord Lytton was more correctly appreciated in Paris where in his last years he much lived. His unfailing presence of mind in physical difficulties or dangers compelled the admiration of all who knew him. A Colonial Secretary himself, he first showed, in the closing chapters of *The Caxtons*, that sense of the greatness of our Colonial empire, to-day a commonplace but unknown up to then.

[93] John Copley, afterwards Lord Lyndhurst, and John Campbell, afterwards Lord Campbell, during their student days at the Bar, both wrote for the London papers, chiefly theatrical critiques.

[94] These figures for the later date are taken direct from Mitchell's Newspaper Press Directory 1897; for the earlier from a note by Mr Garnett in Mr Ward's *Reign of Queen Victoria*; Mr Garnett's statistics being apparently derived from an article contributed probably by Albany Fonblanc to an early number of the *Westminster Review*.

[95] Carried in the January of 1855 a majority of 157 (305 to 148).

[96] Successes of a new sort have been made. The penny newspapers had paid by their advertisements; when the price of the paper on which they were printed exceeded a certain figure, circulation beyond the amount necessary to maintain advertisements was not therefore in itself a paramount object. The new halfpenny sheets realized on every copy sold a profit larger even proportionately than the penny papers had ever made on their copies, advertisements of course excepted.

[97] For the commercial details of newspaper enterprise, the reader is referred to the author's earlier work *England*, etc., where he duly acknowledged his obligations to his editorial chief and personal friend, Mr W. H. Mudford, of the *Standard*; for the fresh facts and figures here given the writer is indebted to Sir Charles Dilke, to Mr H. Labouchere, to an article on *Halfpenny Papers* by Mr F. A. McKenzie in the *Windsor Magazine* for January 1897, and above all to Mitchell's invaluable *Newspaper Press Directory*.

[98] M.P. for Shrewsbury since 1832.

[99] Each reform was followed by a fresh diminution in the death rate.

[100] This lady, in addition to her natural gift of organization, had been trained at the Prussian hospital of Kaisersworth. Accompanied by her friends, Mr and Mrs Bracebridge of Atherstone Hall, and 37 nurses, she reached Scutari November 5, just in time to tend the wounded after Balaclava.

[101] Sampson Low's *Charities of London*, p. 2.

[102] The statistics illustrative of this subject have been derived exclusively from Mr Sampson Low's *Charities of London*, at the places already indicated in the footnotes. For the other facts to complete the little picture, the writer is indebted to friends who have made this subject their special study, such as Lady Priestley, or reluctantly to his own personal experience.

[103] For these statistics, some of them perhaps now given for the first time the writer is beholden to Sir Brydges Henniker, Registrar General.

[104] This most gifted family came originally from Plymouth or its neighbourhood, sending representatives to Bath, Bristol and Barnstaple. The Barnstaple Budd, universally respected, died 1896.

[105] Dr Ferrier's work on the brain, mapping it out according to its functions, appeared 1876 and also perhaps marks an epoch.

[106] Shortly before his death, the late Sir Andrew Clark assured the present writer that his remarks in his earlier work, *England,* on the medical profession were accurate in all respects and applicable to the existing state of things. For the purpose of the present volume when the writer was first contemplating it, and was in occasional correspondence with Sir Andrew, the great physician kindly made a few fresh hints. These, with the information of Sir William and Lady Priestley, have been indispensable to the writer throughout.

[107] Evidence in support of this has been collected by the writer throughout the manufacturing districts, an important fact being that where secularism was most organized, there well-to-do mechanics and artizans are Communicants, and often Sunday School teachers as well.

[108] The Ramsden Sermon, preached before Oxford University June 12, 1892, pp. 10, 11.

[109] These Bishoprics, 75 in America, 4 in other countries, that is 79 in all, control (1897) 4,666 clergy; among the church goers 622,194 are Communicants. The total of Anglican clergy in foreign parts, at the period of the Queen's accession, excluding Bishops, was 897. In 1850 it was 1,193. To-day (1897) it is 4,312. Roughly, therefore, the increase has been 300 per cent.

[110] The most noticeable being the Gorham dispute about *Baptismal Regeneration* 1850, which issued in defining the Evangelical status, as in 1847 Hampden's bishopric had secured the broad Church position. In 1871 the Frome case secured the highest doctrines on the Eucharist. These three decisions practically constitute the Charters of the three chief parties in the National Church.

[111] Not Dean of St Paul's till 1869.

[112] *The Sermon on the Mount,* 1897.

[113] For the information as to the Church of England embodied in this chapter, the writer's thanks are sincerely tendered to the Rev. H. W. Tucker

of the S.P.G. Society; to the Rev. J. C. Cox, D.D., Holdenby, North Hants; to the Rev. A. L. Foulkes, Steventon, Berks; and to Mr G. W. E. Russell. No official statistics of the numbers in the different Churches exist. The basis of the estimate given is supplied by the statistics of the *Federation League Journal*, June, 1886.

[114] This is not the conventional idea of clubs. Thackeray, who knew club-life well, first illustrated this view. An examination of the tariff and general charges at the professional clubs in Pall Mall or St James's would show the absolute truth of the description.

[115] The Honourable Mr Algernon Bourke has a more than amateur experience of modern clubs. While these pages are passing through the press, he gives it as his opinion that nowadays there is practically no play in clubs. All who know anything of the subject would confirm the general truth of that statement.

[116] See *passim* the evidence taken before this Committee printed in the 1844 Parliamentary Blue Books.

[117] The reluctance of referees to interfere is natural and pardonable in view of the fashionable brutality not only of the players but the spectators. A proof of this may be found in a typical instance reported in a daily paper:—A Football Referee assaulted.—A disgraceful scene was witnessed at Lincoln last night after the close of the League match between Lincoln City and Newton Heath. The decisions of the referee (Mr Fox, of Sheffield) gave great dissatisfaction to the crowd, and the hostile demonstration commenced when he awarded the Heathens two penalty kicks in quick succession. After the match he had to seek shelter in the secretary's office for some time, and when he did leave the ground he was badly assaulted by several roughs. The windows of a cab in which he drove to his hotel were completely smashed.

[118] In the diverse materials for this chapter, the writer has been helped greatly by the volume on the Turf in the Badminton Series, but in all which has to do with horses by the Earl of Dunraven, by Lord Ribblesdale, by Mr Leopold de Rothschild; in all that relates to cricket and football by the Hon. and Rev. E. Lyttelton, Headmaster of Haileybury College, and in the football facts by one of Mr Lyttelton's Haileybury colleagues. His chess facts have been given him by a great West of England authority in the game, H. Maxwell Prideaux. For his knowledge of ladies' work he is indebted, as in *England* he was, to Miss F. S. Hollings.

[119] The motion in 1849 for the Sierra Leone reduction was, as Hansard shows, only one of a series of such proposals. Hume's views on the Colonies were much those which Mill had set forth in his famous Encyclopædia Britannica article. Mill may have been against Colonial expansion, but not against Colonial retention.

[120] On this subject see the very interesting and accurate statistics compiled by Mr F. Leveson Gower, and published by the Cobden Club.

[121] A. Cleveland Coxe, then Rector of Grace Church, Baltimore, published his *Impressions of England,* 1856. His Ballads and Carols, ecclesiastical or religious, especially one entitled *In Dreamland,* abound in graceful fancy, and have had a popularity among English and American Anglicans approaching that of *The Christian Year*.

[122] For the facts relating to the administration of law, the writer is indebted to Sir Edward Clarke, and to the Master John MacDonell, of the High Court of Justice. The facts and figures with respect to the Colonies have been drawn from official sources as well as from the very valuable *Imperial Federation League Journal* for June 1886. He is further personally beholden for the local colour inparted to his Colonial descriptions by the private information of Sir Robert G. W. Herbert, Sir Julius Vogel, Mr John Bramston, and other Colonial officials. The privately printed papers of the fourth Lord Carnarvon distributed among his personal friends (1897), opportunely confirm and illustrate the views here given of the Colonial past, present, and future.